# The Tymphaean Symphony

Exploring the Nature of a Greek Mountain

Michael David Jones

Brambleby Books

The Tymphaean Symphony
Exploring the Nature of a Greek Mountain
Copyright © Michael David Jones 2016

The author has asserted his right
under the Copyright, Designs and Patents Act 1988
to be identified as the Author of this Work.

*All Rights Reserved*

*No part of this book may be reproduced in any form
by photocopying or by any electronic or mechanical means,
including information, storage or retrieval systems,
without permission in writing from both the copyright
owner and the publisher of this book.*

A CIP catalogue record for this book is available
from the British Library

ISBN 978 1908241 498

Cover design by Tanya Warren – Creatix
Cover images by the author
Map design by Premier Graphics of Holyhead

First published in 2016 by Brambleby Books
www.bramblebybooks.co.uk

Printed and bound in Great Britain by
Clays Ltd., St Ives plc

# Dedication

For Mary
and all
who made this
Journey possible

Front cover:
The Forest of Ghiol in the shadow of the cliffs of Goura.

Back cover:
Top left to right: *Linum punctatum* ssp *pycnophyllum*; Northern face of Tymphi from the Magoula Meadows, Scarce Swallowtail
Bottom left to right: *Minuartia pseudosaxifraga*; The summit ridge west of Goura, *Globularia cordifolia*.

## About the Author

After a decade working as a museum-geologist and university tutor the author spent twenty-five years organising and leading natural history expeditions, introducing others to the floristic and wildlife wonders of some of the world's wild places of which the mountains of north-west Greece is but one of many. From the arctic to the Sahara and the Cantabrians to the Himalayas, those explorations nurtured a personal affinity with the natural environment seeded during formative years in the English countryside and mountains of Wales. Childhood quests for Emperor moths and Merlin on the Stiperstones and Long Mynd, and for the saxifrages of Snowdonia were the prelude to searches for Musk Oxen and Snowy Owl in the tundra, Houbara and Bibron's Agama in the Sahara and rare rhododendrons and primulas in the Garhwal Himalaya. The author now divides his time between Wales, the east Aegean islands, and Lycian Turkey, the subject of further writings.

# Preface

From a time even before my earliest childhood memories the call of the unknown was an irresistable siren sound. Parental night-time searches would find me asleep between potato rows or nestled amidst stooked wheat sheaves in the neighbourhood fields of those formative years. Not surprisingly, those nocturnal forays led to a fascination with moths so began a lifetime's interest in the natural world and an affinity with the wild. The association has of necessity been a solitary one, but there have often been times when the desire to share with others has prevailed. Now is such a time and in the form of this account of a mountainous enclave in Greece.

For many, remote places offer physical and mental challenges, a provocation to overcome, whether it be to scale and bestride the summits, to navigate the trackless waste or to unmask and expose the previously unknown. Such has its appeal, but there are deeper and more satisfying rewards to be gained from knowledge and experience of place, the satisfaction which comes from a long and intimate association with all that constitutes the whole, whether it be the rocks beneath one's feet, the form of the land or the diversity and interrelationships of plant and animal life which contribute to make a place what it is. The attainment of such a relationship is only possible over time and demands an affinity with place which, in the Greek context, perhaps allows some empathy with the ancient's concept of the *daimon* or *genius* of place; those characteristics greater than the sum of the parts and which manifest the soul or being of a place. If the words of this book convey some sense of the *daimon* of the place called Tymphi I will have succeeded in my purpose, in part at least.

What follows in these pages is a summation of many visits during twenty years, distilled into an eight-day walk across the Tymphaean massif of Zagori in June 1991. That time saw the exceptional confluence of deep winter snows and heavy spring rains, conditions conducive to a remarkably prolific floristic display, one which I was privileged to witness only rarely in my long association with the mountain. All that is described was seen and all events were as experienced, the combined narrative being as true a recollection as the combination of detailed field note-books and memory will allow.

In describing some of the natural wonders of the mountain, the use of taxonomic binomials, especially for many plants, has been unavoidable. Understandably, most Greek plants do not have an English common name equivalent. If the unfamiliarity of these Linnean binomials induces unease do as I have always done, enunciate the words aloud. They are to be savoured, rolled over the tongue and expelled with appreciation of the physical formulation, and of the sound they create – *Eryngium amethystinum*, *Sempervivum marmoreum*, *Hypericum rumeliacum*; recite them repeatedly and they become an incantation, hypnotic and the well-spring of imagination, a siren call of the mountain. Faintly on the wind, *Linum punctatum pycnophyllum* has always summoned my every return, its rarely seen beauty as seductive as the intonation of its syllables.

Having attained an age when change can be contemplated within the context of a lifetime, I view the present state of much of the English countryside as a pale shadow of the bounteous natural world I inhabited as a child. The profusion and diversity which allowed the gathering of wild flowers and even the netting of butterflies or selective collection of birds eggs without deleterious effect has long gone. The plenty of my youth has become the scarcity of more recent years, a contrast which only a lifetime reveals and which one fears will be the experience of succeeding generations as human detrimental influence on species abundance and diversity increases. Whilst reading of the natural wonders of Tymphi and of the manifold influences which have nurtured the mountain, one should be reminded that this is a microcosm of the natural world. It is as vulnerable to ecological degradation as were those lost meadows, marshlands, mires, heathlands and carr woodlands of England. In the absence of awareness alas lies the seed of destruction.

It is customary in most published works to acknowledge the contributions of others, however in this instance I shall not name names, not in deference to any delusional notion of self-importance but wholly to the contrary. Life has progressed to the point of realisation that much of what we accomplish is the result of the influence and prior endeavours of others; we build using the blocks and mortar created by our predecessors, only the form of the edifice is of our making, and even that is largely determined by the influential properties of the materials serendipitously placed at our disposal. Of the materials I have been fortunate to have had available, those listed as 'Sources' are acknowledged as having been in-dispensible. Similarly there are many whose knowledge and companion-ship in its generous sharing has contributed in varying degrees throughout life to that creative process, although to name any would be to deny similarly deserved recognition to those who remained anonymous. They know who they are and share in the dedication of this book to all. Finally, that recognition does not imply any shared burden of blame for error, inaccuracy or any other deficiency in this text; for those, if such exist, are entirely my own responsibility. Even so, I naturally sincerely thank Nicola and Hugh Loxdale of Brambleby Books for the editing of the original text.

# Contents

| | | |
|---|---|---|
| Chapter 1 | The Molossian Way | 9 |
| Chapter 2 | Realm of the Klithi hunters | 50 |
| Chapter 3 | Krevvati's treasure | 86 |
| Chapter 4 | The gift of Goura | 115 |
| Chapter 5 | Karteros and the Bear's cradle | 146 |
| Chapter 6 | The Forest of Ghio | 171 |
| Chapter 7 | The Meadows of Magoula | 202 |

| | |
|---|---|
| Chronology of climatic and associated changes on Tymphi | 225 |
| Principal Sources | 227 |
| Combined Index and Species list | 229 |

# Chapter 1

# The Molossian Way

Stiff from a night on unyielding ground and chilled by a down-draught from snowy heights, I shifted uneasily in my sleeping-bag, reluctant to face the unfolding dawn. Weary limbs reminded me of the previous day's long walk from the plains of Ioannina, to this my overnight resting place below the monastery of Rongovou, on the southern flanks of Mount Tymphi. Whilst climbing the steep slopes of Mitsikeli, with the mountainous bulwark of Albania rising before me to fill the north-western sky, I had paused to gaze reverentially southwards beyond Ioannina towards distant cloud-wreathed Tomaros, guardian of Dodona and of the oracle of Zeus which had guided the ancient world for more than a thousand years. There too, amidst the patchwork of fields spread below me, was the site of Passaron, where in 307-306 BC Pyrrhus, who traced descent from Neoptolemus, son of the Homeric hero Achilles, was at the age of twelve proclaimed King of the Molossians. As I resumed my ascent I had been conscious of walking in the footsteps of those transhumant shepherds who had acclaimed his enthronement. For the route I was following, still used today by their spiritual, if not filial descendents, the Sarakatsani, would lead to the Molossian summer mountain pasturage and the lands of their then Macedonian neighbours, the Tymphaeans.

From the summit of Mitsikeli it had been an undemanding meander towards the rising sun and the depths of the Vikos Canyon, before the ascent beyond Kepesovo and Vradeto to where, on rounding a mountain spur, the magnificent sweep of the Tymphaean massif draws the eye northwards. I had travelled that way before, and would do so many times again, into the realm of Zagori, 'the place beyond the mountain' as the Slavic name enticingly portrays. Here, the land between the Voidomatis and the Aoos Rivers, homeland of the Sarakatsani and Arumani, is a remnant of the natural world where bear, Wolf and Imperial Eagle still survive in an environment nurtured and moulded by the millennial-old pastoral practices of a former nomadic people. I had come, in the early summer of 1991 once more to this Greek mountain fastness, to wander its wooded sanctuaries, karstic slopes and frost shattered summits in awe of its floral wonders, to witness again the grandeur of the Lammergeier's flight, the shimmer of the Swallowtails' wing and to savour those moments of ancestral fear and exultation which only lone encounters with the wilderness can provide.

Below, the waters of the Skamneliotikos flowed swift and clear, not so swift that I could not ford the shallows with ease, but sufficiently so to know the snows on Tymphi had been heavy that winter. Meltwater travels quickly through the cavernous limestones of the mountain, and here, below the village of Tsepelovo, the river was ice cold, even now in mid-June. In the pale light of dawn the distant summits of Kousta and Koziakas lay like blackened beached hulks on a lake of mist above the eastern limits of the valley where Black Pine darkly forested the slopes, whilst to the south Aleppo Pine cast a torn and tattered paler mantle over deeply eroded hills of brick-red shale and sandstone, denuded of ground vegetation and with a meagre soil barely shrouding the lithological skeleton beneath. Before me a patchwork of coppiced hazel and oak scrub, impenetrable but for the incursion of grassy breaks and clearings, rose skywards to the village and curved upstream towards Skamneli, the only other habitation in the valley.

As I lay, still drowsily inert, the sounds of emergent day filtered through the somnolent accompaniment of wind and water. A distant mechanical coughing signalled the reluctant awakening of a heavy diesel engine. Foresters from Skamneli, off for a day's logging above Laista in the upper reaches of the Aoos River, their departure heralded by a cacophany of village dogs. As the rumblings of the lorry faded into the distance, the peace of dawn returned to accompany the call of a Woodlark. Often I have lain at the edge of sleep listening to that wonderful mellifluous song. The unpaired male birds habitually sing before sunset, but it is early morning from well before dawn on warm, windless and often moonlit nights when their performance attains perfection. In the sepulchral silence, those mellow melancholic tones so perfectly crafted into a series of descending phrases, each subtly different from the next, each slowly gaining in volume and tempo, invoke thoughts of Edward Thomas's *The Unknown Bird*, seeming to come from beyond the edge of this world, 'As if the bird or I were in a dream.'

It would be some time before the sun's warmth reached the slopes where I lay, so I was soon up and ready to move on. Shouldering my pack, it was a short descent to the Xatsiou Bridge which carries the *kaldereemee,* the old stone-paved way from Kipoi to Tsepelovo, across the Skamneliotikos. Pausing for a moment in crossing, as doubtless many had done during the two centuries since construction of the bridge, I wondered what thoughts those travellers might have entertained whilst lingering here to contemplate the scene. Merchants upon whose activities the prosperity of Zagori was founded, perhaps returning home from trading in Bessarabia, Constantinople or Moldova, would have been unlikely to have seen much change other than perhaps in the immediate vicinity of the village. The same tranquil natural scene they had left on departure would have been here to greet them on their return. For much of history the pace of environmental change has been sufficiently slow to have appeared insignificant within an individual's lifetime. Cumulatively however, the effects have been profound.

Reappraise the scene with a more forensic eye and within a more extended time frame, and gradually this verdant landscape dissolves in ones mind's-eye into a place of cold, watery, stony desolation, its unremitting greyness broken only by the glassy greens and blues of icebergs newly released onto a melt-water lake. Sounds are elemental, of wind, water and ice in motion. A wall of crevassed ice darkly discoloured by rock-dust, the snout of an eight-kilometre-long glacier sweeping down from the Tymphaean heights through where Tsepelovo is now situated, dams the lake at this very place, creating an outflow torrent of such erosive force that it has cut a deep, narrow gorge through what had been a massive rock barrier, now behind me. Such was the scene 450,000 years before, during the time of the Skamnellian glaciers. Now the Skamneliotikos slides silently and dimly into that same defile, spanned by the arch of a small stone footbridge, and continues westwards into the wooded Vikaki ravine unseen even by the now shuttered eyes of the monastery poised above. Upstream, the smooth rounded limestone boulders and outcrops in the stream bed are welcome stepping stones for negotiating the narrower steep-banked sections, where the waters have undercut the slopes to reveal the sands, gravels and boulders deposited during that glacial episode. Many of these limestone boulders were scarred and scratched during their ice-bound journey and some are impressed into the finely layered silts of the lake bed, having fallen from the melting icebergs which had carried them. The imprint of those times is deeply incised into the fabric of the mountain.

There is as much pleasure in revisiting old haunts as there is delight in discovering that which is new, a motivation which led me downstream from the Xatsiou Bridge on a short diversion. A tributary tumbling steeply down from the springs at Tsepelovo, although much obscured by dense scrub, is the seasonal abode of a spectacular and rarely seen nocturnal amphibian. Carefully searching amidst the more irregularly sculpted streamside rocks I soon found what I was looking for. The intense yellow spots and elongate blotches on a jet black background are the unmistakable and extraordinarily vibrant colouration of the Fire Salamander and a warning of the copious noxious skin secretions which irritate the mouth and eyes of would-be predators. With such a languid demeanour and somewhat doleful facial expression, it is difficult to associate this creature with so much legend and folk-lore implicating it with fire. However, its propensity for taking refuge in the cavities of wet logs would have fed the imagination of many a fireside assembly, witnessing its seemingly miraculous emergence from the flames. Here also, usually concealed beneath the edges of streamside rocks or floating conspicuously with limbs outstretched in shallow pools of the river, is a small warty toad of subdued but variable colour. Catch one, and in the palm of your hand it will voluntarily invert itself to expose a bright yellow or orange belly, another warning of distasteful and irritant cutaneous secretions. Gregarious and often prolific, the Yellow-bellied Toad provides a pleasant choral interlude during spring and summer evenings, wherever there is permanent water on the mountain. Here, however, it must contend with a far superior songster, as the clear liquid phrasing of a Nightingale descends from a streamside thicket below the village spring.

Continuing to the narrow chasm through which the river flows, there is a rock terrace above the footbridge providing an elevated view of the ravine beyond. This is a dark and chilly place during early morning, requiring patience and fortitude from the observer to elicit nature's rewards. Arrowing fast and low over the long deep pool below, a small dark, rather rotund bird suddenly jinks from its trajectory to alight on rocks at the waters edge. Here the white throat and breast beneath a brown head and above a dark chestnut belly confirm it as a Dipper and in affirmation of its identity it dips its body repeatedly and flashes its white upper eyelids in nervous response to my presence. Remarkably, the bird can walk submerged along the stream bed, turning over stones for small insect prey, whilst maintaining progress against strong currents by using both tail and wings for underwater propulsion. I recall vividly that when on a previous exploration of the upper reaches of the Skamneliotikos I heard what sounded like a gunshot, as a Dipper rocketed out of a pool a few metres away, the bird's wings having hit the waters surface with such percussive effect that I nearly fell into the pool in surprise. With perhaps less than a hundred pairs remaining in Greece, this is an infrequent avian encounter.

Although the prospect of coffee at the *magazee* in Tsepelovo was increasingly enticing it was too early to make my way up to the village. This place had for long been in my mind as a suitable location for Otter, as the ribbon of water below, otherwise invisible except from this vantage point, was one of the few deep permanent pools and an ideal place for a chance sighting early in the morning or late evening. I had seen spraint, the characteristic black tarry mixture of scent-gland secretion and faeces of otters, on rocks along the Skamneliotikos and further downstream along the Voidomatis River in previous years, and yesterday in a detour into the Vikos Canyon below the Kokkorou Bridge had found some sufficiently fresh to retain its sweet smelling odour. Otters are solitary most of their lives and often have linear territories of tens of kilometres, feeding mostly at night whilst moving from one lying up place to another between their permanent holts. In Greece, as in much of the Mediterranean, they are not primarily fish eaters, unlike their more northerly relations. Here, the Noble Crayfish, Greek Stream Frog, Dice Snake of which there are many in the rock pools, small mammals, freshwater crabs and a variety of small freshwater invertebrates are the main diet. Only when there is sufficient water flow to allow the incursion of Brown Trout and two species of Cyprinid fish, known to occur in the Voidomatis downstream from the Vikos Canyon, would these be available as potential prey.

With my back to the rockface to avoid creating a silhouette, I hunkered down to watch for a while. The quiescence necessary in situations like this has, for me, never been difficult to sustain. Stillness and silence, coupled with the necessity for alertness to sound and movement, with time, heightens powers of perception. Elsewhere I might listen for the tapping of a foraging woodpecker, the seed-cracking of a desert jird, the rasping breath of a leopard, or watch for the involuntary flick of an antelope's ear, whilst here I waited for the emergence of dark spots on the water which might betray an otter's secretive presence. A state of heightened expectancy can lead to illusory perception. When the wish to see is sufficiently intense, we readily see that which is not there. That sudden swirl at the pool's bouldery edge, that momentary dark shiny undulation in the shadowy undercliff, could so easily be mentally transformed into our desire. Disappointment should not tarnish a vigil unrewarded; all the better to accept the absence of that wonder and exhilaration which a successful outcome would have given.

The dawn mists had now dispersed from the upper valley as I made my way back along the riverside track towards the

Xatsiou Bridge. That single arch of some seventeen metres span, and of utilitarian design, speaks eloquently of those who built it in 1804, even if in name it commemorates only the Tsepelovite financier. The previous day I had taken refuge from the midday sun in the shade of the limestone cliffs which frame the Noutsos or Kokkorou Bridge, further downstream, where the Skamneliotikos emerges from the Vikaki ravine to join the Voidomatis River. As on so many other occasions, I had stood on the adjacent modern bridge in contemplation of the older masterpiece which, in its single attenuated arch, seems to defy the physical laws of this world. With a length of nearly twenty-seven metres, and abutments built on a rock base four metres above the riverbed, the centre of the arch soars thirteen metres and is so slender at its apogee as to seem barely capable of supporting anything of substance. Yet function was not subjugated to aestheticism, as for over 200 years it has borne travellers and merchandise between Kipous and Koukouli. Noutsos Kontodimos, whose wealth brought the bridge into being in 1750, was perhaps a pragmatist who simply wanted to facilitate trade, as the river would otherwise have been impassable during winter floods. It was the *Kioproulides*, the fraternity of master masons, whose collective skills fashioned the creation, who possessed the vision of beauty in form and sculpted it in conformity with its surroundings. Lesser sensitivities would have simply imposed a bridge; they carved out the base of the cliffs on both sides to form a frame for their work of art. There is a wonderful harmony of forces in these structures, such that the resistance and support provided by the abutments and spandrel walls exactly counters the lateral forces from the arch. Without that equality there would either be insufficient pressure to hold the keystones of the arch-ring in place or an excess which would force them skywards, both with disastrous consequences. The location of the Noutsos Bridge also imposed an asymmetry in construction, with the abutment of one side being greater than the other, producing an imbalance in the forces applied to the arch which if not compensated for in some way would result in collapse. This, too, is elegantly resolved, by piercing the larger abutment with an arched aperture, thus reducing the excess mass and consequential force. That the architects and builders devoted the same attention to building the Misiou Bridge two years earlier, a little further downstream, and to the construction of seven hundred other bridges throughout the region of Epirus, is testament to their skills and deep understanding of the relationship of form and structure to physical laws.

Although anonymity is the fate of most artisans, other than the signature which their works inscribe, it seems many of them came from villages whose names, Pyrsogianni, Kipseli, Kotili, suggest a shared origin for their genius confined to the upper reaches of the Sarantaporos River, close to the border with Albania. Why this should be, one can only speculate, as it is difficult to reconcile the nurture of sophisticated technical skills and aesthetic sensibility with such a remote upland region. The builder of the extraordinary thirty-six metre single-span bridge over the Aoos at Konitsa, Ziogas Frontzos, in answer to enquiries of the source of his success, after the failure of Ottoman engineers, attributed all to 'the University of Pyrsogianni', the village from where he and many of his fifty workmen came. Perhaps on dark nights the shade of Thales of Miletus touched the village with his practical genius. To more superstitious minds it was the life of some unwitting and unfortunate passer-by, across whose shadow the foundation stone was laid, which ensured acceptance of the bridge by the *genius* of the place. Better this than the live interment of the master-builder's wife as told in the song of the Bridge of Arta.

Returning beyond the Xatsiou Bridge, one's visual perspective reverts to a more expansive frame as the scene accommodates the slopes leading up towards the village.

Enhanced by the penetrating shafts of light from a low sun, the initial perception is impressionistic, of extensive woodland brushwork in apple and lime greens, contrasting with a meadow foreground of multi-hued floral stippling. Perhaps for many this is how the natural landscape is perceived; as broad-brush splashes of colour with pointillismic indications of finer detail. Only when the eye alights on some incongruous colouration in an otherwise uniform composition is something of interest perceived. Much is unseen except by the eye already attuned and alert to the multitudinous possibilities of what may be there. How else can some wander through such a scene as this and see little, whilst others see so much.

Swaying gently to an intermittent breeze, proud of the meadow grasses, the variously tinted, bright magenta, clustered flower-heads of a *Dianthus* ebb and flow, like flotsam on a turning tide. The deeply serrated petals of the component flowers, flecked with fine white hairs, are spread and reflexed in justifiable assertion of their floristic splendour. I have seen plants like these in the mountains of Bulgaria, Turkey and elsewhere in Greece, and all seem attributable to either a single highly variable species, *Dianthus cruentus*, or else to one of many closely related species. Here the assembly could be apportioned into a generally taller and more robust *Dianthus giganteus* and a slender *Dianthus cruentus* of limited stature, each with subtle but distinct floristic differences. However, some would be difficult to assign to either species. Such are the characteristics of plants which are undergoing rapid evolutionary change; they do not permit definition by immutible criteria and are a reminder that they – and we – live in a dynamic, ever-changing world. Less prominant amidst this floral conclave but imposing in form were the knee-high pyramidal, bristly, densely flowered inflorescences of *Echium italicum*. Reduce your perspective to that of a single branch and you enter a menacing thicket of glassy siliceous spines juxtaposed with pale pink, lilac and ice-blue, frilly edged trumpets of a most delicate hue. The fruit, a tiny intricately sculpted nutlet, was, in a related species, the inspiration for naming these plants *echion* due to the nutlets resemblance to the head of *echis*, a viper. That this affinity was probably recognised in Greece as early as the fifth century BC indicates the discriminatory mores of that time, as the nutlets are only two millimetres in diameter.

The meadow ripples to a momentary gust, revealing the pale pennants of resting Black-veined White, Clouded Yellow and Heath Fritillary butterflies clinging to the taller grasses and flower-spikes. Myriad points of violet, purple and blue appear and reappear within the verdant fray. Many are the violet-blue, wide-eyed bells of *Campanula patula*, the Spreading Bellflower, others the curious mop-headed spikes of *Muscari comosum*, the Tassel Hyacinth. The terminal cluster of violet globular flowers on slender violet-blue stalks are splayed above a column of brown, creamy-yellow-tipped bells and betray the bulbs which have been prized as food in Greece for at least two millennia. Although the hyacinth is ubiquitous in the wild, its abundance in close proximity to a village hints at past cultivation. Even more prolific here are the violet-stemmed spikes of *Anacamptis (Orchis) morio*, the Green-winged Orchid, numbered in their thousands this year but not always so as the plants usually die after flowering, although seeding very effectively and achieving maturity in only a few years. I have seen them from here upward to beyond the village in vast numbers as early as mid-May. For long, the Green-winged has imbued the ancient pastureland of Europe with a violet-purple haze and was for generations of country-folk one of the wonders of springtime. Here the abundance may again reflect past cultivation, as the tubers of several orchid species were used under Ottoman influence to make salep, a nutritious drink, and in earlier times for various medicinal purposes.

A short deviation down to the river led to another group of dark-stemmed orchids, taller and more robust than the Green-winged, growing in saturated ground and with large lustrous carmine pink flowers. Imposing as each spike of *Anacamptis (Orchis) palustris* may be, it is in the detail of the individual flowers wherein lie much of the fascination and beauty of this and so many other orchids. The aesthetic is only as seen through our eyes however and is accidental, a mere coincidental to the prime purpose of procreation, and even that is achieved by deceit. To the newly emerged naive bees which pollinate *Anacamptis (Orchis) morio*, the Green-winged, the flower has the markings, invisible to our eyes, and form of a sage, dead-nettle or similar nectar-rich flower, but as the orchid lacks nectar and offers nothing else to recompense the visitor, the bees move on quickly to another, thereby transferring pollinia and inducing fertilization. The bees learn the true sources of nectar in time, but for the orchid the ruse is successful. Likewise with *Anacamptis (Orchis) palustris*, which attracts the pollinator by ultra-violet patterns on the lip, mimicking those of an unrelated nectar bearing plant, again achieving pollination by subterfuge.

Whilst immersed in such a floristic microcosm, there is little that is likely to intrude, but a short, metallic, high-pitched call from upstream did so. A shrill, staccato utterance is perhaps consistent with the restless, skittish temperament of the Grey Wagtail, constantly flitting, running and jumping amongst boulders in pursuit of winged insect prey which it puts to flight by incessant tail wagging, or delving into shallow water for insect larvae. The birds have young to feed at this time of year; the nestlings hidden in a riverside rock-crevice or tangle of roots. Handsome, lithe and graceful birds, the grey uppers of the adults assume a dark bluish or olive sheen as they move; the undersides lemon-yellow, brightly contrasting with black and white tail, wings and facial markings. This bird has the buff-white chin and throat of the female; the male sporting a distinctive black bib.

After retrieving my pack from a temporary resting place I joined the rutted road which now traces the route of the former *kaldereemee* towards Tsepelovo. This side of the river nothing now remains of the intricately stone-paved surface which had borne away all those far-travelling, enterprising sons of Zagori and returned them in later life, often as men of wealth, culture and learning. Reputedly someone with influence and progressive tendencies had recently contrived to bulldoze the route. Now the track meanders at an inclination which reflects the sensitivities of those who built the *kaldereemee* but in a condition which comments upon the values and times of those who destroyed it. This apart, the landscape does not speak loudly of human activities but whispers of generations who lived in concord with the land, in harmony with its seasons, in conformity with its demands. An expanse of long-abandoned coppiced Hazel, *Corylus avellana*, tells of the ring of the woodsman's axe; dense, intensely browsed thickets of Kermes Oak, *Quercus coccifera*, of the whistles and imprecations of the shepherd and goatherd. The early inhabitants of Tsepelovo had a refined and well-adapted system of subsistence farming based on stock rearing and forest exploitation in which the scarcity of land suitable for crops reduced agriculture to a subsidiary role. What are grassy clearings on these slopes may once have grown wheat, barley, oats and rye, lentils, pea and vetch, some now naturalised still growing alongside plants which were the weeds of those fields. Now, what little remains of those abandoned cultivations provide, where woodland shade would otherwise prevail, havens of light and islands of natural diversity.

A careful search of the edge of several clearings reveals a scarce local variant of the Early Spider Orchid, *Ophrys sphegodes* ssp. *epirotica*, which like most *Ophrys* species normally flower in April, May or even earlier but here close to their altitudinal limit, linger into June. Even with a clear mental image of their form to guide the searcher, they are easily overlooked. It is the much enlarged and conspicuously coloured labellum or lip, a modified petal, which gives most European orchids their distinctive appearance and in *epirotica* this is dark reddish-brown, yellow fringed, with a central lustrous blue double-barred speculum. Attracted by scent identical to that emitted by female bees, male bees of the same species wrongly identify the speculum from reflected ultra-violet light as the wings of a potential mate and alight, orientating themselves accordingly. Although duped into mating activity usually for only a few seconds, the positioning of the insect is so precise that pollinia already attached to its head and acquired from another flower, deposit pollen on the stigma, whilst simultaneously pollinia are detached from the anthers of the host flower, ready but for one final adjustment, for transfer to another plant. The newly attached pollinia are held vertically on their stalks but, as cells on the undersurface of the stalk dry and shrink in minutes, re-orientate into the exact position for contact with the stigma of the next plant to be visited, thus ensuring cross-fertilization. This remarkable mechanism is replicated by most of the species of *Ophrys* in Europe, the main differentiator being that for each the pollinator is a different species of bee, wasp or beetle. Emerging from the concentration necessary to find such otherwise insignificant plants one becomes aware of others visually much more prominent. Here the stony, dry ground is laced with the trailing leafy stems of a rock-rose, *Helianthemum nummularium*, bright with its many delicately petalled, yellow flowers, accompanied by tufts of a conspicuous catchfly, *Silene fabarioides*, each flower a pale, violet-veined, inflated calyx from which tiny white petals protrude.

Leaving the former *kaldereemee*, I turned along a familiar route through the mosaic of coppice and clearings, at times following goat-tracks, at others tractor and forest roads, towards Skamneli. The village does not command the same attention as its larger and more enticing neighbour, Tsepelovo, but the call of voices from the past is stronger here. The derivation of its name implies a 'seat' as befits the natural amphitheatre in which it sits and it looks southwards from an altitude of 1,160 metres over the Selio valley 'the place in the sun'. What more appropriate setting could have been chosen for the extraordinary structure to which I am now drawn. Immersed in a dense dark thicket on the western edge of the village is the Palaiokastro, of three-metre-high stone walls forming all that remains of what was probably a rectangular tower. The limestone blocks of which it is comprised are each of many tons in weight, and are precisely cut and laid without mortar such that the joints will not admit even a knife-blade. Amidst such monumental masonry the sense of 2,800 years accumulated *genius* of place is overwhelming, for this has a Homeric ancestry. No plebeian people of unelevated mind built this. The grandeur of form is the manifestation of a grandeur in concept. Its location is such as to allow surveillance of the valley and to control what must have been an important route across the Pindos range, between what was then Molossia to the west, and Macedonia and Thessaly to the north-east and east. Perhaps the infant Pyrrhus was brought this way during his momentous escape in 318-317 BC into Illyria, as it would have provided a direct route from Passaron to the safety of Macedonian Parauaea beyond the Aoos River. The dramatic event involved just such a river crossing. Centuries before, Neoptolemus, who was reputed by the poet Pindar to have come ashore on the coast of Epirus at Ephyra near present-day Parga, may also have passed this way, on his journey from Troy to the oracle at Dodona and then to his easterly homeland of Thessaly.

Appropriately, the Palaiokastro is one of the few places where I have seen the western form of the Large Whip Snake and the species known from as early as the fifth century BC as 'the guardian of the home', the natural manifestation of the *genius* of the house. Being fiercely cannibalistic, the snake will kill and eat any other snake, including the highly venomous Nose-horned Viper, locally common on the mountain. The *genius* of the house was sacrosanct and never to be disturbed or frightened, even less evicted or harmed, for fear of terrible reprisals to be visited on the perpetrator. Thus the practical virtue of tolerating a snake which would eradicate any other serpent intruder into the home was reinforced by superstitious belief. Perhaps the snake I saw was a descendant of the *genius* of the Palaiokastro.

Standing alone amidst these walls is to invite evocations of this place from as far back as the ninth century BC, the possible time of its construction and a time when Molossian cattle and sheep breeders are known to have established at least one permanent settlement on the Tymphaean massif, at Genitsari near Vitsa ten kilometres to the west, and which they occupied until destruction by fire in the fourth century BC. Their houses were of stone and timber and they were buried in stone tombs accompanied to the afterlife with rich funereal possessions and bronze weapons. Perhaps the defensive walls of this edifice had resounded to their shouts and the clash of their weapons when in 385 BC and again in 360 BC the Illyrians ravaged the region. Such calamities apart, it is probable that life for these farmers was peaceable much of the time and the mountain scene they enjoyed was not dissimilar from that which we see today. The cattle which now crop the riverside vegetation and browse the woodland above Skamneli do so at a comparable altitude to that of Genitsari, whose inhabitants probably utilised the mountain similarly, as the Molossians were famed for their stock breeding. The mountain slopes above and up to the summits were then, as now, largely open grasslands but perhaps with remnant swathes of virgin coniferous forest periodically exploited as a source of timber for which that of *Abies alba*, Silver Fir, and *Abies cephalonica*, Greek Fir, was highly prized. Both tree species were significant components of the forests on Tymphi around 2700 BC, but by the first century BC Greek Fir had disappeared and Silver Fir was greatly depleted.

Vestiges of two defensive stone towers attributed to the third or fourth century BC indicate continuance of occupation at Skamneli possibly as part of the boundary reinforcements of Molossian territory initiated during the reign of Pyrrhus. Further occupation of the village is evidenced architecturally by the remnants of two monasteries, that of Agia Paraskevi built in the twelfth to thirteenth centuries, and of Agios Nikolaos established in 1683 and by a few traditional Zagorian mansions of the eighteenth and nineteenth centuries. These solid rectangular stone-walled and stone-roofed merchants' houses reflect the wealth of those who prospered from the trading dispensations Zagori enjoyed during part of Ottoman rule. Although many of the finest houses from this period were destroyed in 1912 during the Balkan War, some of those which remain still retain the carved wooden ceilings and wonderfully colourful frescoes which adorned the interiors of many Zagorian homes of that time.

The vicissitudes of human existence would inevitably have broken the thread of continuous occupation here as elsewhere on the mountain, as it did in 168 BC when 150,000 Molossians were enslaved into the Roman empire after defeat of the Macedonian forces at the battle of Pydna and in more recent times when the village was all but abandoned during the Civil War of the late 1940s. These depredations apart, it is probable however that a populous existence has been maintained here for most of the last two and a half millennia at least. In 1688, the community was estimated to have been comprised of 1,000 inhabitants with another 800 in adjacent hamlets, whilst later village records indicate a population of 950 in the second half of the eighteenth century. For earlier times it is the vegetational history and the consequential characteristics of the flora of the mountain which suggest the former extent of human presence and activities.

The walk from Skamneli to Tsepelovo is less than an hour, and the steep and narrow stone-paved way curves upwards into the *plateeya*, shaded by a magnificent plane-tree, stepping back in time as the village is architecturally much as it was in the eighteenth and nineteenth centuries. Some of the traditional stone-built mansions have fallen into disrepair, but many have survived intact and are clustered around the church of Agios Nikolaos adjacent to the *plateeya*, in spiritual and temporal duality. Once seated outside Alexis Gouris's *magazee* there can be few who have rested here and not been entranced by this setting and perhaps pondered on the contrast between the restless febrile world outside and this tranquility within. Tsepelovo was reputedly founded in the sixteenth century, although its Slavic name suggests an earlier origin. It became the administrative centre of Zagori in the eighteenth century and, like its peers, has the appearance of having grown out of the meagre soil. All the stone of which it is built has come from the mountain and course upon course of its construction appears as if in stratified congruity with the natural outcrops. There are labyrinthine rocky places high on the massif where, when shrouded in dense mist, the similarly layered natural stone exposures invoke images of ruinous walls and pillars of some long lost civilization. Perhaps the Epirot masons had similar visualizations guiding their work, for those who built the inner walls of these mansions laid *batikes* or binding stones in conformity with those who built the outer, thus creating integral pillars every metre or so to strengthen the high walls. They were clearly very confident of the resistance of those walls as the heavy stone tiles used in roofing were pitched at surprisingly low angles, thus retaining the metre or more of winter snow accumulation apparently without undue stress. Perhaps the masons shared the same faith in divine providence as those gifted iconographers from nearby Kepesovo, who in 1753 decorated the church of Tsepelovo with its artistically acclaimed frescoes.

I had little time to wait before I heard the sizzle of saganaki frying in the kitchen and smelt the aroma of brewing coffee, even less before it was on the table and Alexis was talking enthusiastically about all the rain since Easter and how wonderful the flowers were on the mountain. There had been seventy centimetres of snow that winter, just like the old days, he said, so grazing would be good for the sheep and the shepherds would be happy. This was my fifth consecutive visit to Tymphi, so Alexis knew by now of my obsession with the place and already my regular base-camp in the valley above the village was known as 'the place of the English'. After buying whatever provisions Alexis had to spare, I crossed the *plateeya* beneath the spreading branches of the great Plane tree, still unfurling its spring-green foliage, and followed the steep stone-paved ascent to the imposing guesthouse of my friend Theofanis Tsavalias. Fanis was a kindred soul, a man of the mountain, and knew the secret places where few venture. He would bring me fresh provisions to the Goura Spring in four days time.

Leaving the village northward by the old route in the valley floor, it is not far to where a broad track turns eastwards up the scrub-covered slopes, to meet a stony mountain road constructed to provide seasonal access to the *stanee*, the sheepfolds above Skamneli and Tsepelovo. Before the short climb, I had paused at the dew-pond in the valley meadows to watch the Red-rumped Swallows busy collecting brick-red mud for their nest building and repair. Effortlessly inscribing the air with broad sweeps, long glides and soaring ascents, they can only shuffle precariously when on the ground but sufficiently to scoop up a mud pellet before fluttering skyward. For the villagers these quietly chattering neighbours are the welcome harbingers of summer. Now, although still early morning, the impending heat of a cloudless day was becoming evident and already insect life was heralding that prospect. It was my intention to go no further than the 'place of the English', a kilometre or so further up the valley, as I was still weary from the previous days exertion and longing for the relaxation of pace and contentment which companionship with the natural world bestows. This valley is a place which trekkers destined for Vrisochori or Papingo on the far side of the mountain, pass through in minutes, attending only to the next footfall, impatient for the next vista. Yet for me it was a home-coming, a place where I knew every stone, every plant, every scent and sound, and was my portal to the mountain. It could have been elsewhere as there are similarly worthy places, but serendipitous circumstances had favoured this above others.

Arriving at my old haunt, I was reminded of Alexis's effusive account of the mountain flora, for this was a scene I had never witnessed before at this place and, as subsequent visits would reveal, I would not see again. For now, the normally short grassy sward of the terraced valley floor was ankle deep in flowers, a swathe of multi-coloured forms and textures humming with bees. I knew the flowers as commonplace and widespread in Europe and beyond, but associated and in this profusion the assemblage made a memorable sight. Dense clusters of large pink, red-veined blooms of *Geranium macrostylum* and sulphur-yellow *Potentilla recta*, a cinquefoil, were the suns and planetary giants of this floral cosmos with myriads of the tiny white Daisy, *Bellis perennis*, the galactic stars. There were lesser lights too. The bright reddish-purple discs of a large-flowered form of the Dove's-foot Cranes's-bill, *Geranium molle* ssp. *brutium*, whorls of the minute pale-yellow flowers of a bedstraw, *Cruciata laevipes*, and sprays of a bright pink-sepalled milkwort, *Polygala nicaeensis* ssp. *mediterranea* variously enhanced the scene. More deeply embedded were the reddish-purple funnels of Purple Gromwell, *Lithospermum purpurocaeruleum*, which age to a dark blue, a plant of significance if only because of a close relative first discovered as recently as 1969 high on Tymphi and subsequently on only two other mountains. First encounters with the rare and spectacularly beautiful are never forgotten, so whenever I see a species of gromwell I envisage the azure-blue twinned pin-cushions of *Lithospermum goulandriorum* glinting like sapphire encrusted jewels snagged on the white limestone cliffs which nurture them. Thankfully the plants are accessible only with great difficulty as there are those who covert such gems.

After stowing away my backpack amongst a boulder pile I allowed the surrounding scene once more to exert its influence, thankful there were no fresh man-made intrusions into the landscape. Rumours of plans for ski facilities periodically arise even here, a prospect which induces temporary dread whenever I round the headland above Rongovou Monastery and gaze on the full extent of the southern slopes. I always look for the red and white zig-zag scars which would tell of a new and devastating onslaught, a new roadway tearing into the bleached bones of the mountain, bleeding its blood-red soil. I fear I would turn away on seeing such despoilation, never to return. Ironically however, this meadow is man-made, being the lowermost of a succession of low-walled terraces which without human design would not exist, the thin soil being otherwise liable to transport down the valley during times when snow-melt and rain exceeds the capacity of the subterranean drainage. For centuries the terraces were maintained and cultivated but in the mid-twentieth century were abandoned to seasonal pasturage for sheep and have been occupied by vegetation well adapted to colonising virgin ground. Human intervention then was on a scale which nature could accommodate with ease, not so now.

The valley floor here is perhaps a hundred metres wide and bounded to the west by a sheer-walled limestone barrier which extends northwards for five kilometres with only a single break, to end at the valley head beneath the summit ridge. At its furthest limit this cliff forms the 400 metre-high eastern face of Krevvati, a 2,400 metre-high flat-topped mountain clearly visible against the northern sky. Smoothed and rounded in places by the erosive force of rock debris embedded within glacial ice, the rock face has also been deeply gouged by huge boulders similarly transported, locally creating ledges as here above these terraced meadows, ledges now crowded with flowers. To the east the valley is bordered by the steep slopes of a glacial moraine, rock debris abandoned at the valley-glacier edge, extending southwards from the isolated 2,169 metre-high flat-topped ridge of Kourtetsi at the head of the valley. Once narrowly terraced for cultivation, those morainic slopes are now harvested by the villagers of Tsepelovo for a tea, the soft grey leaves of *Sideritis raeseri*, a plant confined to the mountains of Western Greece.

There are few trees at this altitude of 1,260 metres on the southern slopes of the mountain. Veteran *Juniperus foetidissima* stand in solitude, wrapped in their dark apparel of odoriferous needles, amidst the goat-chewed remnants of scrub oaks above the village. On dank days of low cloud the trees loom from the mist as if the shadowy apparitions of Sarakatsan shepherds in their great black capes of homespun goat-hair. The species of *Juniperus* is now as infrequent a sight in Greece as are the dark-cloaked nomads but there are some well-established stands of the trees, at least elsewhere on the mountain. More evident here are the aged survivors of a onetime extensive scattering of walnut trees, some still flourishing but many exposing gaunt grey leafless limbs which now nurture new life in the form of the nestlings of hole-nesting birds, even as rot and disintegration take hold of their hosts. Within a few minutes of my arrival I hear the scolding of Sombre Tits which habitually occupy a favoured tree nearby, always utilizing the same knot-hole in which to nest. The Walnut, *Juglans regia*, grows naturally as a component of the forests on the upper slopes of the Vikos Canyon, so these fading remnants, above Tsepelovo, could be the progeny of former indigenous forest trees.

Water sources are few on these fretted and honeycombed southern limestone slopes. Here a spring emerges from a sandstone and shale capping, providing a strong flow during spring and early summer following generous winter snow. After replenishing my water supply at the gushing outlet piped down to a trough for sheep from above the adjacent cliff, I set off for a walk in the vicinity. Below the water trough a seemingly barren and unattractive area of stunted scrub extends southwards to a pine plantation immediately above the village. Although visually unenticing, areas like this, invariably adjacent to long established mountain communities and utilised for centuries for animal fodder and bedding, kindling and firewood, often attract enterprising plant species. Perhaps it is the constant disturbance of top-soil and removal of competitors which presents opportunities for such colonisers.

A stony gully just below the lowermost meadow is one of the few locations I know on the mountain for *Astragalus creticus* ssp. *rumelicus*, a spiny shrub which forms dense tussocks covered in clusters of purple-pink pea flowers. Further down the slope another low-growing shrub, *Daphne oleoides*, grew in abundance, its tiny sweet-scented, creamy-white-four-rayed flowers attracting the Silver-Y and other day-flying moths. Appealing as these flowering shrubs are, my attention was primarily focused on finding two orchid species which I knew occur here. However, I am not the only one being attentive and my presence soon elicits loud, ringing calls from that strange bird, the Wryneck, a pair of which habitually breed in the vicinity. Mottled grey and buff-brown, thrush sized and with a long tail, they are oddly reptilian in behaviour, spending much time on the ground where they hop with a jerky gait, crest and tail raised, and with sinuous head and neck movements search for ants which they gather with a flicking tongue. As they also hiss like a snake it is understandable they were known from at least as early as the third century BC as the snakebird and acquired mythological status. To the Molossians the bird was the moon's messenger to Zeus and Aphrodite's love charm. Yet another beneficiary of the ageing walnut trees, the Wryneck lays its white eggs in naturally formed holes and cavities without constructing a nest.

Returning from this distraction, to my quest for orchids, I soon located several dense clumps of the slender, dark-stemmed *Orchis quadripunctata* which here display many tiny intensely violet-pink, long-spurred flowers, the three-lobed lip of which usually bears two or four dark violet spots on a white base. Nearby were a few robust spikes of *Orchis tridentata* with compact conical heads of purple-spotted and streaked, lilac flowers, each with distinctive upwardly tapering, similarly coloured, long-pointed sepals. A passing glance or a superficial appraisal would relegate these plants to the pretty but inconsequential status which is the fate of much of nature to a casual observer, but the reward for a more inquisitive and appreciative sensibility is considerable. These flowers are exquisitely formed intricate structures of great beauty. The outstretched violet-pink sepals and lip of *Orchis quadripunctata* appear as delicate as the finest porcelain and equally vulnerable, even more so the occasional pure white form which sometimes grows here. With the flowers disposed in a lax cylindrical spike, each appears as if an individually mounted ceramic treasure on a presentation plinth. First impressions of *Orchis tridentata* are, however, of the whole composition and only with closer scrutiny does the extraordinary intricacy of structure and form of the component flowers become apparent. Each is an exotic dancer with a flared floral skirt, outstretched arms and hooded peaked headdress.

Just as the behaviour and appearance of the Wryneck suggests a strangeness or other-worldliness even to those who are not particularly familiar with the diversity of birdlife, so is it also true of the flowers of another small spiny shrub which occurs here. Often confined to stony ground and stable screes, the inflorescence of *Drypis spinosa* has a structure unlike any other in that the tiny white or pale pink flowers are marshalled into rectangles which cover the surface of the loosely branched plant in a geometrical mosaic. In that structure can be seen the ranks of the Greek foot soldiers, the hoplites of antiquity, who fought in unison with interlocking shields to such devastating effect. For both the bird and the plant, their strangeness is due to being relict species, survivors of ancient evolutionary lineages, alone in their retention of unusual characteristics as their contemporaries died out.

With approaching midday and a clear sky, there was only a transitory cooling breeze from the snow-covered summits to appease the burning sun. The sweet scent of *Daphne* mingled with that of crushed thyme and but for the hum of indeterminate insect activity all was silent. Looking westwards over the stunted shrubbery of the slopes I had climbed earlier that morning and across the lowermost valley floor, I studied the far cliff face for signs of one of nature's most majestic sights. There is a narrow tree-lined cleft cutting deep into the cliff and it is here at the base of a protruding trunk that a pair of Imperial Eagle had constructed a huge stick-nest the preceding year. It may seem surprising that such birds should nest so close to a village, where sight of human activity must be a daily event, and yet this is a characteristic of the species. Habitually fearless of man the birds have paid a heavy price for that trust as they are near extinction throughout much of Europe, due largely to persecution and even this pair were destined to disappear four years later. Their very presence was unusual as they normally choose lowland habitats to breed. Did one or both come to grief on migration to or from East Africa or attempting to over-winter in the lowlands, or was it at the hands of a trophy hunter or poisoner nearer to home? Whatever the reason the skies over Tymphi will perhaps never again be graced by their effortlessly soaring silhouette and recklessly plunging descent onto unsuspecting prey. For now, I was pleased that my binoculars had helped confirm the presence of one of the birds stolidly perched on a branch adjacent to the nest. I would watch for them later in the day hunting for hares.

Although Imperial Eagle are inclined to rest in the midday heat, there are those for which the sun induces action. I had earlier been following the flight of a large white or pale yellow butterfly in the meadows below and, as it was now ascending the slopes towards me, began to observe it more closely. The flight was not that of a female Cleopatra of which I had seen several during the morning, and now as I saw it periodically glide in long sweeps, pausing only to flutter at the blossom of some remnant fruit-trees, I knew it must be a Scarce Swallowtail. They are seen quite frequently in the valley of the Skamneliotikos and the Vikos Canyon wherever their larval foodplants, Blackthorn and other *Prunus* species grow, the males, with wings closed, imbibing from wet mineral-rich sediment, the females, with wings partly open or fluttering, nectaring from shrubs and flowering herbs. This was a female, which apart from being slightly larger is otherwise very similar to the male. With a wingspan of around six centimetres and a series of six black stripes on the forewing and two on the hindwing, against a pale yellow to white background, they are very striking in flight. Seen closely, the black scalloped edge of the hindwing, which terminates in a slender black white-tipped tail and a blue-centred eye, crescent-edged in orange, displays exquisite detail. These are nature's prima donnas and how well they fulfil their role.

Having found the two species of orchid I had been keen to see, I headed westwards towards the cliffs and to an area of scrub and broken rocky ground where I knew there were other interesting plants which should be in flower at this time. Throughout, the stony substrate was bright with the yellow rockrose, *Helianthemum nummularium*, which I had seen earlier in the day and which appears to thrive on meagre soil as does also a subspecies of St. John's Wort, *Hypericum rumeliacum* ssp. *apollinis* with its large bright yellow flowers crimson-stained beneath. Also here in this seemingly hostile rocky terrain were a few purple-flowered mats of *Aubrieta scardica*, the tiny four-petalled white-eyed flowers so numerous that the pale green leaves were almost obscured. This is a plant more at home near the summits where it forms tight compact cushions, but here less constrained in form, has a place perhaps due to seeds brought down in meltwater. Nearby and vying with it in brilliance of colour were trailing stems and loose mats of a soapwort, *Saponaria calabrica*, with startlingly bright rose-pink flowers, the whole plant covered in sticky glandular hairs. Together this pioneering and restorative quartet wove a colourful and complex pattern into the broken and pallid limestone fabric, tracing and healing the red soil infill of rock fracture and fissure.

It was here too that I encountered a butterfly which, although limited in stature, excels in character and beauty. Disturbed from where it had probably been resting with wings wide open to regulate body temperature, a small bright fulvous brown form suddenly darts upwards and circles in a succession of glides and brief flutterings to land on bare red soil just ahead of me. With wings fully open it is barely discernible, as a complex pattern of black spots, lunules and irregular markings divert attention from its outline already indistinct against the red earth. Wait awhile, however, and its wings may close to reveal an extraordinarily beautiful pattern of shining silver, dark-rimmed spots amidst a tracery of dark veins on the underside hindwing. This was a newly emerged male Queen of Spain Fritillary, one of the characters of the butterfly world as it has an insatiable curiosity for butterflies of other, often wholly unrelated species, erupting from its resting place to greet them as they pass. Females are similar in appearance but often less conspicuous in behaviour as they tend to flutter irregularly, low over the ground in search of violets, the larval foodplant.

The otherwise continuous cliff face is interrupted here, at a point where it has been displaced laterally, allowing a steep climb and access to the mountain west of the rock barrier. A rough but well worn path leads up this incline and through a narrow gully, to emerge above the clifftop. Although now rarely used by anyone other than local shepherds, this path must have been utilised for centuries by villagers for access to pasturage and possibly as the beginning of a route across the mountain to Papingo at the northern end of the Vikos Canyon. In places the way is paved with highly polished limestone slabs and is cut into the rock outcrop suggesting a vintage which could long predate Tsepelovo's origins. In walking this way perhaps I am following in the footsteps of those Molossian shepherds as this would have been one of their few means of access to the high western pastures.

When on the cliff top it was timely to sit and survey the scene from the vantage point often used by Kestrels which habitually nest nearby. The narrow valley enclosing the terraced flower-filled meadows below rises in increasingly high-rise steps between flat-topped Krevvati and Kourtetsi towards the summit ridge, a north-west to south-east oriented, saw-toothed edge linking a fifteen kilometre long line of peaks to form the northern limit of the Tymphaean massif. Beyond lies a precipitous drop into the Aoos valley. None of the summit ridge north-west of Krevvati is visible from here, but further south-east the 2,466 metre-high summit of Goura with its massive cliffs and southerly extension, Kato Tsoeka, dominates the horizon, sloping down to the 2,157 metre-high peak of Tzoumako at the eastern limit of the ridge. Eastwards my gaze encompasses the karstic limestone slopes above Skamneli, and the upper reaches of the Skamneliotikos with the isolated twin peaks of Kousta and Koziakas rising from dark encircling forest. Beyond and extending south-eastwards to flank the headwaters of the Aoos River, the similarly forested mountains of the main Pindos range trace the far horizon. Perhaps those Molossian shepherds paused here too and bartered stories of what wonders lay in those distant Parauaean lands.

Returning to the path, I retraced my steps to where it is possible to scramble down to the terraced meadows below, through a steep boulder and scree-filled gully. Part way down, and secured to the vertical rock-face beneath an overhang, is the remarkable conical nest of Rock Nuthatch which has probably been utilised by successive generations of the same family for decades. I avoided passing too close as it would certainly be occupied at this time and most likely with newly hatched young. The cone is constructed of dried mud, reinforced with feathers, beetle wing cases and other natural debris, protruding some twenty centimetres or so from the rock-face and contains a nest chamber at the end of a long narrow tunnel accessed from the point of the cone. As the cone base is at least thirty centimetres in diameter it is a monumental structure, remarkably constructed by the male bird alone. Soon after I arrived at the foot of the screes the loud trilling call of one of the adults revealed it flitting nervously from rock to rock at the top of the gully, periodically flicking its tail and bobbing like a Dipper. They are dapper, cocky, stout little birds, with a powerful bill and short tail; the body blue-grey above with white to cream underparts, and buff-tinted flanks and vent. A bold black eye-stripe is foremost in drawing ones attention. The short strong legs and long, sharply curved claws enable them to climb rocks and search cracks and crevices for insect prey with ease. It is fascinating to watch them exploring boulder screes in their quest for food, often disappearing for minutes before re-emerging many metres away from where they first entered.

As there were several bushes of *Drypis spinosa* at the base of the screes, I approached cautiously not wishing to disturb any butterflies present, the flowers being especially favoured as a rich source of nectar. A small brilliantly reddish-orange butterfly was transfixed in the pose of imbibing from the pale pink blooms, with wings fully spread to reveal a transient violet sheen. The pale grey undersides of this male Purple-shot Copper remained unseen but would have disclosed a complex pattern of black dots and orange lunules. Similarly contrasting in colour but abundant on the nearby pallid screes were the rich violet-blue salvers of a bellflower, *Campanula ramosissima*, startlingly bright against the white limestone. Being in need of a rest and some midday sustenance, I headed for the dappled shade beneath the fresh-leaved walnut trees at the edge of the meadows. With a tree trunk as backrest and a bed of flowers at one's feet, the joy of solitude amidst a mountain scene like this cannot be quantified, just savoured moment by moment. It can, however, be difficult sometimes to exclude those contrary associations one may have with a place and here I am often reminded of images created by an aged shepherd I met here several years before. We shared little in language, but in graphic mime he told me of how, as a youth, he had narrowly escaped with his life when machine-gunned by a fighter-plane during the Second World War. Only the huge boulders at the cliff base had saved him by providing protection from the ricochetting bullets. He appeared to have survived his experience unscathed and he had the countenance of a man very happy with his lot in life, and I recall a feeling of some empathy as I listened to him talking quietly to his sheep as he led them from the watering trough up the old way and onto the mountain, the way I had walked earlier that morning.

Now I welcomed the soporific influence of midday heat and embraced for a while the role of casual observer, with the full extent of the meadow in my visual compass. In hindsight, events seemed to have been compressed into such a short time span that I must have drifted in and out of sleep as the time appeared wholly occupied by a kaleidoscopic succession of butterflies. The variously ocherous-coloured forms of several species of fritillary, principally Heath, Spotted and Knapweed were most prominent, their upperside wings heavily marked in chocolate-brown, but beneath the hindwing an illuminated medieval stained-glass window with all its delicate tracery and rich shining colours. At times and as if to mesmerise any onlooker, male 'blues', those thumbnail-sized gems of the butterfly world, flashed azure and violet, pewter and powder-blue, confetti-like over the flowery stage. Idas and Mazarine Blue were the lesser thespians, Adonis the greater, a brilliant shimmering cloud of azure and cobalt blue. Itinerant players in bright orange-yellow, black-rimmed apparel, the Clouded Yellows of the cast, settled for a few seconds before exiting rapidly northwards, onwards and upwards to larval foodplants and beyond. Inveterate wanderers, they periodically disperse in yellow clouds from their Mediterranean and North African strongholds into Europe, one of the great migrations being in 1947 when they were observed crossing the Channel to England in huge numbers on a fifty-mile front. Periodically the low fluttering, rather ponderous progression of a largish dusky-white butterfly would also intrude on the scene, this being the Clouded Apollo, another abundant presence at this time of year heading for the southern karstic slopes where the larval foodplant *Corydalis densiflora* grows. A scuffling amongst some dead leaves immediately diverted my attention to nearby stony ground, where a small long-tailed lizard was busy searching for insect prey. The alternating, narrow pale and broader dark, longitudinal stripes indicated this was Erhard's Wall Lizard, which, contrary to that suggested by the name, is a ground lizard averse to climbing.

On resumption of my wanderings, I was inclined to stay on the now shaded side of the valley for a while longer. Here the knee-high leafy stems of an asphodel, *Asphodeline lutea*, elevated dense spikes of bright yellow flowers amidst the rocks and meadow-side trees, whilst an even taller mullein, *Verbascum longifolium* ssp. *samaritanii*, projected its pale-yellow flowered inflorescences skyward to shoulder height from large lanceolate basal leaves. Much of the mullein is covered in a dense coat of yellowish-white filamentous hair which has traditionally been used as a wick in oil lamps. At the other extreme in stature, a tiny grape-hyacinth, *Muscari neglectum*, sprinkled bare stony patches with its pale-blue-tipped spikes of otherwise violet-blue globose flowers. Also here, but showing a preference for the semi-shade beneath the walnut trees, were the large pale yellowish-green campanulate flowers of *Helleborus cyclophyllus* borne in nodding clusters on robust leafy stems above newly emerging segmented foliage. More at ease in woodland semi-shade, its presence here is indicative of former forest.

Whilst moving further along the base of the cliffs, I was about to emerge from the trees when I heard the high-pitched calls of a large flock of Alpine Chough and simultaneously observed them descend onto the uppermost terraced meadows. There were at least two hundred individuals in the flock and their approach was an enthralling sight, a beautifully choreographed undulating stream of coal-black aerial dancers. They are graceful, elegant all-black crows, glossed purple and green, with short yellow bills and red legs, and highly developed social characteristics reflecting their gregarious habits. Listen carefully and the shrill contact calls emitted in flight change abruptly to a double note on landing and then a subdued chorus of chittering, churring and warbling as they busy themselves feeding. What appears to us as just a large flock of birds feeding is in reality a highly structured hierarchy in which females are subservient to unpaired males and both subservient to the high status paired males, and all expressed in the calls they emit. That musical chorus is not the exultation of bliss we might wish it to be; rather it is the mechanistic expression of social bonding necessary for their gregarious existence. If they exhibit some freedom of expression perhaps it is when they indulge in their spectacularly acrobatic aerial displays when flocks glide and soar to great height before tumbling earthward in a frenzy of apparent playfulness.

As I continued to watch the birds feeding, it was soon apparent that there were also a few Chough present, distinguished by their longer, curved bright red bills, vermilion coloured legs and more vivid sheen to their black plumage which flashes a brilliant glossy blue and purple on the body and green on the wings and tail. Their behaviour also differs in that they run, walk and hop with greater poise and purpose and, strangely, can jump sideways. Periodically and for no apparent reason, the whole flock would rise in a chorus of contact calls and float silently a few feet above the ground until breaking out into another chorus followed by silence, before settling again to feed. Throughout this manoeuvre the Chough were almost continuously vocal, emitting their more musical notation whilst also breaking ranks from the otherwise close formation. Such is the fascination of observing nature in detail, every species having its unique characteristics, dependency on the environment and interrelationships with its associates. Choughs use their long bills to probe, Alpine Choughs to search and unearth. Both rely upon extensive areas of treeless upland to provide insect and larval food during spring and summer, and an abundance of berries and grain in winter. Any disruption to the complex dependency these birds have on their food sources and they will disappear.

After watching the flock for some time, I emerged from the cover of the trees, knowing the birds would move a short way up the valley, and continued to where some of the cliff face ledges are accessible. Here the meagre screes are veined with the yellow, white, shell-pink and violet-mauve flowers of the stonecrops, *Sedum acre* and *Sedum album*, of *Thlaspi perfoliatum* and the Alpine Calamint, *Acinos alpinus*. However, it is the rock ledges which harbour most of the more fascinating plants and in compositions which would brighten the countenance of any floral artist. Foremost to my eye are the pendent stems of a knapweed, *Centaurea pawlowskii*, which arise from a tuft of silky-haired basal leaves and terminate in radiating florets of a lovely pale violet. In Greece this is found on only one other mountain. Also spilling over the lips of the ledges are the crinkly edged leaves of a plant which supported by its woody creeping stems, forms a prase-green backcloth to its large pink or mauve-pink blooms. Look more closely and each is seen to be a compact bouquet of smaller five-petalled, true flowers, the outer ones fringing the whole in a circle of protruding petalloid wings. This is *Pterocephalus perennis* ssp. *bellidifolius*, confined to sub-alpine regions of north-west and Western Greece, and Albania. Of lesser bearing amongst the ledge-top vegetation are the white-rayed, many-flowered clusters of a fragrant yarrow, *Achillea abrotanoides*, atop short stems rising from a mass of finely pinnate basal leaves, another highly restricted species found in Greece on only three mountains. In association is a close relative, *Achillea holosericea*, which has dense terminal clusters of pale yellow-rayed flowers above silvery basal leaves and is confined to high mountains in the south and south-west Balkans. Extending yet further this parade of floral distinction are a few tall, much-branched crucifers with numerous pinkish-lilac, yellow-eyed flowers; *Malcolmia orsiniana* ssp. *angulifolia* again highly localised and confined to the Balkans. As visually enticing as this assemblage may be, one's eye is however inevitably drawn to two other far more imposing species which occupy the higher ledges. Here are the huge pure white funnels of the Madonna Lily, *Lilium candidum*, borne on metre-high stems, and the equally substantial violet-blue, yellow-bearded blooms of *Iris germanica*, similarly imperious.

Further up the valley beyond the terraced meadows, the thin stony soil nurtures a vegetation limited in variety but which will soon produce a transformation in colour and form. A fleshy, densely leaved prostrate spurge, *Euphorbia myrsinites*, already attractively blue-green with bright yellow-green bracts, is generously interwoven into the ground cover everywhere. Less conspicuous is the spiny-toothed foliage of *Eryngium amethystinum* with newly emergent, similarly spiny, thistle-like flowering stems. Within a few weeks the spurge will turn a darkening salmon-pink and the eryngo inflorescence a brilliant metallic blue, colouring the slopes progressively almost to the summits. Crossing to the eastern sunlit slopes, I climbed to the high ground of the morainic ridges which run south down towards the Skamneliotikos and the Selio valley. Beyond, shadows were beginning to infill the hollows and sharpen the edges of distant ridges and summits far to the horizon. With the sun now low over the heights of the western massif, any movement on the slopes and in the valley below would be accentuated and minutely discernible. It was whilst scanning the wooded slopes below Skamneli that I first caught sight of the familiar form, unmistakable even at that distance, of the Short-toed Eagle circling and hovering above the stony ground adjacent to the river. With powerful downbeats of the long, narrow fully extended wings, only the dark upper plumage was revealed, rendering the birds progress difficult to follow across the shadows. Only during the often prolonged bouts of hovering, as it searched for reptilian prey, did the white underparts appear, flashing brilliantly as the high-angled wings were momentarily caught by the sun. A mature adult seen at close quarters in flight appears pure white beneath, although flecked and barred dark brown, whilst many are dark-headed as if enveloped in a hood. When observing the beautifully sinuous, hovering wing motion, with the rippling wingtips inscribing a figure of eight, it is impossible not to envisage that traditional dance of the eagle, the *Zeibekiko*, in which the often lone dancer, with arms outstretched, slowly encircles an imaginary antagonist. Perhaps those very same Molossian shepherds who had acclaimed Pyrrhus their king had also so often gazed in wonder at this hovering avian apparition and instinctively extended their arms and similarly stepped to the music of their time. It would have been a fitting presentiment as Pyrrhus was to be known as the 'Eagle', the one who swooped unerringly on his enemies.

It is moments like this, when events elicit speculation of former times and of former inhabitants, that one wonders how this scene would have differed from now and how those people perceived the landscape and conceptualised their relationship with it. We so easily forget that what we see is what we think we see and that visualization is largely culturally derived. At the end of the fourth century BC, those Molossian shepherds would most likely have experienced a physical landscape much as it is now but with a mosaic of pasture and deciduous woodland extending further up the slopes than it does now and similarly so into the upper reaches of the Skamneliotikos where presently there is almost continuous woodland. From the upper limits of the woodland to the summits it would have been largely herb-rich grassland on karstic limestone pavement much as it is today. The success of the Molossians in animal husbandry was in part attributed to an ability to pasture their cattle and sheep in the mountains during spring and summer when lowland meadows were parched and lean. For them the Selio valley with its spring-fed river would have been a prime location in this otherwise largely waterless terrain. If a stock-raising settlement could be maintained by the Molossians at Genitsari for several centuries it seems probable they would have done so here too and what better place than at Skamneli where fortifications were long established. The indications of former terracing, now overgrown, in the valley between Skamneli and Tsepelovo suggest land which was at least capable of pasturage in Molossian times even if the terracing is later. Although terracing was practiced in lowland Greece from before the fourth century BC, there is no evidence of it being applied in mountain environments at such times.

As livestock farmers the Molossians would have viewed the mountain as a source of sustenance for their animals, even with the constant threat of wolves and bears to contend with, but beyond that any resemblance to our present-day perceptions of the landscape ends. The over-riding reality was that the mountain, the *oros*, for they spoke a Greek dialect, was the domain of the gods and pre-eminently that of Zeus, reinforced in the Molossian mind by the proximity to Dodona the principle oracle of the god. To be on the *oros* was also to expect an encounter with the great god Pan, albeit far from his Arcadian haunts, to be ensnared in an Oreads whirlwind or beguiled by a Nereid, and pity the man who offended the Dryads of the forests or the Naiads of the waters. All that was encountered was imbued with metaphysical meaning and all events were considered manifestations of the supernatural. The *oros* possessed, for them, a significance which we can theorise but not experience and yet being here, alone, devoid of most of the trappings of modern living, there are moments when it seems possible to hear faint voices and share thoughts from that distant past. Unshackle the imagination and temporarily suspend all notions of contemporary understanding of the world and the existential gulf between now and then seems lessened.

Much has been surmised about the quality of the light in Greece, of its intensity and of how it imparts a vitality and uniqueness to everything it touches. Colours seem more densely saturated, pure and vivid, objects appear elevated and more sharply defined, as if backlit by an intense source of illumination. All that you thought you were familiar with can suddenly appear as if seen for the first time, revealing qualities of which you were previously unaware. Perhaps it is the high incidence of reflection from the white limestone, so evident in much of Greece, which produces these effects, but whatever the cause the consequences can be an unsettling challenge to the senses. In response it is not surprising that so much in the natural landscape was bestowed with the mythical powers they were and why in Zagori until recent times it was said of the three great Fates, who inhabit mountain caves, 'one Fate spins the thread, the second apportions good fortune and the third bad'. It was a brave or foolish man to be out on the *oros*, especially at night and alone, a thought I quickly put out of my mind in view of my intentions.

Despite the ever-lengthening shadows I was still inclined to wait in anticipation that an Imperial Eagle would launch an evening foray. Although they are known to be partial to large snakes, lizards and even tortoise, their preference here is probably for Brown Hares and for medium-sized ground birds such as Rock Partridge. Although normally nocturnal browsers, hares are often active during the cool of early morning and late evening throughout the summer months and have several litters, so they are a ready source of prey. It was not long before I saw one of the birds circling upwards out of the valley above Tsepelovo and turning eastwards over the ridge directly below me towards the great expanse of karstic grassland above

Skamneli. Perhaps because of the low sun the distinctive pale yellow crown and nape appeared silvery-white against the dark upper plumage, as did the pale off-white base of the tail. As its trajectory was direct, the flight was fast with several powerful downbeats between short glides. Only the hands of the wings and tips of the primary flight feathers were upturned and the tail slightly splayed. The bird was gone as quickly as it came and, although I waited in the hope it would begin to search the slopes below, it did not return. It would quarter the mountain grasslands methodically, with short downbeats and long glides on flat wings, until suddenly drawing in its wings to dive or drop with feathered legs extended and talons spread onto its luckless prey. The shrill scream of distress is the only sound a hare makes, but the end is swift, impaled on long crescentric claws in a bone-crushing grip.

The exhilaration that follows such an event helped speed my descent, so I was soon back in the valley meadows with time for my overnight preparations before nightfall. It had remained cloudless and calm throughout the day and with just a little cloud now spilling over the northernmost summit ridge there was promise of a clear night sky. I would make my resting place for the night, beneath the lip of the eastern morainic ridge, where there was a good view of the western sky, well above any cold down-draught from the snow-flanked summits. With a clear sky, even at this moderate altitude, the temperature falls dramatically when the sun dips below the horizon. After securing a bag of food high in the branches of a tree I climbed to the ridge summit and prepared a place for the night. Already there was a dull red glow where the sun had been above the western horizon, and the sky was darkening beyond the peaks of Kousta and Koziakas in the east. In the meadows below, the white-furred wands of the mulleins appeared ghostly in the gathering gloom. Soon the silence was interrupted by different sounds to those of the day, as the denizens of the dark began to stir. A Woodlark recited its now familiar liturgy from a treetop above the village and another more distant, perhaps the same bird I had heard at dawn, struck up in rivalry as dusk drew its mantle across the landscape. Abruptly, a Nightjar began its strange unworldly undulating churring call, always difficult to locate but seemingly emitted from high in a nearby tree. Later I heard the periodic clapping produced by vigorous overhead impact of its wings as the male bird traced a circular flight over its territory. There will be a scrape of bare earth nearby in which the female will lay a clutch of speckled and spotted eggs. Being familiar with the place and its natural inhabitants I was not surprised when a Scops Owl in clear ringing bell-like tones began its metronomic monologue. In mid-June at this altitude and location the birds are probably incubating, this being a male proclaiming its territory whilst the female is lodged in a treed nest-hole. Although the female can emit a similar call, it is higher pitched and less persistent. Whilst some find the repetitiveness of the male's call rather trying, as it can continue without a break for thirty minutes or more, and be maintained until the small hours, I find it pleasantly soporific. Nature's substitute for counting sheep.

I was, however, far from contemplating sleep, as the first indications of a spectacularly starry sky were beginning to appear and from this elevated position I had a far more expansive view than that of the previous evening when adjacent to the Skamneliotikos. Now, a thin crescent moon, burnished by the receding sun, was brightening in the west, just clear of the clifftops and beneath the brilliant shining orb of Venus and the lesser one of Jupiter. Although I searched with binoculars for the faint red glow of Mars which would have formed the apex of a triangle, of which the other two planets were the base, it was undetectable at this time. That revelation would wait for a vantage point at greater altitude from where such a 'Grand Conjunction' of the three planets would be clearly visible.

Observed from here all would be below the horizon within half-an-hour. Having settled for the night, what better canopy could there be than this celestial array, and none more appropriate than the brilliant star Arcturus soon to be directly overhead, for this would have been a guiding light for those Molossian shepherds. They moved between plains and mountains in part according to its progression and would also have gazed knowingly from beside their nightime fires at the Pole star now above the head of the valley and the Great Bear crowning the summit of Krevvati. Perhaps that knowledge of the constancy of the stars provided some reassurance to counter fears of godly caprice, sufficient to allow them an untroubled sleep, a state of composure I was soon able to share.

# Chapter 2

# Realm of the Klithi hunters

The western clifftops were already sunlit when I awoke amidst the dissolving shadows, so I was quick to move onto the ridgetop for that welcome warmth. The far away descant of a lone Woodlark and the gentle churring of a neighbourly Nightjar were my sole audible companions. I was thankful not to have been disturbed during the night by the barking of village dogs, distant as they were, as speculative forays by wolves sometimes cause raucous pandemonium when alien scent arrives on the wind. Not that such an occurrence would merit much concern as my few observations had always been of solitary animals loping across the southern slopes late in the evening, there being insufficient numbers to support roving packs. However, my precautionary measure of placing provisions well away from where I slept was in recognition of these and other potentially unwelcome night-time visitors.

As I intended completing the initial ascent during the coolest hours I was soon on my way through the scrub below the terraced meadows towards the old, partly paved way to the clifftop but had not gone far before disturbing a male Red-backed Shrike which had adopted a leafless branch on one of the walnut trees as a vantage point. The bird is neatly attired: blue-grey crowned and mantled above, rufous backed with a white throat and pink underparts. Although attractive in appearance, there is an air of malevolence too as it habitually rotates its long white-edged black tail whilst perched, watching and waiting. It has a heavy, black, hooked bill and a black facial mask, curiously in character as it is a 'highwayman' of the bird world, waylaying the weak and vulnerable and impaling them in a thorn bush larder. Here its prey will be largely grasshoppers and beetles, but if they become insufficient to feed its young then other birds and their nestlings will be imperilled. The female is probably now incubating eggs low down in a nearby juniper bush.

A little further and as expected, the ever-watchful Wryneck unleashed a ringing tirade upon the valley. Why they should advertise their location so loudly and do so when perched conspicuously on the very tree in which they have eggs or young is bemusing. However, whilst pausing to watch and listen for a while, it did alert me to another of the birds which are so dependent upon the walnut trees, for there fluttering in the canopy of one of the larger trees, picking insects from the leaves, was the sparrow-sized Lesser Spotted Woodpecker, a black and white, barred and streaked bird, just as frequently occupied creeping along branches in search of prey. Unlike other woodpeckers, it has a small insubstantial bill and requires well-rotted wood, both for extracting larval food during winter and for nest hole excavation, so is reliant upon these aging trees. During this temporary halt a persistent rustling from beneath a nearby tangle of vegetation disclosed the rather battered and scarred hulk of a large and venerable Marginated Tortoise. With a strongly flared rear margin to the elongate carapace and pale yellow centre to each of the otherwise black plates, these are creatures of distinction. This is about as far north as their range extends and, being such ungainly animals, one can only admire their ability to survive in such a harsh rocky environment.

Whilst climbing the path to the clifftop I had paused in the hope that the Imperial Eagles were evident but, seeing the regular perch unoccupied, I assumed the male at least was away hunting as is usual early in the day. Beyond the spring which provides the piped water supply to the troughs in the valley below, the way turns abruptly up a steep bank of rapidly eroding shale to where it is more stable and at this time of year covered in a grassy sward. Here were the robust densely flowered spikes of *Dactylorhiza sambucina* in the two colour forms typical of this orchid, one various shades of yellow and the other a vivid magenta. Amongst them were a few plants with purplish-red, less compact flower spikes resembling *Orchis mascula*. With so few other flowers present, these strikingly colourful orchids understandably commanded attention. However, it was to the drier, more exposed margins of this shale and sandstone outcrop that I was drawn, where scattered on loose mats of tufted foliage were the exquisite bright pink flowers of *Dianthus haematocalyx* ssp. *pindicola*. The serrated almost frilly-edged petals are straw-yellow beneath and arise from a purple calyx on short procumbent stems, a composition for which the bare brown, shaly substrate provides a most appropriate setting. This beautiful plant, here clinging so precariously to life, is known from only a few mountains in northern Greece and Albania.

My route now followed what in places was a distinct path but more often was lost in the wandering trails woven by sheep and goats over the centuries. As I knew the terrain intimately, direction was not a concern, so I meandered between limestone crags and grassy hollows drawn by whatever colour and form was of interest whilst progressively rising towards the northwest and the Megas Lakos, a major tributary of the Vikos Canyon. From there I would follow the southern lip of the tributary ravine to an overnight destination on the eastern edge of the Vikos. The terrain for much of the ascent is very stony with sparse vegetation and little topsoil, most of what remains being confined to solution hollows and clefts in the limestone. It was not always like this. In a few places where recent erosion has cut deeply into the substrate there are vestiges of a more generous soil with the remnant roots of what had been substantial trees. What is now a great expanse of treeless, almost barren, stony and rocky hillside rising westwards from the village was, in part at least, once forested. Of the few plants which do remain here most are more usually associated with woodland clearings and margins. Both of the orchid species seen on the shale outcrop are so inclined as is also a third, *Orchis ustulata*, the Burnt-tip Orchid, of which there is a single colony of fifty or so plants, the objective of a deviation from my otherwise direct route. The compact cylindrical spikes of small white-lipped, scented flowers are crowned with dark burnt-red unopened buds, hence the common name. Look closely and you will see a throng of purple-spotted, white-costumed pierrot with outstretched arms, such are the intricacies of the flowers.

Although by now the sun's progression had long subdued both Woodlark and Nightjar, all was not silent, as the distant call of a Hoopoe drifted up from the valley below. This, the territorial call of the male is as exotic a sound as is the appearance of the bird, with a purity and clarity of tone which belies the monosyllabic *poop, poop, poop* of its utterances. Few could hear this call and not be intrigued by its source and none be enthralled more on a first encounter. In flight it alternately spreads and closes its wings, exposing and hiding the black and white barring as if a huge butterfly with a cinnamon-pink body, whilst on the ground it periodically fans a black-tipped long-feathered majestic crest. With a long curved bill with which it probes for insect larvae and pupae, it is one of the wonders of the avian world. Requiring naturally occurring cavities in trees for its nest sites, it too is reliant upon the old and decaying walnut trees of Tsepelovo.

Within an hour most of the ascent was behind me and when I came to a familiar narrow gulley fringed by columns and walls of finely laminated limestone I knew it would not be far to the Megas Lakos. Here the thinly layered rocks provide in their cracks and crevices ideal anchorage for the plants of natural rock gardens, a white-washed canvas upon which nature exercises its inexhaustible palette. Hanging in festoons were the palmate leaves of *Geranium macrorrhizum*, beset with clusters of large, rose-pink flowers vivid in the slanting rays of the early morning sun. The true glory of this plant appears elsewhere on the mountain, amongst boulder screes and shaded fissures and crags where the stout branching rhizomes are free to erupt into great billowing masses, often metres in extent. Revelling in this freedom, the plant has evolved an endless variety of subtle shades of pink, red and purple and is similarly adventurous in both form and structure too. Back in the gully, wedged tightly into shaded crevices, were the dark green, rugose leaves of *Ramonda serbica* forming rosettes from which arise large violet bells on leafless stems. This and four other closely related species found in Europe are the sole representatives of their kind from warmer pre-glacial times, their near relatives now being largely confined to tropical climes. Also tucked into cracks and crevices here and on most crags at this level were numerous greyish-green compact leaf rosettes beneath the short, stout, nodding reddish-purple flowering spikes of *Saxifraga porophylla* ssp. *federici-augusti*, a saxifrage confined to the Balkans. Here too adding contrasting hues to this already colourful scene were the bright yellow-rayed discs of *Doronicum columnae* and the creamy-white, red-spotted floral sprays of another crevice saxifrage, *Saxifraga paniculata*, above clustered rosettes of lime-encrusted, obovate leaves.

Emerging from the upper end of this enchanting cleft, it is not far to the edge of the Megas Lakos where a well worn sheep-track is intercepted and followed south-west to a small dew-pond, at this time frequently attended by House Martins busily collecting mud for nest construction. They will have a colonial nest site on the cliffs of the Vikos Canyon. After climbing one of the nearby crags I sat for a while, this being the first opportunity for views westwards down the full length of the Megas Lakos to the Stouros, the limestone plateau west of the Vikos and north-westwards to the massive bulk of 2,436 metre-high Astraka. The dry stream-bed of the Megas Lakos some 200 metres below was earlier in the year fed by meltwater running southwards from the slopes east of Astraka and the peaks of Karteros and Gamila on the main Tymphaean summit ridge. From my vantage point the ravine turns abruptly westwards, falling a further 650 metres over a distance of five kilometres to its junction with the Vikos and the Voidomatis, in a canyon with near vertical walls for much of its 800 metre depth. One's senses need time to adjust to this magnitude of scale, perhaps more so because of the absence of trees in the foreground. There are trees, forests of them, but at such distances and depths that they have the appearance of a uniform sward, a dark green verdigris on the pewter-grey limestone. It is only the dusting of isolated trees on the slopes at the upper forest limit which provide some comparative measure. Returning to my immediate surroundings, I knew that this and other crags in the vicinity were home to many of the crevice- and cliff-inhabiting plants already encountered and many others too. Here were large leaf-clusters of *Ramonda serbica* in full flower, but also tucked away on well shaded, often north and north-west facing rock walls, were dense hard cushions of the lime-encrusted foliage of *Saxifraga marginata*, covered in compact sprays of white-petalled flowers on finger-length stems. Most were in decline, with fading and falling petals, but still an impressive sight and indicative of what awaited at higher altitude for, although an uncommon species, there are many other localities on Tymphi where this saxifrage flourishes. Also, wedged into cracks and crevices, were the fleshy-leaved rosettes of *Sempervivum marmoreum*, some of which will produce stemmed clusters of pinkish-purple rayed flowers a month later.

Beyond the dew-pond I followed the edge of the Megas Lakos ravine wherever the terrain allowed access to the fringing crags and outcrops, as the established route habitually followed by sheep and goats meandering through the hollows, although requiring less exertion, offered limited incentive. The varied views of the ravine and tantalising glimpses of inaccessible hanging rock-gardens were a compensatory reward for the effort. Many of the plants in flower were of species seen elsewhere, some revelling in the cooler, shadier, more northerly facing aspect, especially the pinkish-violet cushions of *Aubrieta scardica* and rosy-pink curtains of *Geranium macrorrhizum*, although mats of *Pterocephalus perennis* ssp. *bellidifolius* were yet to flower. Sharing this preference for craggy vertigenous aspects, some flowers not previously seen or not sufficiently conspicuous elsewhere warranted attention. Pendulous masses of the strikingly bi-coloured trifoliate leaves of a cinquefoil, *Potentilla speciosa* var. *discolor*, locally festooned the rocks. The pale-yellow flowers, although attractive, were too sparse to outshine the foliage, a bright lustrous green above and white-woolly coated beneath. Here too were leafy clumps of a dead-nettle, *Lamium garganicum* with white and pink-flushed flowers, sufficiently variable to merit recognition of two or three subspecies on the mountain, this one closest to subspecies *laevigatum* with its many-flowered clusters. Far less conspicuous, although protruding abundantly from rock crevices, was a catchfly, *Silene parnassica*, forming dense tufts of linear foliage from which arose numerous slender shoots terminating in flowers with enrolled petals, white above and green beneath.

With the sun now sufficiently elevated to banish much of the early morning shadow from even the deepest parts of the Megas Lakos ravine, movement, however insignificant, was seemingly magnified when viewed from this lofty position.

Even the progression of Clouded Yellow butterflies far below could be traced as they alternately appeared bright against the greenery and then dissolved fleetingly into the pallid background of the limestone. There were other butterflies also: Orange Tip and Mountain Small White, but too distant to differentiate, and perhaps even a rare Eastern Orange Tip. Nearer at hand, the stillness of the gently undulating grassy slopes falling away southwards from the ravine rim was interrupted by the feeble flutterings of a solitary Apollo butterfly.

For the remaining distance to the confluence of the Megas Lakos with the Vikos, it was the prospect of the grandeur of that scene which drew me on, despite the many temptations to linger and explore the immediate surroundings. Besides, it was hot and tiring carrying an additional burden of several litres of water, knowing that there was none where I was bound, and under a cloudless sky it would be a welcome relief to reach my destination before midday. Between occasional pauses to scan with binoculars the flanks and floor of the Megas Lakos, I was increasingly drawn to the ever-widening view south and west. In walking westwards, I was completing half a circle and could look down on the route I had followed since crossing the Mitsikeli ridge two days before. Now the long spine of Mitsikeli occupied much of the southern horizon, an imposing reminder of its effectiveness in isolating the mountain enclave of Zagori from the Ioannina plain beyond. A tiny notch in the skyline towards the north-western limit was where I had crested the ridge, a crossing place which had been used by Molossian drovers and Sarakatsani shepherds for millennia, and from where the route down to the Voidomatis was clearly visible etched into the mountain side. From my elevated position the great expanse of ridged and deeply gullied terrain between Mitsikeli and Tymphi was now also partly in view, much of it newly forested but still scarred by the intense erosion to which this unstable shale and sandstone substrate is so susceptible. In the foreground, was the gullied extremity of the Mazaria Ravine, which at first runs south and then turns abruptly west to curl around the village of Vradeto tucked into the mountainside below, to a confluence with the Vikos. It would be difficult to find a more challenging location than that of Vradeto, bounded as it is by defiles on three sides and until the construction of a tortuous modern road only accessible by a stone staircase, the *Skala*, which climbs the wall of the Mazaria Ravine. The village owes its existence to an isolated water-retentive veneer of sandstones and shales which feeds the springs on which the settlement depends.

With my destination now in sight, I headed for the most prominent of the rocky shelves bordering the Vikos from where I would have the most extensive views of the canyon and of the immediate surroundings. Tracing the edge of the Megas Lakos accustoms the senses to the grandeur of this landscape, but even this does not lessen the awe and wonder engendered by a first view of the Vikos from such a vantage point. Perhaps inevitably, immediate attention is drawn to the thin, white ribbon of water-scoured limestone marking the course of the Voidomatis along the otherwise densely wooded floor of the canyon. Even with the heightened flow from the heavy snows of this last winter, most of the riverbed at this time of year is dry in this part of its course. The still considerable subterranean flow only appears intermittently, in rock pools, before surfacing as substantial springs towards the lower, northern end of the canyon. Whilst such detail may be the object of attention initially, it is the enormity and proportions of the whole which eventually transcends all else. From here, where the course of the river turns north-west from its north-south orientation upstream, there is a clear view of the whole eight-kilometre-long lower section of the canyon, incised up to a 1,000 metres, sheer-walled, through the flanks of the

Tymphaean massif with the bulk of Astraka rising another 1,000 metres above to the east. Massive screes long-stabilized since their accumulation during a period of severe cold between 28,000 and 24,000 years ago and now well wooded, sweep down from the base of 700-metre-high cliffs to confine the river locally into a secondary ravine as the process of down-cutting continues. From my vantage point, the western wall of the canyon is perhaps 900 metres distant, as the canyon narrows to half the width of its more northerly section and continues to constrict upstream for a further eight kilometres to where I had crossed two days previously. I had on that occasion sufficient time to walk downstream alongside the river to rock pools beyond the Misiou Bridge and so, as I settled down for a rest in the heat of midday, my thoughts were of what I had encountered during that detour.

It had been hot then too in the confines of that white-walled chasm, the still air, throbbing with the hum of insect life, in accompaniment to the soft undertones of the river. Upstream, near the village of Kipoi, the cold waters of the Skamneliotikos emerged from the Vikaki ravine to join those of the Voidomatis and passed beneath the arch of the Kokkorou Bridge and the parallel road bridge in a broad, gently flowing expanse of clear cerulean blue. Narrowing through a series of shallow pools, much of the water soon disappeared through the cobble- and boulder-strewn riverbed and into subterranean channels leaving little at the surface beyond the Misiou Bridge during summer months. As I made my way over the rocks alongside the river I was conscious of the soft, aerial chatter of the Crag Martins which habitually nest on the adjacent cliffs, now wheeling and cavorting in the shadows above the Kokkorou Bridge. My attention was, however, drawn more to what I anticipated ahead, and at a place where the path abuts the craggy slopes I found the magnificent but unobtrusive orchids which remain unseen by so many who pass this way.

The metre-high spikes of perhaps only a dozen plants were each crowded with up to fifty flowers, white and heavily veined and tinted in royal purple, each a finger-nail-sized hood, from beneath which extrudes a three-lobed lip, the centre a finger-long, cork-screwed, bifid tassel projecting outward from the main axis of the inflorescence. This is one of the lizard orchids, *Himantoglossum*, attributable to species *calcaratum* or *caprinum*. Nearby, immersed in the already sunburnt vegetation of rock ledges were the large white trumpets of *Lilium candidum*, the Madonna Lily, more accessible than those on the cliffs above Tsepelovo but still best viewed from below, as hornets regularly nest on these crags and will defend their territory aggressively. Far less evident and revealed only to an informed eye were the inky-purple spathes of *Arum petteri* shaded beneath adjacent scrub oaks. Here too, hidden in dense wayside growth, were the emerging stems of what will shortly be the knee-high floral towers of *Acanthus balcanicus*, an architectural construction of thirty or more flowers, each a purple-veined helmet overarching a short corolla tube with a projecting three-lobed white lip, subtended by a broad spiny green bract. The flowers resemble canopied balconies, each with a billowing white sheet draped over the retaining rails of a futuristic steely spiked tower. Callimachus the sculptor, of fifth-century BC Athens and Corinth was perhaps similarly impressed, as he used the form of the acanthus leaf as inspiration for his design of the capitals for Corinthian columns.

In places where the canyon floor is wider than the present river channel, one walks on the sandy, pebbly surface of an extensive former floodplain, the Klithi terrace, some three metres above the present riverbed. Strolling through this now idyllic grassy parkland of flowery meadows and woodland clearings, the many attractions which appeal to the senses understandably obscure the significance of that which is underfoot. But there lies a story with implications which extend far beyond these confines for the sands, gravels and pebbles which comprise this terrace were derived from the sandstones and shales exposed in that deeply gullied terrain seen extending south from Tymphi to Mitsikeli. Tributary streams of the Voidomatis carried the rock debris in times of flood during a three-millennial-long period which began around 4,250 years ago and continued until the terrace surface became sufficiently stabilised to support permanent vegetation around 850 years ago. The erosion was probably initiated by deforestation for timber associated with increased settlement in the region. As the oracle at Dodoni dates from at least 4,000 years ago and the Thesprotians settled the lowland area soon after, from that time onwards there would have been continual demands on the forest resources of the region. Throughout that time anyone intent on crossing this upper portion of the river would have been confronted by a sinuous, silt-laden torrent in all but the driest summer months, flowing through a broad, bare, stony floodplain. Woodland would have been confined to the canyon slopes. It is only in the last 850 years or so that the terrace has been colonized by trees and shrubs, with portions formerly cultivated for growing cereals and legumes later utilised as meadows for grazing and harvesting of hay, a practise maintained even to the present day. So now I pass in the shade of grey-haired Downy Oak, *Quercus pubescens*, and shiny-leaved Macedonian Oak, *Quercus trojana*, whilst all around Eastern Hornbeam, *Carpinus orientalis*, unfolds its soft, vernal-green foliage from smooth-barked branches. Dense thickets, isolated shrubs and some mature trees of the evergreen, spiny-leaved Kermes Oak, *Quercus coccifera*, are here too. These and their associates are trees which favour the drier sunnier upper slopes of the canyon further downstream, whilst the depths are forested with species better adapted to a shaded, humid environment subject to harsh frosts during the colder months.

The sandy terrace soils are very favourable to orchids, and this is one of the few places where the rose-pink sepalled and petalled spikes of *Ophrys scolopax* ssp. *cornuta* can be found, extending loftily amidst the grasses. With pronounced horn-like projections from the sides of an intricately marbled chocolate-brown lip, this Horned Ophrys is one of the more extreme variations of a very attractive species. It was whilst searching for the orchid that I disturbed what I assumed was a Balkan Whip Snake, since all that I saw was the whiplash of a yellowish-brown tail as it sped away through the grass with disconcerting rapidity. They are not venomous but, like their near relative, the western form of the Large Whip Snake which can reach three metres in length and also occurs here, their astonishing mobility is very disturbing to the unwary. The momentary awareness of a presence not clearly seen perhaps activates ancestral responses to a perceived threat. Whatever the reason for my brief disquiet, I was relieved by the compensatory sight of several Lycaenid blue butterflies sent skyward by the commotion. My chief motivation for this detour and at a time of day when a quest for shade would be uppermost in most minds was to see some of the many butterflies for which the canyon is such a rewarding location, so this initial offering was eagerly pursued. There are a great many species of small 'blues', some readily identified but many requiring very close inspection especially of the complex pattern of spots, lunules and venation on the undersides and even then only sufficient to make a tentative determination. One of those that had been disturbed into brief flight settled obligingly enough for me to recognise the deep violet-blue, black-bordered form of a male Zephyr Blue, the *sephirus* subspecies of which I knew occurred locally from having identified it on previous visits.

Arriving eventually at one of the more floriferous areas of grassland, I was content to sit for a while and watch the progress of whatever was in flight. With a lifetimes experience of watching the natural world, recognition of something different and therefore intriguing, is instinctive and only then prompts further and closer investigation. From my resting place, those tiny butterflies flashing alternatively silver and pale sky-blue whilst flying around nearby bushes and up into ivy-clad boughs I know are Holly Blues. Whereas, a subtle indefinable difference in flight, indications of similarly pale underwings and a preference for the scrubby Kermes Oaks, leads instinctively to a different conclusion, that of Ilex Hairstreak. Now my attention returned to the open grassy meadows towards the river as several larger distinctly black and white butterflies rose and fell lazily above the elevated mauve flowers of a scabious, *Pterocephalus plumosus*. These I know will be Marbled Whites with perhaps a few Balkan Marbled Whites if they have emerged a little earlier than normal this year. If the opportunity arose, I wished to take a closer look at these handsome butterflies which have an especially attractive and pronounced black scalloping along the outer margins of the former and prominent ringed ocelli on the underside hindwing of the latter. But now my attention was drawn elsewhere, for there was the unmistakable form of a magnificent butterfly, soaring dark-winged down through a break in the trees and with powerful wingbeats, towards the meadow before me and then onward as quickly as it came, heading further upriver. If it had alighted, with open wings, the distinctive velvet purple, maroon-tinged, creamy-edged splendour that is the Camberwell Beauty would have been displayed. Look closely and there is a row of powder-blue spots along the inner edge of the broad cream border which shine with great intensity from a velvet backcloth. The butterflies appear mysteriously, dark winged, seemingly from the depths of the canyon and the sallows on which they lay their eggs.

Feeling somewhat re-energised by this encounter, I continued, passing through a floral abundance, similar to that on the slopes below Tsepelovo, including the Green-winged Orchid, *Anacamptis (Orchis) morio*, although here well passed their best. Even more evident were the densely compact conical flower-heads of *Anacamptis pyramidalis*, the Pyramidal Orchid, the tiny bright pink flowers of which have a long filiform spur accessible only to butterflies and moths, having a proboscis sufficiently elongated to reach the nectar within, whilst simultaneously achieving pollination. They were in greater profusion now than in any previous year, no doubt due to the heavy springtime rainfall in what is normally a very dry part of the canyon floor. This thought gave me renewed hope of finding a very elusive orchid, but in continuing to search the grassy areas where I most expected to find it I was constantly disturbing Small Heath butterflies which have the habit of sitting quietly on grass stems with wings closed. Ignoring these as being of lesser interest, I was inclined to look for their more interesting cousin the Pearly Heath, another butterfly ever reluctant to reveal its upperside. However, as it is the underside which is most distinctive and attractive, with a bright orange-brown forewing and broad milky-white band edged with a row of beautifully ringed ocelli on the hindwing, I was pleased to confirm their presence too, alongside their duller neighbour. The orchid meanwhile remained elusive but there would be other opportunities to find it further downriver.

Arriving at a place where some of the subterranean flow surfaces as springs below an otherwise dry area of riverbed, I approached cautiously so as not to disturb any butterflies which might be imbibing moisture at the water's edge. Such places, where mineral rich seepages emerge, often attract large numbers and in that I was not disappointed, for, amassed at the source of a small rivulet, jostling for advantage, were fifty or more 'blues' beneath a cloud of others vying for position. I have seen larger gatherings before but it is always a wonderful sight, invariably dominated by the colourful males, a shimmering array of azure, cobalt and violet, here seemingly levitating above the brightly sunlit limestone. The violet-tinged, shining azure blue, black-edged splendour of Amanda's Blue was especially evident. Yet there were some of a more brilliant azure, devoid of any violet and with a distinct black margin broken into spots on the hindwing, which I knew to be the *dalmaticus* subspecies of Escher's Blue. Others which were smaller and a deep violet-blue, with pronounced broad black borders and conspicuous white fringe were most probably the *magnagraeca* subspecies of the Idas Blue, although very difficult to differentiate from the Silver-studded Blue which also occurs here and elsewhere on Tymphi. Further on, beyond an expanse of pebble- and cobble-strewn dry riverbed, onto another area of river terrace, I resumed my search for the elusive orchid and after close scrutiny of a considerable area found as anticipated, a single plant, for I have never seen it otherwise. *Ophrys sphegodes* ssp. *helenae* lacks the complex markings of its cousins but is still handsome, with a large orbicular lip of rich velvety maroon or chestnut, beneath violet-tinted, yellowish-green sepals and petals. Even with as many as eight flowers on each spike, it can be very difficult to find when associated with tall grasses but provides generous reward for the effort.

Renewing my search for butterflies, I made my way across the terrace to where I had seen a scattering of the mauve-flowered scabious *Pterocephalus plumosus*, a source of nectar favoured by many species. In the vicinity were robust plants of *Salvia verticillata* with dense whorls of violet blue flowers clustered on tall stems and of *Salvia sclarea*, a strongly aromatic relative, with whorls of lilac and cream flowers somewhat obscured by large pink and mauve bracts which impart a very attractive appearance to a statuesque form. During my approach I had again been prompted by that sense of seeing something distinctly different as a seemingly insubstantial and undefinable butterfly with a rather erratic but strong flight came into view and passed sufficiently near to betray a hint of orange-brown markings as it sped onwards. Only one species here could conform with those characteristics, the Nettle-tree Butterfly, the only representative in Europe of its kind. It has highly cryptic colouration and an irregular wing margin which ensures that when at rest it is indistinguishable from the dead leaves amongst which it hibernates for long periods, hence the apparent absence of definable form and substance during flight. The Southern Nettle Tree, *Celtis australis*, on which its caterpillars feed, is a slender, graceful tree of the forested upper slopes of the canyon. Arriving at the terrace, the unmistakable coppery and fulvous-red colouration of several male Spotted Fritillaries was immediately evident, these being the *meridionalis* subspecies which here, on Tymphi, is in both sexes much darker and heavily spotted and barred with black than other subspecific forms. The underside hindwings are white or cream, patterned with black spots and lunules and two irregular orange bands, creating a very striking contrast to the uppersides. There were others here too, a few male Amanda's Blues, apparently attracted by females laying eggs on *Vicia cracca*, their preferred foodplant, and a single Persian Skipper, a small olive-grey butterfly with prominent white markings, very localised in distribution. Another which could so easily be disregarded in view of the dull dark blue-brown uppersides were a few Chequered Blues which, in addition to the chequered fringe, have very bold black spots on the white underwings and a prominent orange band on the underside hindwing. This is as far south as its range extends.

Knowing that it was not far to the Misiou Bridge and being intent on continuing further to some rock pools, I regained the path which follows the eastern riverbank and walked on. Ahead, a ridge descends the western slopes marking the route of a *kaldereemee* from the village of Vitsa down to the bridge, which would before the advent of modern roads have provided the main means of contact for that community with Koukouli, Kipi and other villages east of the Voidomatis. It is tempting to surmise that prior to the fourteenth century when Vitsa was founded, the same route was used by the ninth- to fourth-century BC inhabitants of the adjacent Molossian settlement at Genitsari for access to the river and then to the southern slopes of Tymphi and the valley of the Skamneliotikos. Wherever the terrain offers a route and allows access to natural resources available for exploitation, men would surely have followed. The Misiou Bridge, constructed in 1748, spans the river where it passes between two rock buttresses in two slender stone arches accessed on the eastern bank by a massive paved ramp and on the west by the *kaldereemee* descending from Vitsa. A principal arch spans the main river course in a leap of eighteen metres, a secondary arch the remainder in seven metres, the two supported by a buttress which has a triangular base pointing upstream. It is a splendidly harmonious structure framed by the first of the towering cliffs which appear on entering the main part of the canyon.

My route now followed the riverbed, mostly dry except for a deep pool beneath the bridge, and because of the need to step from boulder to boulder demanding of concentration. It was, however, this requirement which led to the discovery of fresh otter spraint deposited conspicuously on prominent rocks at intervals along the rivermargin. Even with only an intermittent surface flow the river still offered them food, as I knew would be evident in the rock pools not far ahead. Fortunately the boulders did not require my continuous attention, otherwise I might have missed the large yellowish butterfly which swept down from above the tangle of trees and shrubs bordering the river, for I recognised instantly the characteristic flight and form of this, one of the rarest and most handsome of Greek butterflies, the Southern Swallowtail. If this one continues upriver, perhaps it will pause for nectar at the *Salvia* or scabious, resting with feet on the flowers whilst fluttering rapidly to support its own weight. It is then one would see the black and dusky-blue banding, bold against the buttercup yellow background and the intricacy of the scalloped black-edged hindwing, short-tailed, with an orange and blue ocellus. Having seen them regularly in the canyon, sometimes flying with the similar but more heavily marked Swallowtail, they are presumably well established and hopefully well protected here.

It was not long before the proximity of the rock pools became evident. A chorus of resonant *kek* and *croax-croax* calls rising and falling erratically in volume signalled the presence of Marsh Frogs, which as I approached promptly plopped noisily into the deep green water. I had taken the precaution of surveying the rocks around the pool with binoculars from a distance in the hope of seeing a Montpellier Snake of which there are some very large representatives in the canyon. As they feed predominantly on lizards and other snakes, including the many Dice Snakes living in these pools, this was as likely a place as any in which to have a close but cautious encounter with this often aggressive reptile. Brown Trout are also often stranded here by falling river levels but are unlikely to survive the first visit by an otter. These apart, my chief motivation for visiting this location was the hope of seeing another of the very special butterflies which frequent the canyon and in that I was not to be disappointed, for crowded around one of the mineral-rich seepages and gliding gracefully under the overhanging trees was an assembly of twenty or more Southern White Admirals. The white spots and submarginal row of powder-blue lunules on both wings appear startlingly bright against the blue-black background which glows with a faint iridescence as they float on flat wings in and out of the dappled shade. With wings closed, they are transformed. A bold silvery-white basal band appears, shining pale blue in the changing light, as an addition to the pattern of white spots, all on a ground of rich red-brown. Experiences such as this are to be savoured, so I sat and watched this wonder of nature for what seemed a timeless duration before reluctantly starting an overdue return.

The walk back was not without its rewards, although inevitably when striding out much of nature withdraws to let the intruder pass. Empathy with the natural world and rapid progression are not compatible. I did, however, encounter a solitary Hermann's Tortoise ambling unconcerned across my path, an apposite meeting in view of my preceding thoughts. Whilst constantly scanning ahead in the hope of seeing the Southern Swallowtail again, I also allowed myself a short detour in pursuit of another of those intuitive sightings. Even from a considerable distance, the alternate fluttering and gliding motion of a medium-sized, yellowish butterfly persistently low over rough grassland suggests festoon, and so it was. The Southern Festoon is an especially attractive species, with black scalloped margins, black veining and barring to both wings, and red lunules on the hindwing, all on a straw-yellow background. The undersides are even more intricately patterned, with prominent red bars on the forewing. Fortuitously the same detour led to a local variant of the common Kidney Vetch, *Anthyllis vulneraria*, this one, subspecies *bulgarica*, having large golden yellow flowers on ankle-high ascending stems. It appears to flourish on the dry open stony ground of the canyon, one of the few known localities in a distribution which is confined to Greece.

Without the assiduity of mind demanded during the outward walk, the return allowed some freedom for mental ramblings prompted by the surroundings, and it was recollection of those thoughts which were now my preoccupation as I surveyed the canyon two days later from my lofty viewpoint. That visualization of a torrential Voidomatis meandering through the barren stony floodplain of the Klithi terrace 4,250 to 850 years before, was in such contrast to all that I had seen during my brief detour into the upper reaches of the canyon, as to thrust the significance of environmental change once more to the forefront of my mind. In that particular instance the environmental contrast underlined the consequences of what may have been at least in part, human deforestation of the rivers catchment area. Dramatic as those effects may have been, they were however insignificant compared with earlier naturally induced events. Evidence of much greater change is preserved in the vicinity of the Kokkorou Bridge, where I began the detour, for there in a road cutting are the remnants of another river terrace, the surface of which is 56 metres above the present riverbed. The sands, silts and gravels which constitute the Kipi terrace, as it is known, were deposited between 160,000 and 140,000 years ago by the Voidomatis, flowing at a level considerably above the present canyon floor. Indeed, the river must have then occupied a broad floodplain and only in the vicinity of the Misiou Bridge did it enter a discernible canyon. At that time much of the chasm I had walked did not exist. The sediments of the Kipi terrace contain a high proportion of components derived from igneous rocks, for which the nearest sources are well to the east and within the catchment area of the more easterly tributaries of the Aoos. This rises in the mountains around Metsovo, 40 kilometres south-east of Tymphi. It appears that the upper reaches of the Aoos must have flowed into the Skamneliotikos at the time the Kipi terrace was formed, transporting this igneous debri in times of flood and only later were these upper tributaries captured by the present-day Aoos as its headwaters eroded southwards.

So standing now on the edge of the Vikos Canyon, it is possible to envisage the scene which must have existed at that time when the Kipi terrace was formed. Flowing some 60 metres above the present canyon floor, the Voidomatis would have been a very impressive river, especially during the spring and early summer when its already substantial volume, fed by an extensive eastern catchment area, was supplemented by meltwater flowing into the Skamneliotikos from valley glaciers on the southern flanks of Tymphi. For that time saw a return of the mountain's permanent ice fields. From my previous night's resting place above Tsepelovo I would have seen, 150,000 years ago, the ice-front of these, the Vlasian glaciers, in the valleys above me, the surrounding slopes permanently snow covered or stripped to bare rock by the wind. Only in the Selio valley below, occupied by the gravel- and sandbanks of a broad braided torrential Skamneliotikos, would there be substantial vegetation, perhaps of willow thickets and an ephemeral flush of grasses, sedges and short-lived annual flowering plants. Beyond I would have seen the upper reaches of the river and its tributaries extended far into the spine of the Pindos Mountains and flowing through similarly arctic terrain. All would have been exposed to deep and prolonged seasonal snow cover and destructive scouring by erosive meltwater. Returning to my present Vikos edge viewpoint, it would have been the lowlands of the Kalamas River basin, just visible west of the Mitsikeli ridge, which alone would have offered a more inviting scene. For it is there and in similarly favoured areas that even in the most severe phases of that 20,000 year-long cold Vlasian episode, woodland of deciduous oak and other temperate forest species would have survived amidst a great expanse of undulating seasonal grassland. During less severe climatic interludes, Hazel and species of elm and pine enhanced the woodland diversity, with forests of the firs, *Abies alba* and *A. cephalonica*, clothing the western slopes of Mitsikeli. Even then these lowland areas would have been snow covered during winter.

These scenes of mountain glaciers and meltwater torrents, of forest and rolling grasslands, were just part of an ever-changing landscape ebbing and flowing in response to the vicissitudes of climate for a period of some 200 centuries. That length of time alone is difficult to comprehend, even with the many and varied scenes and series of events which one can envisage being encompassed by it. How much greater the challenge to comprehension when extending the time scale back to that of the Skamnellian glaciers which dominated the mountain between 423,000 and 460,000 years ago. Between the climatic extremes of the Skamnellian and Vlasian glaciations, which left their indelible scars on the mountain, there passed an immensity of time no less significant in its manifestations of change but leaving a far less evident signature. At the height of the Skamnellian glaciation when the ice-dammed lake in the Selio valley overflowed, to resume the course of the Skamneliotikos through the Vikaki ravine and into the Vikos, the floor of the canyon below my vantage point would have been some 170 metres above its present level. At that elevation the river meandered through a floodplain almost as broad as the 900 metre width of the canyon as revealed before me and no less impressive with sheer canyon walls almost rivalling their current grandeur. With an amelioration of climate, the glaciers retreated and forest trees which had survived in lowland enclaves began extended their range into the former grasslands at lower altitudes and then into the mountains. The firs *Abies alba* and *A.cephalonica* appear, from the abundance of their pollen preserved in lake sediments, to have dominated the various phases of forestation in the Tymphaean region for much of the next 50,000 years, perhaps at times clothing the massif to the very limits of its summit ridge. Other species favoured the broad expanse of the Vikos Canyon floor, an association of deciduous oaks, the elms *Ulmus* and closely related *Zelkova* and the hornbeams *Carpinus betulus* and *Ostrya carpinifolia* probably being predominant. At times when the climate was especially warm and dry the evergreen oaks became a significant component and at others, species of lime *Tilia*, hazel *Corylus*, box *Buxus* and alder *Alnus*, flourished. Throughout, the constituent tree species were constantly changing in relative proportions, but cumulatively this was the longest episode of extensive and continuous forest cover ever attained in the region within the last half a million years. As befits an event of such longevity and magnitude, it is known as the Dodoni Forest Period, the time of the great Dodoni Forest.

With the return to a cooler climate around 370,000 years ago, the forests retreated in favour of the mountain grasslands and alpine vegetation which was better able to withstand the harsher environmental conditions then prevailing. For short intervals pine woodland may have encroached into parts of the massif, from the lowlands where it formed extensive open forests in which the deciduous tree species that had predominated in the great Dodoni Forest now occupied local enclaves. Treeless grasslands and sparsely vegetated terrain were, however, predominant and this remained the situation for a further 30,000 years until once again the climate favoured a return of the temperate deciduous forests. This alternation between temperate forest and boreal grasslands in response to climatic fluctuation occupied the whole of the period between the Skamnellian and Vlasian glacial episodes. Some of the intervening cooler phases may have culminated in snow and ice accumulation in the summit corries of Tymphi but insufficiently so for a return to the extremes of the two glacial periods. Of the warmer interludes, the presence of species such as wild olive, *Olea*, and of others intolerant of frost, indicate periods when the climate was at least as mild as that of today, whilst incursions of the evergreen oaks and of *Juniperus* suggest summer aridity. Throughout, the environment was in transition and subject to an ever-changing mosaic of forests, open woodland, meadows, copses, clearings and grasslands, which migrated between mountain and lowland as the climatic changes dictated. This ensured the survival of many plant species which might otherwise have died out during the extremes of the glacial periods as the physical landscape was sufficiently diverse to provide ecological refuges for those which were vulnerable. It was with such thoughts that I was able to look down upon the great ribbon of forest that clothes the floor and slopes of the Vikos Canyon today, knowing that I was contemplating one of the richest assemblages of forest species existing anywhere in the Balkans.

During this restful interlude I was mindful of the other inhabitants of the canyon which I hoped to see and whilst continuously scanning the length of the floor it was not long before the distinctive black and white form of an Egyptian Vulture appeared, circling lazily on outstretched wings. The distinctive wedge-shaped white tail and buff-brown tinge to the head and scapulars was clearly visible even though it was several hundred metres below me. Any pride in one's visual acuity this might imply pales into insignificance compared with that of the bird, for it can differentiate a fist-sized food source from a height of one kilometre! There are several pairs nesting on the canyon cliffs, especially at the southern end where they are a frequent sight during spring and summer, cruising above the roads and villages for carrion and discarded food scraps. I once inadvertently rescued a tortoise from an Egyptian Vulture which had overturned its victim on the road near the Kokkorou Bridge and whilst holding a leg in its bill was attempting, unsuccessfully as it turned out, to take off. The tortoise continued unharmed after my intervention.

Looking northwards, beyond the rim of the Megas Lakos ravine, the slopes of Astraka rise above a conspicuous horizontal rampart created by a massive layer of limestone, which if not evidently a natural feature could be imagined as some ancient fortification encircling a mountain citadel. Follow the rampart around the flanks and it becomes apparent that it is inclined gently southwards and in conformity with all the other layered outcrops wherever one looks, for that is the substructure of the mountain, a vast multilayered crustal block of limestone tilted to the south. Diverting one's gaze westwards across the Vikos Canyon, the same multilayered sequence is evident in the Stouros plateau, an extension of the Tymphaean massif isolated from it by the canyon. An irregular band of woodland darkens the slopes above the canyon walls, fringing the tonsure of deeply eroded limestone which crowns the plateau. That capping is an extraordinary maze of many hundreds of house-sized solution hollows which, although now largely devoid of dense vegetation, remains wooded and impenetrable towards the southern limits, above the villages of Monodendri and Vitsa. It is a landscape of the most inventive imagination, at once both a hellish cratered battleground and an enchanted fairytale labyrinth.

Those Molossians who in the ninth century BC founded the settlement of Genitsari, chose a location 350 metres beneath the southern edge of the Stouros plateau and some 200 metres above an enclosed depression of cultivable land to the west. From this lofty position they looked south-west from their stone and timber dwellings, over lush lowland meadows extending north and west from the Pamvotis Lake, beyond royal Passaron, to the valley of the Thyamis River, receding distantly to the coast at Kestrini. That view encompassed most of what was then Molossia. Later in the five centuries of their occupation of Genitsari, the extensive lands of Chaonia to the north-west and Thesprotia to the south came under Molossian control, to create by 400 BC, during the reign of Tharypas, a well organised and prosperous state. At an altitude of 1,030 metres, Genitsari would have been snow-bound during winter months, so a seasonal migration of both animals and stockmen to and from the lowlands was an essential aspect of life. When in residence, access to the southern slopes of Tymphi would have been feasible by descending into the canyon along the present-day route of the *kaldereemee* from Vitsa and traversing the then treeless Klithi terrace upstream to the slopes which lead to the Selio valley and the contemporary settlement at Skamneli. Looking now, along the southern narrows of the Vikos chasm to the site of Genitsari, the imagination readily imbues the slopes with the white braids of sheep trailing their Molossian shepherds down to the river, destined for high Tymphaean pastures. Except for the more challenging river crossing, the natural scenes which confronted them on their journey would have been similar to those we see today.

That was not so for some of the earlier human incursions into the area, for the Vikos Canyon was a seasonal base for hunters during the harsh climate following the third and last glacial episode to leave its mark on the mountain. During this, the Tymphaean glacial phase, permanent ice accumulated mostly in the corries above 1,800 metres with maximum extent between 28,000 to 24,000 and again around 21,000 years ago, accompanied by a return to climatic and environmental conditions similar to those of the earlier Skamnellian and Vlasian glacial episodes. A very extensive floodplain terrace, the Aristi terrace, now some twelve metres above the present riverbed, formed during the earlier 28,000 to 24,000 year maximum, especially in the lower more northerly part of the canyon, as a result of intensive meltwater erosion of the southern slopes of Tymphi. Most of the terrace deposits are consequently of limestone gravel and some flint but with significant glacial clay and silt derived from the older glacial moraines. A second floodplain terrace, the Vikos terrace, between two and ten metres above the present riverbed, formed at the later 21,000 year-old maximum. Although this included much limestone, the finer grained components came from the river catchment further east and south of Tymphi. The earliest human intrusion into the area, for which there is evidence, was around 25,000 years ago, at the height of this Tymphaean glacial phase. It is, however, not until the period 16,500 to 13,000 years ago that there is abundant evidence of sustained, though seasonal, occupation of rock-shelters in the northernmost extension of the canyon, from which there were probable incursions into the Tymphaean massif.

From my vantage point, a group of eight hunters would have been some 13,000 years ago just visible on the then treeless floodplain of the canyon floor below, moving cautiously across the open, sparsely vegetated terraces when not impeded by gullies and secondary channels from the main river. Fording the torrent would have been hazardous, as springtime snowmelt and glacial meltwaters contributed to a considerable flow. Even in shallow but fast flowing water, the smooth surfaced limestone cobbles would have presented difficulty underfoot, especially in water turbid with glacial silt and clay. Binocular-aided scrutiny would, however, reveal them using their long wooden spears to assist their crossings, the sharpened flint-edged and barbed tips glinting aloft in the afternoon sun. Clothed in ochre-stained hides of Chamois and Ibex skin, sun-tanned, tousle-headed and decorated with strings and beads of perforated shells, they would have been a commanding sight. Having travelled some nine kilometres from their rock-shelter encampment downstream, six of their band would spend the night in one of the rock-shelters below, warmed and reassured by the protective glow of a fire and nourished by the Ibex meat they had brought with them. Two would continue a further five kilometres to the rock-shelters beyond the future site of the Misiou Bridge, to the encampment of a second and related group. From there a combined force would set out at dawn to round the Mazaria defile on the slopes leading towards the eastern end of the Megas Lakos ravine and to a rendezvous with their compatriots who would have scaled the ravine floor. All were familiar with their surroundings and with the seasonal routine, for they came every year, always at this time, the time when the Chamois and Ibex gave birth and grazed high on the mountain, for then the adults were most vulnerable when protecting their young and with little concern for their own safety. The elders of the hunting group had led them this way every fourth or fifth day since the last full moon, but now, with the moon brightening again, the newly born animals were getting stronger and more agile and soon climbed to inaccessible places on the cliffs and crags accompanied by the adults, so kills were more difficult. Spear throws were only effective at close quarters or from above and a miss frequently stripped the weapon of its precious flint barbs and points on impact with the rocks. A broken or irretrievable spear was even more calamitous. They would, however, persevere for as long as the animals continued to graze and seek refuge at this height.

One of their companions, especially skilled in making the flint points and barbs, had remained at their rock-shelter base to craft a surplus which the group would take with them when they moved camp to the lowlands. They knew that the grey flint could always be found amongst the gravels and cobbles which formed a flat-topped terrace well above the river, although large pieces were infrequent and often of poor quality, shattering or cleaving unevenly. Using a large block of limestone as an anvil and a quartzite hammerstone, one of his few permanent possessions, the craftsman would produce as many finger-sized, elongate, narrow and thin flakes as was possible from the flint core-stone. These blanks were then carefully retouched, either to produce a single cutting edge along one of the long edges, or two cutting edges ending at a sharp point at one or both ends. This was then broken by a transverse fracture either to remove an unwanted butt-end or to produce two finished points or barbs. The angle and orientation of that transverse fracture was crucial as it would determine how readily the point or barb could be embedded in a wooden or bone haft or spear and remain secure. Whoever developed that transverse fracture technique 16,500 year ago was not only technically skilled but must also have possessed a degree of mental and visual preconception beyond that of others, for the technique was maintained at that rock-shelter and, as far as is known nowhere else, for over 3,500 years.

Flint tools for butchering, for chopping, whittling and boring wood and for scrapping and piercing animal skins were also essential for survival, so the skills of the flint-knapper were paramount in their society. Their very presence in the canyon depended upon the accumulation of flint within the Aristi terrace deposits. They could not have functioned otherwise, without importing quantities of ready-made tools from elsewhere. So as the small band of hunters in the canyon below watched their two colleagues disappear upriver they were content to know that all would be well back at their home encampment. The young children and their mothers would be safe in that communal gathering, busy rendering the remaining animal carcasses down to the last morsel of bone-marrow and sewing the soft chamois-skins into clothing with bone-needle and sinew. Close by, the river would sound a reassuring presence accompanied by the chattering of children and the methodical tapping of the flint-knapper. All that mattered in their lives depended upon the maintenance of continuity, the passing on from generation to generation of the accumulated lore of their kind, the preservation of the established ways. They followed the animals. In the lowlands they followed the Aurochs and the Red Deer. Here in the mountains it was the Chamois and Ibex and for as long as the elders knew it had always been so and would continue that way. Even so, there were times when the oldest amongst them told stories of how things had been different in the past, not that the others thought much of these yarns other than as an opportunity for ridicule and hilarity. It had been difficult making progress in the lower part of the canyon that day, due to dense thickets in places, and they had been forced to climb high onto the massive and unstable screes to get round these obstacles, something the Old One said was not necessary in his youth. He also said that the woodcutting Beaver was more abundant now than in the past and there were many places around their rock-shelter which had once been open grassland but were now thick with young trees. It all troubled him as it was becoming more difficult to find ways through to the bare mountain where the Ibex and Chamois gathered for this brief time, and when the animals returned to the lowlands they dispersed into the more impenetrable areas of woodland. This came about because the days and nights were getting warmer, he said. Some of his colleagues listened and pondered confusedly, more from respect than understanding, as he was the keeper of the bones on which he made cut marks for purposes they could not comprehend. This would be their last hunting foray to the heights of the mountain this year, after which they would do as they had always done and drive any animals they could encircle on the lower slopes into the range of spearmen positioned above a narrow gully leading down to the river below their camp. Soon, however, they would leave the protection of the rock shelter and follow the sun and the Old One to a lakeside encampment from where they would hunt the Red Deer.

Diverting my gaze from the depths, to the scene beyond the northern limits of the canyon, I could see a little of the terrain those hunters would have had to negotiate after leaving their rock-shelter of Klithi, as it came to be known. The region has changed considerably in the intervening 13,000 years, due to tectonic uplift of some parts and subsequent erosion of soils, producing a variation in relief, which they would not have encountered. Their route, after an initial climb away from the river, would have required a gradual descent into the basin enclosing the Gramousti Lake, through well vegetated grasslands, perhaps bright with yellow flowered hawkweeds and hawkbits, and the mauve, lilac, purple and blue of knapweeds, asters and fleabanes. The hunters were apprehensive when in the open but the Old One always stopped for a while on the high places to survey the ground ahead, sometimes stooping to pick a handful of the scented wormwood which grew abundantly on the poorer soils, breathing in the aroma as he turned to gaze on the great bulk of Nemerska which climbed to where the North Star would appear. Lions and the dreaded Spotted Hyaenas, which always pursued the herds, would sometimes follow the Red Deer even to these cold uplands and wolves were always not far away so the group had to be vigilant and stay together. From beyond the high point they would see the lake nestling in a depression, beneath limestone slopes to the north and a sinuous line of willows marking the course of an outflow stream, snaking its way south. Much of the ground around the lake was marshy and fringed with sedges and willow thickets. The group would, as always, return to their habitual encampment in a gully at the foot of the limestone slopes, where they had some protection from both wind and predatory animals and a good view of the lake margins, where they would endeavour to encircle and kill their prey. Summer was when the Red Deer herds came through with their newborn calves, on their way to the high pastures of the Nemerska slopes. Herds of small horses, the European Wild Ass, also came, on their way to summer grazing to the north-east, and sometimes the northern summer migration of the great Aurochs, which like all cattle depended heavily on water sources, also reached the lake. The horses were too wary to allow an approach in the open and the Aurochs too powerful unless a calf could be isolated and brought down, so the hunters relied on the Red Deer for their survival here.

In time the Old One, seeing the flowers fade to seed and blown by the increasingly cold wind, would listen for the distant bellowing of the red stags in rut and lead the hunters downstream to its confluence with a larger river and the wooded protection it provided. From there they would follow the herds south, leaving the river where it turned towards the setting sun and the sea, to follow a tributary upstream, out onto the plain leading to the great lake and marshlands in the shadow of the Mitsikeli ridge. That route, from leaving the Thyamis or Kalamas River as it came to be known, to cross the now extensively cultivated plain to the Pamvotis Lake, was there now spread out before me. One could not help but feel fearful for that tiny band, so exposed to the danger of predators, trekking across such an expanse. Their safety lay in reaching the southern limit of the lake for there they would be united with others, at the cave of Kastritsa, the place they had left in the early springtime. The gathering, perhaps a hundred strong, for that was as many as the hunting could support in the region, would follow the Red Deer south, as winter here, surrounded by snow-covered mountains would offer an uncertain and precarious existence for any who stayed. Within a few days the riverside route would lead them to the marshlands of Ambracia and to the great coastal plains which then extended westwards to what is now the island of Kerkyra or Corfu, for then sea level was much lower. There on the wide open expanse of grassland the herds of deer, horses and cattle would congregate throughout the winter. There too, the Tymphaean hunters would be reunited with others of their tribe, perhaps no more than five hundred in number, many having returned from similar forays as far inland to north, south and east as the hunting could sustain. Together they would pass the winter gathering whatever food they could from the sea-shore and hunting the plain's animals before once again trekking inland to their springtime hunting grounds, following the migrating herds as they had always done.

With the western canyon wall now extending a shadow across the forested floor, my vigil was renewed in the hope of seeing one of the most secretive birds I know to inhabit the region. Although the Black Stork is one of the largest, it is also one of the most elusive of birds, choosing to site its huge stick-nest as distant from human presence as possible and always extremely wary when searching riverside pools and shallows for the fish, amphibia and other prey on which it feeds. Having spent days stalking them along the wooded rivers of the Fagaras mountains of Romania, I know the exhilaration of observing these birds at close quarters. The long scarlet legs and bill are in such contrast to the white underparts and metallic purple and green sheen of the black upper plumage, that an elusory existence would seem impossible. Yet when the bird is in statuesque pose beside a woodland stream the human eye seems unable to discern a recognisable outline. Only when the bird moves is the form revealed. Now I watched the alternating wingbeats and long glides of its trajectory far below as it headed upriver to a nest high in the Vikaki ravine. The lengthening shadows of late afternoon also herald the return of another avian inhabitant of the canyon, but one which has no propensity for secrecy and for which the rapidly declining numbers indicate an imminent extinction in Greece. As I scanned the western cliffs for signs of its rock-ledge nesting site I knew that the colony of old has long gone and that one or two pairs are all that remain of the Griffon Vulture in these mountains. The single juvenile, now fully fledged and ready to fly, was easily located above the white-stained cliff face accompanied by one of the adults. Soon they would be joined by the other parent, arrowing in on tightly withdrawn wings, instantly fully extended and flapped to slow the sudden upward approach to the nest. What they lack in appealing features they compensate for in their aerial mastery. With a timing seemingly designed to challenge this last assertion, the gentler sounds of a warm evening were suddenly enveloped in a rush of wings and the loud communal chittering of a flock of Alpine Swifts, the pre-eminent masters of the skies. For an hour or more, before they settle to roost in their cliff face colony, they congregate in an aerial display, mesmerising in its convolutions and awesome in its choreography. In their adaptation for flight they must be the ultimate avian proponents, their scimitar-shaped wings and powerful wingbeat propelling them up to a thousand kilometres in a single day when gathering insect food for their young.

Withdrawing a little from the edge of the canyon to where I had chosen to spend the night, I settled down to await the suns progression towards the distant mountains of southern Albania, which were just visible above the expanse of the Stouros plateau. It had been cloudless and hot throughout the day, but now cloud was spilling over the edge of the Tymphaean summit ridge and distant thunder warned of a storm to the north. I was hoping for a clear night sky as this was the most advantageous place from which to see the planetary conjunction which I had glimpsed from above Tsepelovo the previous evening, so the prospect of a possible storm was troubling. Nevertheless, I was not too perturbed as accumulations of cloud in the forested basin of the Aoos south of the great bulk of Smolikas often drift against the massive north-eastern cliffs of Tymphi after hot days such as this. Only if the cloud rose over the summit ridge sufficient to flow down the southern slopes would vision be obscured. Soon the western wall of the canyon assumed a dark violet hue and what little cloud then remaining above the summit ridge glowed pink, as a fiery sunset silhouetted the mountainous horizon. Violet darkened to purple, purple to indigo, as the rockscape once more dissolved into night.

I had positioned myself, facing west, in a small grassy hollow, sheltered I hoped from any cold down-draught from the summits. The crescent moon, brightening as the sun disappeared below the horizon, was now alongside an already glowing Venus, riding on its shoulder with a more subdued Jupiter at arm's length. A brief search with binoculars failed to locate Mars, but as the lunar and planetary conjunction, now some thirty degrees above the horizon, would be visible for another two hours before it too followed the sun, I knew the red planet would soon appear to complete the planetary triangle. As if to mark time before the planet's appearance, a solitary Scops Owl began to call from the canyon followed soon after by the deep sonorous, bitonal call of an Eagle Owl, my sole audible companions for the night.

# Chapter 3

## Krevvati's treasure

The shadow of Kazarma, the high ground immediately east of my overnight resting place at the edge of the Vikos Canyon, had provided an unwelcome chill that morning. Droplets of dew had gathered on the scalloped and fluted limestone slabs and the air smelled earthy and vernal. A diaphanous blue haze filled the canyon floor. As I retraced my route of the previous day, eastwards along the rim of the Megas Lakos ravine, the slopes of Astraka were already bathed in an enticing glow and it would not be long before I shared that pleasurable warmth. The threatened thunderstorm of the previous evening had dissipated and it was a cloudless sky which now proclaimed the promise of another parched Tymphaean day. In that initial stillness and quiet any sound was comparatively amplified and so it was that I came to pause at the head of a precipitous rocky gully on hearing faint melodious calls drifting up from the depths. Listening for a while, the clarity of tone and the repetitive short phrasing indicated the song of the Blue Rock Thrush, so I moved to where I had an uninterrupted binocular view of the craggy slopes below. The male bird, invariably perched on a prominent rock, would be an elusory subject with dark dusky-blue plumage melding into the abyssal shade. Unable to locate the bird, I was about to move on when the song suddenly increased in volume and length of phrasing as simultaneously the fluttering form launched out into the ravine, returning in circular flight to silence and obscurity. In these mountains the Blue Rock Thrush is an infrequent and ephemeral inhabitant of impenetrable places such as this and is seen by few. Prompted by this good fortune, speculative thoughts of other possible encounters reminded me of another elusive species I had seen briefly above Vradeto a previous year, and now led me to search some of the rough grassland on the southerly slopes before moving further away from the canyon. Rock Sparrows are inconspicuous greyish-brown, streaked and spotted birds with a markedly cream and brown-striped crown. They nest in the canyon cliff face and at this time of year would be foraging for caterpillars and grasshoppers with which to feed their young. Whilst systematically scanning the nearby grassy slopes I eventually located a bird with the distinctive frenetic behaviour which the Rock Sparrow often exhibits when searching for live food, energetically jumping and hopping with a very upright stance before dashing to grasp prey in its hefty bill. Soon it took flight on powerful wingbeats and disappeared in a bounding swift trajectory towards the canyon edge.

After an hour's brisk walk I came to the crags at the eastern end of the Megas Lakos and climbed to a vantage point for a departing glimpse of the ravine and the western limits of the mountain. I thought then of those Palaeolithic hunters who had spent a night, sleeping fitfully perhaps, in their canyon rock-shelter beside the river, alert to every sound should it be the harbinger of danger or, equally dread, a messenger from the unknown. Those times were still formative years in the development of human consciousness and perhaps, whilst huddled around their campfire that night, the Old One had plied them with the reassuring mythologies of their time. Those voices, which habitually repeated the hunters cries and imprecations in the narrower confines of the canyon, what were they if not the manifestation of other beings fated to forever mimic the utterances of the living. By the time those Molossian shepherds frequented the mountain the myth had evolved to become the voice of the nymph, Echo, condemned by the great god Pan to forever repeat the last words heard.

By sunrise the hunters would have toiled up the ravine beneath me and would now be hidden amongst these very crags waiting for the combined band of their kith and kin to drive any Ibex grazing the lower slopes into an ambush. The Ibex would instinctively make for the crags. Bounding through a purple haze of the flowering grass *Phleum alpinum*, a relict species still growing on the mountain, the animals would be unaware of danger ahead, unless a cold draft from the icy summits brought a scented warning. For the waiting hunters there would be only a brief opportunity to make a kill as the escaping Ibex would not stop until the relative safety of the Astraka cliffs. If fortune favoured the hunters the carcass would be decapitated and dismembered where it fell and seemingly, from the skeletal evidence remaining in their rock-shelter, apportioned to favour the Klithi hunters with the right-handed half of the torso. Did the Old One distrust the sinistral, even then? Whatever the outcome of their ambush, the hunters would press on in pursuit, with the added quarry of the Chamois which, with young to protect, habitually favoured the heights. The treeless slopes towards Astraka and beyond to the Tymphaean summit ridge allowed unhindered visibility for the hunters, so they could plan their onslaught carefully. Animals which attained the summit ridge would escape with ease but those which could be diverted to occupy the crags and cliffs of isolated Astraka would be more vulnerable. It would be exhausting and dangerous for the hunters on the sharp-edged weather-worn, icy rocks, but there were ways to gain height and launch spear throws from above the animal's favoured sanctuary. From there the Old One would lead his band back to Klithi down the north-western slopes, skirting a marsh-fringed lake into the ever-encroaching woodland, whilst their companions retraced their own familiar well-trodden way back to the southern limit of the canyon.

After descending the crags I continued my way north-eastwards towards the distinctive flat-topped summit of Krevvati and out across the intervening karstic slopes, an enticing labyrinth of limestone walls, tables and hollows in clear sunny weather, but an eerie, treacherous, unworldly place when enveloped in low cloud and mist. Even in times of torrential rain or rapid snowmelt, surface water is transitory. It disappears rapidly through the deeply creviced limestone and into numerous sinkholes and shafts, the few open ones often dangerously snow-capped even now, as late as June, but most others disguised by fallen rocks at the base of flowery hollows. With the summit ridge now dominating my field of view for the first time, I was reminded of the need to be vigilant, for one of the greatest of all the avian masters of the skies had appeared there only four years before, gliding and soaring on the updraft from the Aoos valley beyond. Knowing it to be a rare and rapidly disappearing bird in Europe, apart from the Pyrenees mountains where I had observed it many times, that appearance of a pair of Lammergeier had sustained the hope of a return. With a wingspan of just under three metres, it is always a mesmerising sight, soaring effortlessly on fully extended flat wings, bowed slightly during a fast glide or drawn in scimitar-like for descent and rarely flapped except briefly during take-off. A pair will sometimes lock talons at great height and cartwheel earthward to part in a final plunge and upward sweep when only a few metres from the ground. A male will sky-dance in an undulating sequence of rapid dives and soaring climbs or glide at great velocity rolling and angling its wings in a display of extraordinary aerial agility. To witness such mastery is to see a pinnacle of nature's evolutionary genius, and yet this bird is disappearing from so much of the world's skies. In the Himalayas the Lammergeier accompanies transhumant peoples and their flocks, consuming the bones and whatever flesh remains from discarded carcasses and has no cause to fear man. Perhaps those Molossian shepherds welcomed this bird too and marvelled at the enormity of its stick nests built in cave entrances high on the canyon cliffs and at its ability to swallow whole the leg bones of a sheep. They might also have gazed skyward uneasily at times, knowing the bird's propensity for carrying large bones and even tortoises to great height and dropping them onto rocks, to render them into edible portions. In later years perhaps they had heard of the death of Aeschylus, rumoured to have been killed by a tortoise falling from the sky, and had nodded knowingly of the truth of the matter. Were the birds I had seen to be the last of their kind to shadow the Tymphaean slopes? All that was evident now was a distant solitary Raven making its way back to a nest high on the canyon cliffs.

There were flowers in abundance here, induced by the melting snow which still infilled many of the hollows and persisted as drifts against crags and shaded rock walls. Some were protruding through the winter blanket, as on the edge of a snow-filled depression, where the pale lavender-blue and lavender-pink goblets of *Crocus veluchensis* were progressively emerging. They clustered in their hundreds around all of the shrinking snow patches, white-throated, with golden anthers and frilly orange style enclosed in segmented cups. Others accompanied them. Sprays of slender-stemmed *Gagea pusilla*, with six-petalled flowers, bright yellow within and green-striped without, were scattered amidst the similarly formed and striped white stars of *Ornithogalum oligophyllum* which carpeted the ground in short-stemmed clusters. Less conspicuous, but a constant companion, were the compact mauve-pink sprays of *Corydalis densiflora*, with intricately constructed long-spurred flowers amidst delicately divided foliage. On slopes from where snow had long gone, the violet and mauve, white-flecked floral clusters of *Acinos alpinus* were woven into the grassy fabric everywhere, seemingly all of the small-leaved, procumbent form typical of the subspecies *meridionalis* which predominates at these higher levels. Bright yellow sprays of *Alyssum montanum* ssp. *repens* and the brilliantly blue, large-flowered forget-me-not, *Myosotis alpestris* ssp. *suaveolens*, further enhanced the colourful assemblage.

With the reassurance of time unhurried by extraneous demands, I was content to meander from one flowery enclave to the next whilst remaining alert for any movement or sound which might betray other early morning presences on the slopes. Several avian visitors have regular breeding territories here and being extremely watchful at such times will already be aware of the intruder. They will be evasive and retiring until I stray too close to a nest or to offspring. Habitual diversionary behaviour will then reveal their presence. On approaching an expanse of stony ground with scattered low grassy tussocks, I was alerted by a high-pitched rather plaintive lingering call, apparently from the direction of low rock outcrops ahead. Stopping to listen more attentively, the calls changed to a series of barely audible anxiety notes and, just as I had binocular sight of the bird's upright alert stance amongst the rocks, it took off in a steep fluttering silent ascent. Well above me and with the sun still low, the white underparts and black white-edged tail were clearly visible as it circled, gliding with wings and tail widely spread, in a series of undulations. It was singing now, high-pitched and urgently in sibilant tones, accelerating into a finale of trills and liquid chittering which ended abruptly as it closed its wings and dropped head-first to where, close to the ground, it flew for some distance back to its original rocky outpost. The bird was now clearly visible; a long-tailed lark, greyish-brown, flecked with white and streaked black above, white below, with the face and upper breast strikingly decorated black and pale yellow. This was a male Shore Lark, so named because the North Eurasian race, which breeds in the high Arctic, regularly winters on the coasts of eastern England. Here, the *balcanica* race breeds only at the highest altitudes of a few mountains in Greece and elsewhere in the Balkans, dispersing to lower levels for the winter. There are other southern races, as in the mountains of Morocco and from Turkey eastwards into Asia, generally favouring high altitude stony slopes and plateaus where there is abundant insect food for their summer brood. It seems likely that these are relict populations which have remained in place since the last glacial maxima, whilst others moved progressively northwards to their present breeding grounds in the arctic tundra. This is a bird which those Palaeolithic hunters would probably have encountered on their mountain forays and I wonder how they would have contemplated its strange characteristics, for this is a bird with horns. After moving closer I could see the facial markings more clearly. From a broad black crescent across the upper chest there is a continuous thick black stripe curving upwards beneath the eye to the bill, above which is a black stripe across the forehead. This stripe extends backwards into lateral headbands, the extremities of which are feather tufts which in this bird, a male, are erectile projections. Seeing me approach even nearer the bird adopted threat behaviour, strutting about its rocky perch with slender horns raised very conspicuously, and jerking its head up and down above an arched back. Abruptly it took flight and silently, with fast deep wingbeats which alternately present pale and darker surfaces, flickered low over the ground to another vantage point at some distance. It was leading me away from the shallow scrape in the lee of a grassy tuft, where the female sits on a recently constructed nest of grass, fine rootlets and leaves, lined with knapweed down and, curiously, with an entrance path of small stones. In compliance, my route led directly away, as these are scarce birds here, vulnerable to disturbance.

After an hour of gradual ascent I arrived at an escarpment edge sweeping down from the main summit ridge and forming the western limit of an embayment, which to the east rises in massive screes to the basal cliffs of Krevvati. Clusters of the tiny, bright yellow flowers of *Draba lasiocarpa*, arising from dense tufts of minute rigid linear leaves, coloured the stony ground, whilst on the nearby slopes there were isolated spikes of *Orchis pallens*. Topped by a dense cylindrical cluster of pale yellow, elder-scented flowers, this rare orchid is more at home in the shade of open woodland, so its occurrence here is perhaps an indication of the former treed extent in what is now exposed alpine grassland. Looking westwards and down across the broad basin which drains into the upper reaches of the Megas Lakos ravine, to the great mass of Astraka, I was reminded of the changes which those Palaeolithic hunters of 13,000 years ago would have had to contend with and of the Old One's concerns about the encroaching forest. His observations were prescient for in time his people would abandon their springtime occupation of the Klithi rock-shelter as the mountain grasslands receded and hunting became increasingly difficult. It appears, from the stone artefacts they left behind, that the hunters reoccupied the shelter around 10,400 years ago when there was a return to colder climatic conditions and a retreat of woodland from the mountain, but that was a short-lived episode. Within 500 years oak and pine had invaded the lower slopes and during the next 2,500 years an open oak woodland with a considerable variety of other tree species occupied all but the exposed summit ridge and the unassailable cliffs. Further climatic fluctuations then favoured a change, first to an association of Silver Fir, *Abies alba* and Greek Fir, *Abies cephalonica*, then to a dense forest of the hornbeams, Eastern Hornbeam *Carpinus orientalis* and Hop Hornbeam *Ostrya carpinifolia*, which, with many other tree species, predominated until 6,200 years ago. A return to a much more open, perhaps lightly wooded landscape followed, persisting for some 1,200 years to when a mixed deciduous and coniferous forest rapidly colonized and occupied the slopes. This prevailed until around 4,400 years ago when human activity began to exert its influence.

Following the escarpment edge eastwards, I soon came to the breach which allows a steep but comfortable descent into the valley below. If ever confronted by the need to find this place in dense cloud or mist, I know I can rely on the Alpine Chough to be my guide, as the way is beside the cavernous vertical shaft in which they congregate to nest and raise their young. Their communal vocalisation is audible for some considerable distance. Today was an opportunity to rest for a while and enjoy the idiosyncratic behaviour of these characterful birds as they flaunt their aerial prowess and ingenuity during descent into their colonial chasm. Some approach low over the surrounding ground and turn in a leisurely half roll to parachute into the Stygian depths, but many seemingly hurl themselves in reckless abandon, twisting, rolling and girating into the abyss. The exhibitionists amongst them plummet vertically from great height or tumble in disorderly squabbling twos and threes as if more intent on altercation than arriving safely and all amidst the conflicting trajectories of a hundred others. Their nests are in cavities and on ledges fifty metres and more from the surface, and their exit is assisted by an updraught from an opening in a cliff face far below.

After descending the scree-slope, which leads to the valley floor, I was drawn to some of the nearby crags and stony hillocks as these are wonderfully floriferous rock-gardens at this time of year. Many of the plants are deep-rooted, woody-stemmed perennials with foliage closely moulded to the rock surface. When tightly and intimately interspersed, the colourful mosaics which result are exquisitely refined. Most participants were familiar from previous encounters, but the blue-violet, lobed trumpets of *Edraianthus graminifolius* nestling in rosettes of linear leaves, were a striking addition. Elsewhere on the rocky slopes there were solitary stems elevating the scented, frilly-edged, pink flowers of *Dianthus sylvestris* and tufts of the much paler pink or white thrift, *Armeria canescens*. Entrancing as these rock gardens were, it was however the hollows in the floor of the valley which offered the most appealing attraction as they provided a density of floral abundance far beyond any I had seen before in this locality. The deep winter snows and subsequent heavy rains which Alexis had described must have initiated this profusion. Swathes of violet-flowered *Viola epirota* were foremost in abundance amongst the assemblage with the glossy yellow orbs of the buttercup *Ranunculus sartorianus* shining through the dense foliage and the delicate dark blue bells of *Campanula rotundifolia* swaying above the sward. Most visually riveting of all, however, were the dark-veined, deep purplish-red salvers of *Geranium cinereum* ssp. *subcaulescens* which on Tymphi have a large intensely dark purple stain at the base of each petal. Even as here, competing with others, they appear to glow with a strange quality but when isolated against the whiteness of the limestone they impart a luminous effluence and seem to float, as if detached from the background. They epitomise all that is surmised about the apparent uniqueness of the light in Greece, of how it reveals obscurities and otherwise hidden truths.

As I intended to make a detour to explore the screes beneath the western face of Krevvati I stowed my pack temporarily amidst some boulders and set off up the valley. Thankfully there was a cool downdraught from the snow-capped summit ridge, as with a cloudless sky it would otherwise be a hot and exhausting climb. Following the succession of flowery hollows which interrupted an otherwise boulder strewn route I had not taken before, I was surprised to encounter several stands of the tall yellow toadflax, *Linaria peloponnesiaca*.

The dense terminal columns of spurred flowers on knee-high, leafy wands seem somewhat out of place amidst such exposed rocky surroundings, as indeed they are since they are another species more at home in open woodland but one which has adapted to environmental change as former forest cover retreated. Similarly for another erect-stemmed plant, *Asyneuma limonifolium*, of which there were several scattered over the slopes, this with an interrupted spike of lovely pale blue to lilac five-rayed flowers. Far less visually assertive but fascinating as an extreme example of its kind were the tiny single-flowered stems of *Dianthus integer* ssp. *minutiflorus* appearing everywhere its mats of linear tufted leaves could take root. The purple tinged, cylindrical calyx provides an appropriate contrast to highlight the white flowers amidst the limestone. Whilst there were many other more familiar species too, I was inclined to press on as an earlier binocular-aided scan from the escarpment suggested an unexplained whiteness to the screes ahead which was not remnant snow. It was my intention to climb towards the summit ridge as far as was necessary to be able to contour back across the screes to the foot of the western-facing cliffs of Krevvati. After working back at the base of the cliffs I could then descend the screes to my starting point in the valley floor. As I climbed, the palmate-leaved masses of *Geranium macrorrhizum* tumbling in cascades over the boulder piles became ever more extravagant, flaunting their roseate, pink, and purple floral acclamation to the morning sun. There are few botanical sights to compare with this exuberant plant. Not to be outshone, however, and as the acclivity steepened, there in close proximity were two of the mountains most spectacular species of thyme, *Thymus boissieri*, a carpet of pinkish-purple, and *Thymus leucospermus*, drapped like a chlamys cloak of royal purple as if discarded by Pyrrhus himself.

Pausing for a while to admire these floristic wonders, I became aware of intermittent resonant and melodious calls, at first difficult to locate as they were reverberating from the adjacent cliffs but seemingly originating from the escarpment opposite. There were long pauses between the mellow, fluted phrases which were more fluid than that of Blue Rock Thrush and, searching the craggy edge, the characteristic outline of a male Rock Thrush with its short tail and upright chat-like stance came into view. It was too distant and shaded to differentiate the strikingly coloured plumage, but as it turned and dropped into the boulder pile below, there was a glimpse of the white back patch and a flash of orange undersides. The mottled brown female will probably have eggs in a neat cup of grass, rootlets and moss beneath a boulder or in a rock crevice nearby. Although much depleted in numbers throughout the mountains of southern Europe, they are consistent summer visitors here, so I was confident of seeing others during my walk.

Continuing my ascent, I was approaching the lower limits of the screes and could now see that the whiteness I had previously discerned was, as I had thought, a profusion of flowers emerging from beneath the rock debris over most of the slope up to the cliffs. There were abundant sprays of white-flowered *Berteroa obliqua* on the slopes below but the plant on the screes was different. Arriving at the first of these, I recognised them as *Cardamine carnosa*, a species I had seen in previous years in rocky hollows just below the summit of Goura at the south-eastern limit of the main summit ridge. The flowers, each thumbnail sized and with a yellowish base to the otherwise pure white obovate petals, were so liberally scattered above the fleshy segmented foliage as to impart a seemingly snowy coverlet to the slopes. As was so amply demonstrated, this is a species admirably adapted to life amongst the rocks of a stable scree-slope, for the plants have extremely lengthy, slender and flexible rhizomes. Although this profusion alone was remarkable, I soon realised that the swathes of flowers before me was only part of the floristic exposition for there, too, in equal abundance but secreted between the rocks, were the exquisite flowers of *Viola albanica*. I had found similar plants a few years before, in the screes at the base of the great cliffs which plunge from the summit ridge of Tymphi into the Aoos valley but had been uncertain of their affinity. They did not conform to the species as described from the adjacent peak of Smolikas, one of only a few mountains in north-west Greece and Albania where it grows, reputedly only on serpentine and schist substrate. On Tymphi the plants flourish on limestone, the flowers differ in colour and the leaves and stipules only approximate in their proportions. The flowers are a rich lilac, the lowest petal shallowly bilobed, with a yellow, white-rimmed basal eye from which arise three dark violet streaks. The downwardly directed spur is long, slender and dark violet-purple. Set amidst the glaucous and celadonic foliage, the elements of which are more slender than in typical *albanica*, here amidst the heights of Tymphi they are an inspirational sight. Whatever binomial epithet is appropriate, this is a plant of exceptional beauty, and exhibited in such glorious array, will hopefully remain inviolable in its mountain stronghold.

Following the margin of the screes brought other floristic surprises as I moved further up the slopes. A high altitude form of the Horseshoe Vetch, *Anthyllis vulneraria* ssp. *pulchella*, appeared in places where substantial boulders gave protection, the large variously coloured pink-flushed flowers held aloft on ascending leafy stems. Secreted amongst the screes but abundant also on the grassy slopes from where snow had only recently receded, were the bright yellow cups of *Ranunculus brevifolius*, an alpine buttercup with fleshy, somewhat angular leaves. Having gained sufficient altitude, I then contoured back across the screes to the base of the western cliffs of Krevvati which appeared from my earlier binocular-aided scan to have a few accessible floral masses clinging to the sheer-walled southern limit. Most of these were found on closer observation to be the rather loosely compacted cushions of *Minuartia pseudosaxifraga* which were studded with five-petalled white flowers, many still in bud. This is known from only one other mountain, that of Nemerska on the border with Albania. Others, however, in some abundance at the base of the cliffs, were densely flowered clumps of a chickweed, *Cerastium decalvans*, which, with its white-felted foliage and stems, and large white flowers, is a most attractive sight. Also here, tucked into sheltered and shaded corners was a catchfly, *Silene chromodonta*, with tiny bifid-petalled white flowers on slender very fragile stems, also known from only one other mountain, that of Olimpos where it grows in deciduous forest at low altitude. This is another species indicative of the former extent of woodland on the mountain.

After retrieving my pack from the valley floor, my route was through a breach in the rock wall forming the western flank of the valley above Tsepelovo and some three kilometres from my earlier overnight resting place above the village. There were substantial drifts of snow blocking the mountain track which winds up the slopes beyond Tsepelovo to this its highest point in the valley and then climbs the southern end of the Kourtetsi ridge to meander eastwards down into the valley beneath Goura and thence to Skamneli. Hollows only recently relieved of snow were coloured with the now familiar *Crocus veluchensis* in abundance but here accompanied by a profusion of violet-blue *Scilla bifolia*, the six-rayed flowers in finger-length sprays brilliant against the frosted bleached backcloth. Elsewhere clusters of the white-starred *Ornithogalum oligophyllum* were emerging in multitudes from a newly revived grassy sward with scattered leafy clumps of the large-flowered bright blue *Myosotis alpestris* ssp. s*uaveolens* making a welcome reappearance. With a few Clouded Yellow butterflies determinedly heading north beneath the midday sun, I emulated their single-mindedness by climbing a short scree-slope to the crags which shade the eastern side of the valley. Here, beneath some wonderfully floriferous purple cushions of *Aubrieta scardica* clinging to the cliff face, is a plant assemblage nurtured by the partial shade and protection afforded by the rocks. Retiring in habit and unobtrusive in appearance, the nodding, green bells of *Fritillaria thessala* ssp. *ionica*, delicately tessellated in purple or pink, appeared above pale green foliage. Far more evident were the dense clusters of minutely pink-flowered *Valeriana tuberosa* crowning tall solitary stems and the lovely Pheasant's Eye Narcissus, *Narcissus poeticus* ssp. *radiiflorus*, pure white, with a yellow, vermilion-tinged cup-shaped eye, amidst glaucous leaves. Following the line of crags a short distance up the valley side, some splendid clumps of *Doronicum columnae* displayed brilliant yellow, radiating discs, shining brightly from the deeply shaded alcoves they favour.

After descending from the crags I turned eastwards along the track leading to the ridgetop and then traced the crest northwards onto the slopes of Kourtetsi, an inclined karstic plateau bounded by the narrow uppermost section of the Tsepelovo valley to the west and by the broad Goura valley to the east. As the two valley-heads merge in a great cirque beneath the main summit ridge, Kourtetsi is thus confined on three sides by depressions and isolated as an elevated tabletop rising to a 2,169 metre-high summit at its northern limit. Being in need of a rest, I chose a suitable vantage point on the southern rim of the plateau and settled down in the midday sun. Mitsikeli and the more distant extensions of the mountainous skyline to the south and east were shimmering hazily in the heat, but the broad extent of the Tymphaean southern slopes were in sharp focus, undulating down to the Skamneliotikos, in the Selio valley far below. The ridges and gullies, hillocks and hollows of those slopes appeared as insubstantial components of the landscape yet, being remnants of glacial moraines are significant vestiges of momentous times and extreme climes.

My walk from the edge of the Vikos Canyon, if undertaken at the height of the Skamnellian glacial phase some 450,000 years ago, would have been a daunting challenge in a lifeless and bleak landscape of ice, rock, sediment and meltwater. Viewed from the crags above the Megas Lakos ravine, the cinereous rock walls of Astraka and Krevvati would have framed an ice-field blanketing the intervening slopes up to the summit ridge. Below, a glacial tongue extended into the upper reaches of the Megas Lakos ravine. Following the edge of the ice-field, it would have been a tiring walk across a morass of sandstone blocks and saturated silt, interlaced with meltwater streams which were rapidly eroding down to the underlying limestone. From the escarpment edge the challenge ahead would have been clearly visible, with first sight of the Goura glacier sweeping round the southern edge of Kourtetsi to coalesce with the glacier occupying the Tsepelovo valley, a two-kilometre wide expanse of ridged and crevassed ice at the confluence. Crossing that glacier would have been hazardous, but once onto the heights of Kourtetsi the full panorama of the glacial landscape on the southern slopes of the mountain would have been apparent. Looking out over the expanse of ice directly below, its continuation as a kilometre wide glacier, curving just east of where the village of Tsepelovo is now located, would have dominated the scene down to the floor of the Selio valley. There the glacier blocked the outflow of meltwater, forming the substantial ice-dammed lake I had first envisaged when crossing the Xatsiou Bridge. The glacier's former channel is now largely obscured by moraine deposited during retreat of the ice-front, and even the valley evident today above Tsepelovo, which would have been part of that channel, was probably re-excavated by meltwater from the subsequent and less extensive Vlasian glaciers. Diverting my attention eastwards across the slopes, a second offshoot of the Goura glacier would also have been apparent. Of similar magnitude to the Tsepelovo glacier, this ploughed a course through where Skamneli is situated and was the source of icebergs floated onto the melt-water lake. Perhaps the reverberating roar of rock-falls and avalanches from the heights of Krevvati and Goura into the then ice-filled corrie behind me would have been superfluous in emphasising the severity of the Tymphaean environment at that time.

In contrast, recollections of so many plants seen during the day favouring shelter and shade, invoked images of times when environmental conditions on the mountain were far more temperate. For much of the 6,000 years immediately after those Palaeolithic hunters finally abandoned their seasonal rock-shelter home, the mountain was, as previously envisioned, forested to varying degrees, and my walk from the edge of the Vikos Canyon at any time during that period would have been a pleasant meander from clearing to clearing through open woodland or beneath the densely canopied cover of more ubiquitous forest. Arrival at this plateau edge would be coincidental with emergence above the treeline, revealing a scene of summit crags and cliffs rising from an otherwise largely arboreal landscape. That so many of those woodland species survive on the open mountain to this day is a reminder of those former times and the fluctuations between arctic and temperate environments a testimony to the inevitability of natural climatic change.

As it was my intention to spend the night here and in the meantime explore the plateau and its surroundings, I was thankful for the opportunity to wander unencumbered for a while. There was water at the Goura Spring not far away, so I would make a detour there later to replenish supplies. Before setting off, however, I wanted to search the slopes below in the hope of repeating a reptilian encounter I had made the previous year. Then it had been a surprise which had quickly escalated into excitement with the realization that I had found a species of snake not previously recorded on the mountain or anywhere else in northern Greece. Conditions were now ideal, with the slope having been in full sun for several hours so I began with an expectancy only slightly constrained by experience. Orsini's Viper is a somewhat lethargic species, so a methodical search of the slopes, surveying the ground a few metres ahead, should be successful in finding any which were basking in the sun. Yet, after half an hour of pacing an extensive area, including the exact locations where I had found two individuals the previous year, I reluctantly accepted defeat and resigned myself to recollections of that earlier experience. At that time my immediate response to seeing the coils of a stout-bodied viper sunning itself on a rock was Nose-horned Viper, which I knew to be present on the mountain. Even so, a momentary appraisal was sufficient to discount that possibility as the head was too small and elongate and lacked the distinctive nasal structure. Also this snake appeared to be extremely docile and as I soon realised was feigning death, having uncoiled to adopt a zig-zag form and a rigidity which allowed me to turn it over to expose a white and rose-pink underside. As it was so obliging, I took the opportunity to record details of the head scales and other features necessary for identification, a rather disconcerting experience when confronting those malevolant, lustrous, vertically-slit eyes in such close proximity. That was sufficient to confirm it as a Greek subspecies of the Orsini's Viper, previously only known from a few locations in the southern and central Pindos Mountains of Greece, and more recently from a single site in southern Albania. As all occurrences are confined to isolated areas between 1,750 and 2,000 metres altitude, it may have been a more widespread species at lower levels in times of cooler climate, obliged to move to higher and more restricted areas as the climate ameliorated.

Although the limestone which comprises the mountain is almost everywhere deeply and variously eroded, this is especially evident in the vicinity of Kourtetsi. Here there are extensive areas of rock pavement, where the surfaces of gently inclined strata are deeply incised, in places for several metres, by two or more sets of parallel vertical fissures intersecting at high angles. The fissures, originally formed during the early stages of rock formation as incipient planes of weakness, are vulnerable to percolating water and especially when covered in humus-rich soil as they would have been when the slopes were forested. Decaying humus raises the carbon dioxide content of rain-water and consequently the effectiveness of limestone dissolution, thus widening and deepening the fissures, a process which accelerates as the surface area of limestone under attack increases. With loss of the forest and much of the associated ground vegetation, the soil is vulnerable to erosion and may be removed entirely or, as on these more gently inclined slopes only partially, leaving sufficient within the fissures to support plants which thrive in such shaded and confined spaces. Gazing into these clefts is to enter another world, one inhabited especially by arctic-alpine ferns, of which the palmately dissected *Asplenium fissum* and rectangular-pinnuled *Asplenium trichomanes* ssp. *inexpectans* and *Asplenium viride* are the delicate minutia, whilst the Holly Fern, *Polystichum lonchitis* and Hart's Tongue, *Phyllitis scolopendrium*, are the more robust. The conclusion that many of these are relicts from colder times is reinforced by the presence of the temperate and subarctic species Baneberry, *Actaea spicata*, the densely white-flowered spikes of which can also be found protruding from some of these fissures.

Although only two kilometres or so to the northern end of the Kourtetsi plateau, the fissured and sharp-edged rocks underfoot require attention with each and every step. The resulting slow and measured progress is nevertheless conducive to a more receptive appreciation of one's surroundings than might otherwise be the case. My first stop was on hearing a sound resembling that of two quartz pebbles being ground together, subsequent to a short warble, the unmistakable phrasing of a Black Redstart. Several pairs regularly nest in rock fissures in the surrounding crags and will have young to feed at this time of year. Ever watchful, as soon as it came into binocular vision, it was gone with a flash of russet-red rump and tail into the rock piles at the plateau edge. Here too, erupting from fissures replete with a generous red-soil infill were several compact shrubs of a dwarf rose, mostly deep pink, some pale-pink-flowered, with red prickles on zigzag stems and attractive grey-green elliptic leaflets. This is *Rosa heckeliana* ssp. *heckeliana* which is quite abundant on the slopes below Kourtetsi and otherwise confined to the Balkans and Sicily. The rose was not alone for there were other flowers, already familiar, with some such as the pink or white thrift *Armeria canescens* and the white-flowered *Dianthus integer* ssp. *minutiflorus* especially abundant, even in this relatively exposed environment. Even some of the taller species such as *Achillea abrotanoides* and *Valeriana tuberosa* were here too, although more localised and somewhat stunted compared to those seen at lower and more sheltered locations. The valerian is an attractive source of nectar for butterflies and here had detained a single Painted Lady on what would otherwise be its energetic migration northward. These are boldly coloured and patterned butterflies when freshly emerged, as this one appeared to be, presumably being one of a local brood derived from earlier springtime immigrants from North Africa. Although denied a view of the bright terracotta, black and white-spotted uppersides as it was feeding with closed wings, the undersides have a more subtle beauty. That of the hindwing, with its delicate tracery of white veins and row of ringed ocelli on an intricate buff and white patterned background, is mesmerising in its detail. Of the forewing there is a rosy-red base to the inner angle which never fails to seduce the eyes before these are drawn to the buff, white, black and terracotta intricacies of the remainder. That these exquisite wings carry millions of its compatriots from the desert fringes of North Africa to the furthest reaches of Europe in annual mass migrations is, as I can testify from encounters in the Sahara, one of the wonders of nature.

As these rocky slopes lead only to an inconsequential summit, they are part of the untrodden ways even for the Sarakatsani shepherds and their flocks, except when pasturage on the mountain is so meagre that even these barren acres are grazed. Such unfrequented places are the preserve of ground nesting birds, and here it is the Rock Partridge which favours the area. Scanning the ground ahead for movement, as the birds habitually run from perceived danger, the distinctively marked head of a male appeared amongst the rocks as it periodically paused to view the intruder. The white throat, rimmed by a black necklace which passes through the eye and across the forehead of an otherwise blue-grey head, is simultaneously both a bold display and an effective camouflage, as the markings detract from any perception of outline. A series of black and chestnut-brown stripes on creamy-buff flanks do likewise for the body, so until it moves the bird is very difficult to locate amidst the differently shaded and sunlit blue-grey rocks. Female birds are more subdued in colouration and less boldly marked, and will probably have young chicks at this time, hatched in a shallow sheltered scrape and now foraging for insects and larvae amongst the rocks and vegetation. Later they will adopt a diet of leaves, shoots, buds, seeds and fruit which will sustain them for most of the year, the young birds only descending to lower levels when snow blankets the mountain.

Knowing that the Rock Partridge would rapidly outpace me and soon disappear, I continued on, accompanied by the aerial song of several Skylarks, circling invisibly in the blueness above, a reminder that they too were nesting somewhere on this plateau. Enchanting as that song is, I was hopeful of a vocal rendition from a much more elusive songster which nests in the crags here and which sometimes performs in response to invasion of its territory by a human intruder. The male Rock Thrush I had encountered briefly during the morning had delivered a few phrases of its perch-song but that was only a brief sample of its repertoire. After approaching an area of rocks at the plateau edge where a pair had nested in previous years, I sat and waited. If in residence, and despite being very retiring when breeding, the male bird should appear in time. Even in the silhouette it presented initially there is an unmistakable form to this bird, upright, short-tailed and heavy-billed, an identity affirmed characteristically by upward flicks of its tail. Dropping to the ground, its long hops ensured rapid progress to a prominent rock which it surmounted with two full downbeats of its dark wings and momentary chestnut flashes from the underwing. Seen, as now, in bright sunlight, a breeding male is a remarkably colourful bird, with bright orange-chestnut undersides, blue-grey head and mantle, and a white back intermittently revealed between flitting wings as it nervously appraises the intruder. Suddenly it launches low from its rock perch and then climbs silently and steeply with powerful wingbeats, bursting into song as it flutters butterfly-like with fanned tail flaming bright orange-red in the afternoon sun. The song is a torrent of resonant fluting phrases mingling with mimicry and warbling subsong, reaching a crescendo at the pinnacle of ascent where the bird soars and flutters, then plunges silently on spread wings and tail back to its rock perch. After a brief appraisal of the intruder, it was gone with a flash of white, over the rocky plateau edge.

It was several minutes before I felt any inclination to move on, being preoccupied with the aftermath of this encounter, and later still before other aspects of the surroundings began to impinge on awareness. Underfoot the bright pink flowers of *Prunus prostrata* were bursting from crimson tinted buds on freshly leaved woody branches tightly clothing the rocks, whilst elsewhere another procumbent shrub, that of *Iberis sempervirens*, contributed clusters of its tiny white flowers above evergreen foliage. A multi-rayed, bright sky-blue composite, *Lactuca intricata*, also occurred sparingly, its intricately branched stems appearing above rosettes of pinnate basal leaves on taproots wedged deep into the rock fissures. Surprisingly for such an exposed location, isolated clumps of the tall stemmed *Tulipa australis* were adding their bright yellow, scarlet-tinged, stellate flowers to the scene, perhaps another relict from former forested times.

As I was following the eastern edge of the plateau, now narrowing towards the northern summit crags, the broad extent of the Goura valley was becoming ever more evident beneath the towering mass of Goura peak beyond. From that 2,466 metre-high summit, a spur, the Kato Tsoeka ridge, slopes gradually southwards in conformity with the inclined strata and occupies the skyline before plunging steeply down to the slopes above Skamneli. That ridge would be my route tomorrow. For now it was sufficient just to appreciate the grandeur of the scene with the frost-shattered cliffs of Goura rising from massive screes bordering the snow-pocked expanse of the valley beneath. When approaching the northern limit of the plateau the scene widens further as the head of the Goura valley sweeps westwards into the great cirque, an amphitheatre backed by the saw-toothed summit ridge connecting the Goura and Krevvati peaks and leading into the upper reaches of the Tsepelovo valley. From my vantage point the floor of the depression, the *megala leethareeya* or Place of the Great Stones, lies some 300 metres below, still partially snow covered amidst the many huge limestone blocks from which it is named. If those Palaeolithic hunters had ever ventured this far they would have gazed upon a permanent ice-field filling this amphitheatre with short glacial tongues extending a few hundred metres into the Tsepelovo and Goura valleys to left and right of their elevated location. The great stone blocks destined to be abandoned on the floor would have been evident on the ice-field surface.

As I intended making a detour down to the Goura Spring I was climbing over rocks looking for a possible way down when a small slate-grey bird suddenly flew out with a short rippling call which seemed strangely disembodied, as if emitted from elsewhere. This was instantly recognisable as an Alpine Accentor, a bird I have encountered many times in mountains from the High Atlas to the Himalayas and which is well known for its ventriloquistic skills. Beloved by many who frequent high places, this is a bird which has hopped onto my boots looking for insects or seeds I might have disturbed from beneath the snow, even in mid-winter. Now, perhaps with a moss-lined nest of grass and leaves hidden in a rock crevice, it is far less confiding. However, after moving away a little and sitting quietly, I was rewarded when the bird reappeared with little runs and hops amongst the rocks, stopping briefly to flick and jerk its wings and tail in anxiety. This is the *subalpina* race of the Balkans and when seen closely in good light is far from the dull grey bird it might seem to be from a fleeting, distant encounter. It is beautifully coloured and patterned, the head, breast and undersides a lovely pale ash-grey, with a blue or brownish ever-changing sheen, and rufous-streaked flanks. The chin and throat are white, patterned with semi-circular necklaces of delicate black spots, and the feathers of the back, wings and tail a dark brown, variously tinged, streaked and edged in rufous, black and white in a beautifully intricate composition. When nature combines such plumaged refinement with a confiding and trusting demeanour it offers us a very special privilege.

After retracing my route a few hundred metres to a break in the plateau edge, I began to descend into the Goura valley, inevitably a tortuous route as there is a series of escarpments to negotiate. Most present only a two or three metre drop, that being the thickness of the resistant limestone layers, but still sufficient of an obstacle to require a detour to find a safe way down. I had not gone far before being alerted by a cacophony of sharp, staccato, *chack* calls, the characteristic alarm response from adult Wheatears, in this instance accompanied by several juvenile birds. They are normally shy and wary but here with young to protect were adopting a distraction display, the male being especially forward, standing boldly upright on a prominent rock, flicking its wings to expose a white rump and black-barred tail whilst constantly bobbing in extreme agitation. This is the *libanotica* race, which has pale blue-grey upperparts and creamy-white underparts, with contrasting black wings and black cheeks beneath a white eye-stripe. The female, less bold in this display, is also restrained in colouration being brown above and pale buff beneath but with the same distinctively marked black and white tail as that of the male. Those Palaeolithic hunters would have been familiar with this encounter as those birds which now breed in the Mediterranean region are perhaps relict populations, whilst others have extended progressively northwards to breed in Europe, the Arctic and central Asia as the climate ameliorated. They mostly winter in sub-Saharan Africa, so are early summer visitors to their breeding grounds.

There were few other surprises on my approach to the spring, this being floristically poor terrain, perhaps due to the centuries of concentrated grazing by sheep from the seasonally occupied *stanee* a little further down the valley. *Crocus veluchensis* and *Scilla bifolia* still appeared in sufficient quantity to border the receding snow with colour, to be followed by a few other familiar early flowerers, but with the flocks soon to arrive from their wintering pasturage in the lowlands little else is able to flourish here. The Goura Spring erupts as a steady stream from the valley floor and flows for only a short distance before returning underground and, as befits any such source on an otherwise waterless mountain, is traditionally honoured by the inhabitants of Skamneli, in this instance with visitations during wedding celebrations. The water's seemingly miraculous appearance and disappearance has no doubt been an object of wonder for millennia, reinforced perhaps by the equally surprising emergence of hundreds of Yellow-bellied Toads some of which aestivate beneath the winter snows and breed with such evident success during early spring. Although the Yellow-bellied is known from many other localities at high altitude, that is less so for the Green Toad, a pair of which were busy mating and laying spawn in the ice-cold waters. Thoughts of the night-time chorus combining the high-pitched liquid trill of the latter with the monosyllabic but musical utterances of the former, briefly offered the temptation to relocate my overnight camp to the vicinity.

My return route lay along the Goura valley for a short distance before it was necessary to head upslope towards the southern end of the Kourtetsi plateau, again having to negotiate the sequence of escarpments but less of an obstacle from below as the rock walls were clearly visible during the ascent. Perhaps attracted by the enhanced feeding potential provided by large concentrations of sheep adjacent to grassland-nesting habitat, there are always Ortolan Buntings to be seen here during summer months. These rely on insect and other invertebrate larvae to feed their young but revert to dependence on seeds out of the breeding season. Male birds were already proclaiming territorial rights in ringing tones from their rock perches and progressing from one eminence to the next in fluent undulating flight which reveals white edging to the dark brown tail. With rufous brown uppers streaked black on wings and back, orange-chestnut underparts and olive-toned head and breast with yellow throat, the male is an attractive bird. The duller female will have a grass- and leaf-lined nest in a depression on the nearby slopes.

On regaining the plateau and after retrieving my pack, I chose a suitable overnight resting place and settled down for the evening. It had remained a cloudless day and, as the northern summit ridge appeared innocent of obscuring any impending storm clouds, I was hopeful of an unimpeded view of the southern night-sky. The planetary conjunction would also be visible westwards through the gap south of Krevvati and above the southern slopes of Astraka. In the meantime, I was happy to observe the progression of light and shade across the landscape and to watch and wait for any surprises which nature might present. True to habit, one of the Imperial Eagles must have left the eyrie from above Tsepelovo for an evening sortie, as I was alerted by the shrill alarm calls of a Kestrel in aerial pursuit. Presumably the eagle had flown up the valley too close to the falcon's cliff nest site, as now they were engaged in riotous progress across the slopes below me with the smaller bird launching mock attacks against the larger. In such confrontations nature appears to exhibit an instructive element of constraint. Both birds are lethally armed, but any injury to either would threaten their continued survival, so they are behaviourally conditioned to offer only threat and counter-threat until the territorial integrity of each is restored. At that point the Kestrel wheeled away and winged its way homeward, whilst the Imperial Eagle resumed its hunting foray.

Gradually a pink glow emanating from the face of Goura, retreated in deference to an indigo haze advancing eastwards from Krevvati, as the great amphitheatre became overwhelmed by shadow. Only the serrated skyline of the summit ridge, briefly flaming gold and bronze, remained illuminated but soon faded as the sun sank further towards the slopes of Astraka. In the silence of a windless evening the slightest and most distant sounds seemed enhanced, as now even the amphibian chorus from the Goura Spring became faintly discernible. More evident was the occasional clatter of a falling rock, a consequence of contraction imparted by rapid cooling as shade replaces sunlight and night displaces day. Every diurnal temperature change assists gravity in dismantling the mountain; nothing is permanent.

Soon the western sky dimmed to disclose the now somewhat corpulent crescent of the waxing moon adjacent to a brilliant Venus, with Jupiter a lesser light, now a little detached from the planetary association. Within an hour the red glow of Mars had emerged to accompany them on their descent to the horizon. The clear, shrill contact-call of a Little Owl arose briefly from the valley above Tsepelovo reverberating from the cliffs where a pair habitually nests. Absorbed in watching the emerging panoply of stars, magnificent in the darkness of a now moonless sky, my intention of prolonging wakefulness to witness the celestial progression must have lapsed, for it was clearly much later that I awoke abruptly and very alert. Overhead the splendour of the Milky Way ran from north to south, an indicator of early morning hours. Some sense of a potential threat had perhaps penetrated sleep, so I lay listening intently. A sharp clink of stone on stone suggested movement on the road below. That part of the road cuts through fine-grained porcellanous limestone which rings bell-like when struck or dislodged. Raising myself sufficient to scan the slope down to the road with my binoculars, the silence was suddenly shattered by a sequence of explosive spitting and loud high-pitched cries as two, dimly visible, substantial feline forms disappeared into the darkness. Although normally solitary animals, there was no doubt that they were Lynx. They are known to occur very rarely in the well-forested Aoos valley where Roe Deer are their main prey but apparently range onto the open mountain in search of hares, Rock Partridge and Chamois. Elated by this encounter, I lay back in awe of the brilliant starry pathway extending overhead to the southernmost horizon. Above me the lovely blue star, Vega, shone brightly alongside Altar and Deneb, its companions in the Summer Triangle, set amidst the myriad stars of Cygnus and Aquila. Beyond lay the magnificent star-clouds of Sagittarius towards the centre of the galaxy and further still the glorious array of bright stars in Scorpius with brilliant red Antares just visible above the Mitsikeli ridge. A little to the east, Saturn hung low above the mountains of Metsova. It was a feeling of profound contentment which accompanied me once more to sleep.

# Chapter 4

# The gift of Goura

It was the reassuring *chuck chuck chuckara* of Rock Partridges which was my early morning alarm call on the Kourtetsi plateau. The male birds are inclined to welcome the first hint of dawn with enthusiastic vocalization in affirmation of their territorial claims, an instinct which lessens as the day progresses but is often reinvigorated in the evening. Now the calls seemed as emblematic for this stony Balkan wilderness of clint and gryke, of crag and cliff, as is the *coulee* of the Curlew for northern bog and moor. As my overnight resting place was shaded by the Kato Tsoeka ridge, I moved to the sunlit slopes and walked down to where the road was partly blocked by snow in the hope of finding tracks left by the overnight visitors. Lynx leave surprisingly large imprints, but on this occasion there was nothing to be seen. Retracing my steps, I crossed the ridge and followed the road down towards the southern end of the Kato Tsoeka ridge which was to be my route to the Goura summit. A male Stonechat was busy exhibiting slavish adherence to mechanistic behaviour with a display of demented wing and tail flicking, whilst flying erratically between perches and chacking loudly, all to divert my attention from his offspring who would have been unnoticed but for this display. I stopped to admire his smart attire of black head and throat, white collar and bright chestnut breast. The drab female, habitually more subdued in behaviour, was a mild understudy to the histrionic lead actor. They are frequent summer visitors to the lower slopes of the mountain and to the grasslands which provide the abundant insect food on which they rely. The similarly dependent Ortolan Buntings were also very evident in their early morning foraging, an activity which I was observing carefully in the hope of seeing a much more elusive species which is very similar in appearance. This is near the altitudinal limit for Cretzschmar's Bunting, but having seen a few pairs here in previous years, they appear to be regular visitors to these slopes, attracted by the abundant insect prey and grass-seeds, adjacent to rocky terrain suitable for nesting. As they are exclusively ground feeders, seemingly never mounting rocks or tussocks, they are much less obtrusive than many species even though relatively tame and confiding. After scanning a few contenders looking unsuccessfully for the grey head and bright orange-chestnut throat which differentiates them from Ortolan, I abandoned the search knowing there would be other opportunities.

Access to Kato Tsoeka is by way of a steep morainic ridge after which the acclivity lessens and it is possible to follow a rocky crest above the westward-facing cliffs overlooking the Goura valley. Stony slopes plunge steeply south-east to extensive grasslands around the isolated 2,157 metre-high summit of Tsoumako at the eastern end of the Tymphaean massif. Some craggy outcrops at the commencement of the crest provide anchorage for wonderfully floriferous compact cushions of *Minuartia pseudosaxifraga* with their starry white flowers surpassing those of Krevvati in abundance. Many of the rock plants seen elsewhere are also here despite the exposed position. After climbing to a height sufficiently elevated to survey the scene now unfolding on all sides, I settled down for a rest in the warmth of the sun. From up here the southern slopes of Tymphi appear more benign than is apparent underfoot when negotiating its fretted rocky surface, such detail being absorbed into the undulations of hill and hollow which impart a gentler face to the landscape when viewed from above. These slopes are the pasturelands which have drawn shepherds and their flocks since at least the ninth century BC, when the Molossian settlement at Genitsari was founded, and probably much earlier, for there is evidence of pastoral influences well before then. Around 4,400 years ago there was, locally, a significant increase in plant species which favour the nitrogen-rich, disturbed substrates, typical of intensive stock rearing and enclosure. That this was accompanied by an abrupt decline in forest trees, increased erosion and an insurgence of grassland species further supports the probability that human influence and the incursion of domesticated animals was significant at that time. A similar interlude also appears in the vegetational history of the mountain some 6,000 years ago, which would be contemporary with the apparent early spread of animal husbandry within Greece. Whilst it would be speculative to suggest a continuous history of animal pasturage on the mountain since that early date, it would be much less so for most of the last three millennia. The Genitsari settlement was active for 600 years, after which it seems likely that pastoral practices would have been maintained under the then powerful Molossian state at least until its destruction by the Romans in 168 BC. The Molossians were famed throughout the Greek and Roman world for their animal husbandry. When the Roman legions departed they took 150,000 Molossians with them into slavery and reputedly left seventy cities and settlements in ruins. Although this devastation was probably confined to the more populous lowlands, the resulting economic decline and collapse in demand for timber may account for the apparent resurgence of pine forest on at least part of the Tymphaean massif during succeeding centuries. As pine appears to favour the northern and north-eastern slopes however, it seems likely that the grasslands of these southern slopes retained their open aspect.

At some time in this sequence of events, nomadic shepherding communities enter the scene and, of the ethnic groups which have filled that role in recent times, the Sarakatsani appear to be of greatest antiquity. Their pure Greek dialect, and cultural and artistic affinities, indicate a regional provenance sometime within the third millennium and an ancestry perhaps arising from the transhumant shepherds of the Molossian era. But Sarakatsani are not only confined to this, the Epirus region of Greece. In the mid-twentieth century they were also established in the other northern provinces of Thessaly, Macedonia and Thrace, with a few further south in the northern Peloponnese and Euboea, cumulatively some 80,000 strong. Being wholly nomadic, there would have been few constraints to the practical necessity of exploiting the most productive pasturage available and, as that of Tymphi was apparently considered some of the best, it seems likely to have been continually and long favoured as a summer destination. In the 1950s there were over 30,000 sheep and goats belonging to Sarakatsani *stanee* grazing the summer pastures of the villages of Papingo, Vradeto, Kepesovo, Tsepelovo and Skamneli, constituting most of the southern slopes of Tymphi from the Vikos Canyon in the west to the valley of the Skamneliotikos in the south and east. The numbers may have been even greater during the earlier half of the twentieth century, as it was in 1938, when all semi-nomadic shepherds were required by law to register as citizens with the village authorities of either their summer or winter pasturages, that the consequent constraints on nomadic life began to impinge on the 4,000 or so Sarakatsani who then favoured Zagori. Their citizenship enabled them to acquire property and, although their rights to pasturage were also now given some legal protection, slowly they were assimilated into village life and a more settled existence. Consequently the number and size of flocks gradually declined.

Now, as the eye wanders over this pastoral domain, thoughts of the impending demise of those ancient transhumant ways are accompanied by feelings of sadness at their loss. Sheep continue to graze here, but the nomadic way of life of the Sarakatsani is drawing to a close. The few flocks I have seen climbing the slopes of Mitsikeli on their journey from the lowlands have never been more than a few hundred strong, perhaps 500 at most, and apparently that of a single family with their belongings strapped to mules. Some families have maintained vestiges of the celebratory customs long associated with these migrations, the women in embroidered skirts and bodices, the men in black woollen suits and the mules with coloured saddle-cloths. But more usually the procession is so depleted in numbers both of animals and personnel that such refinements are abandoned in favour of convenience. The assembly is always accompanied by two or three brutish guard dogs. Often these animals include a canine monster which itself attests to the Sarakatsan pedigree as the dog breed is probably descended from the Molossus, formerly prized by the Molossians and famed throughout the world of antiquity for their formidable abilities as guard dogs. I have been confronted by similar animals in mountains from the Fagaras of Romania to the Lycian Taurus of Turkey and whilst their aristocratic heritage is the last thought in mind during such intimidating encounters, their pugnacious character and bulk seems consistent with such an ancestry.

Flocks destined for Tymphi sometimes rest for a day near the village of Kepesovo above the Vikos Canyon, following an overnight crossing of Mitsikeli. On arrival, often before dawn, a temporary pen is set up and the ewes are milked before being allowed to graze until mid-morning. Then they lie in the shade throughout the heat of the day. Meanwhile, the women turn the milk into a feta cheese for family consumption. They also bake bread and tend to the goats which may constitute a fifth of the flock. In the evening the sheep are milked again and a second batch of cheese prepared whilst the flock sets out on the last overnight leg of its journey led by the head of the household, usually with a second shepherd bringing up the rear, accompanied by the dogs. It is a raucous assembly when the shepherds and dogs are in full cry but musical when they are not, for sheep and goats alike are temporarily attired with bells to assist in locating strays. When moving unseen through the stillness of an evening the throng sings an ethereal song, of metallic trills and tremulations from the sheep, to an accompaniment of tinkling brass from the nannies and sonorous tolls from the billies. Soon this ancient voice, which for millennia has filled the night air on its annual journey from the shores of Parga and the Gulf of Arta, will fall silent.

After lodging my pack amidst a rock outcrop, I continued to follow the crags which mark the crest leading to the summit. Although lacking the floral diversity seen elsewhere, the rocks still had promise of much to come, with the silver silky-haired basal foliage of *Achillea holosericea* locally abundant, amidst tufts of linear-leaved *Armeria canescens* and the fleshy spathulate-leaved rosettes of *Saxifraga porophylla* ssp. *federici-augusti* lining every crack and crevice in a verdant tracery. Soon all would be in full flower. The adjacent slopes, now immersed in the early morning sun were more colourfully endowed, a gentle breeze rippling through pale blue wands of *Asyneuma limonifolium* and the more robust spikes of *Valeriana tuberosa* topped with pink-flowered clusters. Familiar as these were from previous encounters, they are an arresting sight when amassed in swaying unison in a soft light. Just as this profusion was an exceptional response to an exceptional combination of winter and spring precipitation, so also was the accompanying abundance of *Viola epirota*, now colouring the slopes with a violet suffusion. Here too were the white-flowered sprays of the evergreen candytuft, *Iberis sempervirens* and another dwarf shrub, that of *Daphne oleoides* but yet to flower, both seen sparingly elsewhere although apparently flourishing and abundant in this higher altitude location. Whatever circumstances favoured these shrubs, perhaps they also accounted for the abundance of a dense cushion-forming legume, *Astragalus sirinicus*, with lilac and purple-tinged, cream pea-flowers amidst compact spine-tipped foliage. It is tempting to surmise that the dearth of such shrubs elsewhere on the mountain is due to burning to enhance grazing. Whatever the reason, it is an environment favourable to some as I had not gone far before disturbing a covey of Rock Partridge chicks, nine animated balls of tawny down, scuttling in follow-my-leader procession through the shrubbery. Remarkably the accompanying adult remained passively alongside the chicks, squat and moving close to the ground, all fight or flight instincts suppressed even though I was within only a stride of the group.

Continuing on I was soon reminded of one of the many dangers facing those Rock Partridge chicks and other ground nesting birds, when passing close to one of the crags, an explosive hissing alerted me to a thick-bodied snake coiled at the base in full sun. Nose-horned Vipers appear frequently on these slopes. I had tried to catch one once, an experience which demonstrated that the textbook description of temperament, 'rather phlegmatic and not very irascible', does not apply to the Tymphaean contingent, even less when the animal is provoked. After an initial bout of ill-temper it unleashed an air-borne attack from a coiled posture, which for a heavy sixty-centimetre-long snake was most impressive. I reminded myself of its highly venomous credentials and withdrew suitably chastened. Vipers are, however, fascinating creatures and this species more than most because of the extraordinary horn-like scaly upward extension at the tip of the upper jaw. The vertically slit pupil in an otherwise lustrous golden eye, beneath a heavy brow, is alone sufficient to impart menace, but the horn, which is very pronounced in some individuals, suggests an unknown faculty in the apparent furtherance of evil intent. After satiating my fascination at a respectful distance I continued on along the crest with other objectives in mind. Already several Skylarks could be heard, lost in the blue overhead and the distinctive abrasive refrain of a Black Redstart emanated from the rocks ahead as the bird dived over the edge to the cliffs below. Always when on this route, I head for a featureless place on the crest where, if I have anticipated the flowering time correctly, there is to be found one of the floristic wonders of the mountain. The approach invokes heightened anticipation and today I am not disappointed for there the floor of a shallow hollow on the lip of the crest is paved in a mosaic of the gorgeously blue salvers of a procumbent flax, *Linum punctatum* ssp. *pycnophyllum*. The extreme density of the tiny linear leaves, as indicated by the subspecific name, provides an appropriate infill to the spaces within the white limestone substrate onto which the three-centimetre-diameter flowers are liberally and closely impressed. In defiance of the ferocity with which winds scourge and scour this crest, the woody taproots penetrating deep into the red-earth-filled grykes, have kept these plants in place perhaps for centuries. Now their unyielding fortitude gives life to forms of great beauty. The flowers open as wavy-edged goblets which soon splay their five broad petals to form shallow bowls of violet-tinged cobalt blue, shading inwards to a delicately dark-veined white eye. The plant grows sparingly elsewhere on the slopes of Goura almost to the summit but nowhere does it display a comparable floristic abundance and prostrate form as here. Amassed in their hundreds amidst grey-green foliage and marble-white pebbles, this floral display is an incomparable sight, an invitation to linger and meditate on the wonder of nature. Whilst others, quite commendably, strive to recreate such wonders in the gardens of the world, this can never be accomplished as without the *genius* of place a vital essence is missing. All that is before me in this place is uniquely of this place and can neither be replicated or transposed; once lost it is lost forever.

From the flowery carpet at my feet, it is four kilometres southwards to Skamneli and a further two kilometres to the waters of the Skamneliotikos, 1,000 metres below my present elevation. Distant as that may be, the clarity of the early morning air allows one to discriminate of detail, especially using binoculars, which belies the disjunction. Two Egyptian Vultures appearing black and white at this distance were occupied with mobbing a Black Kite, presumably contesting interests over the rubbish dump adjacent to the village as both birds are inveterate scavengers. The kite is of very infrequent occurrence here and is probably a non-breeding bird on an exploratory foray. What it lacks in colouration, being a dingy brown, it compensates for in aerial prowess with a fluidity and suppleness of movement which is a joy to watch. It can side-slip on arched wings, to pluck food from the ground and rise again without alighting, a manoeuvre which few other birds can accomplish. Soon it abandoned the confrontation and disappeared to reconnoitre the river downstream towards Tsepelovo.

Resuming my climb, it was not far to another place on the cusp of the ridge which I habitually favoured. This shallow gully etched into the craggy cliffs below, is the regular nesting site of one of the most spectacular birds on the mountain. It breeds elsewhere, both in the Vikaki ravine and the Vikos Canyon but is there extremely elusive. Here, with patience, it can be observed so closely as to obviate the need for binoculars. So I settled down amidst the rocks at the head of the gully to wait. Framed by the walls of the gully is a portion of the Goura valley, far below and still exhibiting the well-worn web of sheep tracks from the previous year's occupation of the *stanee*, the sheep-fold of the Sarakatsani, now obscured from view. Sometime soon the medley of bells will herald their coming on the night-time air and they will return to their home in the mountains, for home is how they have traditionally perceived it; their winter in the lowlands is an estrangement and an exile. Always when rounding the mountain shoulder above the Rongavou monastery and seeing again the great expanse of Tymphi opening magnificently before me, I surmise what thoughts and emotions those returning shepherds might experience when arriving at that same place and on seeing their summer homeland again. The few who continue to tread these old ways may have only a vague notion of the ancient footsteps they follow, but they will have a profound and unquestioning sense of belonging here. They could have no finer entree and I envy them that epiphany.

Traditionally the Sarakatsani flocks left their winter quarters soon after the Feast of St. George, April 23rd, and would arrive at their mountain *stanee* sometime in early May, but on Tymphi that has not been so for decades. The few I have seen usually arrive during June and this year, with prior knowledge of the heavy winter snows, probably late June. It was customary for the flocks of each *stanee* affiliated to Skamneli to be apportioned two blocks of grazing from amongst the three areas of the mountain administered by the village, of which the Goura valley and the slopes up to Goura summit were a single area. The extensive pastures of Tsoumako to the east were the second, and the wooded region around the place known as Yiftokambos, north of Tsoumako, the third. In times when the demand was intensive, flocks were apportioned pasturage supposedly to ensure equality of benefit, so no *stanee* was advantaged or disadvantaged with a disproportionate share of good or poor grazing. Such controls may also have contributed to a sustainable use of the pasturelands and prevented overgrazing of the most desirable areas of which

Goura was foremost. The rich grassland flora on the mountain today is largely a consequence of those customary ways.

Absorbed as I was in thoughts of the Sarakatsani, the sudden appearance of my avian quarry flitting butterfly-like across the gully was more of a surprise than it should have been, as I rarely fail to encounter it here. An observer having no preconception of the Wallcreeper can be prone to disbelief if the sole visualisation is a fleeting glimpse of the bird in flight. Alternate splaying and closing of flight feathers creates seemingly dramatic and rapid changes in size which, accompanied by bold and vivid carmine flashes from the upperwing surfaces, effectively confuses the onlooker. An often erratic flight trajectory, deceptively desultory but with the power to make rapid and steep ascents and manoeuvres on rock faces, adds further novelty. The combined effect is one of delight and curiosity for this is a bird of beauty and idiosyncratic behaviour. Having flown onto a sunlit expanse of rock only a few metres below me, where it was preoccupied searching for insects and spiders, I could not have wished for a more accommodating subject. Male Wallcreepers are unusually confiding in the presence of human company close to a nest site, a behavioural response which may have evolved as distraction of an intruder from the female with eggs or young. The bird's riveting appearance and incessant activity is certainly most effective in maintaining one's attention. Whatever the reason, it is an endearing reaction and greatly facilitating of a close encounter. At a distance of two metres, which is perhaps the nearest I have been, the predominantly dusky-grey body plumage and matt black face, throat and breast, provide a perfect foil to the dark-carmine of the upperside forewings which is exposed during persistent flashing of open wings as it progresses across the rocks. The broad black tail, and black undersides and trailing edges of the wings, accentuates this contrast. When very close, prominent white spots are also evident near the tips of the primary wing feathers. Captivating as this colouration may be, the birds behaviour is also enthralling as it sidles up to a crevice before adopting a creeping posture and suddenly flashes its wings and hops jerkily forward to extract an insect with its black needle-like, long, curved bill. As this is accomplished on even vertical rock faces, the wonderful versatility of the bird's large and long-clawed feet becomes apparent. As if to emphasise that facility, it may take a long measured walk up a seemingly glass-smooth rock surface perhaps following a crack, which it examines with sinuous reptilian head movements constantly interrupted by wing flashes, presumably intended to startle any prey into movement. After what seemed an age but was only a brief interlude, the bird was gone in an erratic descent on flashing wings, back to its mate and a moss and lichen nest amidst the crags. I was only sorry not to have heard a departing melodious and fluting whistle, even though this is the time of year when the bird is often silent. With so few of its kind remaining in Greece and most of those in these uplands, it is another endangered voice of the mountains.

Resuming my ascent towards the still distant but steadily looming summit of Goura, the eastern slopes were now fully in view beneath the snow-capped ridge which arced downwards from the peak, towards Tsoumako and the forests of the Skamneliotikos headwaters beyond. Those forest edges would be where some of the Chamois would retire overnight and after emerging at first light would now be grazing the slopes up towards the snows. The young are born in May to early June and usually the mothers and young associate with immature females in small groups which can be seen high on the snows during the heat of the summer, resting in relative safety. Any perception of threat, primarily human, as the former one from Wolf and Lynx is now negligible, and they retreat to the cliffs and crags of the northern face of Tymphi. Their remarkable agility even on the most vertigenous cliffs ensures safety against most predators, although Lammergeier are known, rarely, to dislodge them to certain death, and there is always the ubiquitous hazard of illegal hunting. The 120-130 individuals on Tymphi are a fifth of the total population in Greece, but despite those numbers it requires vigilance to find them in the expanse of the massif. The tawny pelage, streaked dark brown on the legs, undersides and spine, renders the animal almost indistinguishable from the parched hillside vegetation of summer. Only movement of the partly black and white facial stripes of the head will betray location, using binoculars to verify the characteristics of hooked horns. Today I am rewarded by a group of twelve (four mothers, each with a single youngster, and four juveniles presumably less than four years old) emerging over the skyline in single file on the glistening snow. Their proximity to the Goura summit is even more remarkable knowing, as I do, that there the snow curls over the lip of the northern cliffs which plunge 800 metres into the Aoos valley. I have a special affinity for these and their kindred inhabitants of the high places of the world, born of the time when I emerged onto the icy summit of Toubkal in the Moroccan High Atlas during mid-winter with the temperature ten degrees below freezing and encountered two Aoudad, that extraordinary and so nearly extinct ancestor of the goat-sheep lineage. As they plunged over a precipice which would have been daunting even to the most proficient rock-climber, I knew I was witnessing one of the most remarkable feats of natural agility possible. Ever since, I have been drawn not just to the Chamois, Ibex and Moufflon of European mountains but to those many elusive and evocatively named brethren of more easterly ranges, the Serow, Goral, Markhor, Bharal, Himalayan Tahr and others of their kind. In their physical prowess and affinity with the most inhospitable and inaccessible of places, they are nature's equivalent of the *genius* of place, that which embodies the spirit of the *oros*, the mountains of the world. If by human depredation they disappear from the wild places, we lose not just their animal form and substance, but most preciously an essence of the mountains themselves.

As I was intrigued as to where the little band of Chamois would go, the route west from the summit of Goura being a dangerous frost-shattered arête, I stood and watched for a while but, seeing them lingering on the snow, I continued on. Soon they would be alert to my presence and return to safety beyond the summit ridge. During my preoccupation with the Chamois I had also become aware of bird movement on the slopes in the foreground to the snow and realized that Shore Larks were here too. From their flight patterns and behaviour they were clearly male birds on breeding territory, reassuring evidence that they were not just confined to where I had encountered them the previous day. Underfoot, those gloriously shining discs of *Geranium cinereum* ssp. *subcaulescens*, which had so graced the valley west of Krevvati, were now just beginning to emerge and would soon be carpeting the ground in their thousands, but it was towards some bright yellow masses wedged in nearby crags to which I was now drawn. As anticipated, these were the tall, leafy-based clumps of that Leopard's Bane, *Doronicum columnae*, whose large, yellow-starred flowers were secreted in the crags of Kourtetsi. Here, 300 metres higher and on an exposed crest, they seemed out of place but no less welcome, a startlingly bright splash of buttery-yellow against the silvery-white limestone. As if to compound the notion of misplacement, what appeared to be the tip of a rocky pinnacle further along the craggy tops, moved and then took flight, immediately followed by another. I had disturbed a pair of Little Owls which, although commonly hunting around dawn and dusk, will frequently perch, as these had done, in elevated locations fully exposed to the sun. If I had been more watchful and seen them before they saw me I might have observed them resting with one eye closed and then bobbing comically as an expression of anxiety on detecting my presence. Little Owls are usually encountered at much lower altitudes than this, so these were the adventurers of their kind.

With the lowermost snow-filled hollows on the slopes not too distant, a rest felt appropriate before the remaining ascent. Although there was a pleasant and cooling downdraught from the snows, the mid-morning sun demanded a measured pace. So whilst seated for a while, I began scanning the surroundings for whatever might be of interest. Far below and seemingly above the Vikaki ravine, three raptors were circling in close proximity. Three together suggests at this time of year either a pair and a loner of the same species or a pair perhaps mobbing or otherwise defending territory from the intrusion of another species. At this distance it was difficult to identify any distinguishing features other than those which implied that all three were Buzzard-like in appearance and flight. Then one bird, whilst still circling, began gaining height above the other two, until when significantly higher it drew in its wings and gathering speed in a downward curve, rose steeply on now outstretched wings, until when almost stalled it raised its wings vertically into a rapid quivering motion. Only one species exhibits such behaviour, the Honey Buzzard, a bird which breeds very rarely in Greece but which I knew to be present from previous encounters. The bird repeated the manoeuvre several times, progressively loosing height in a circular descent towards the other two, one of which then flew off westwards over the Vikos Canyon. From its flight path on distinctly raised wings this departing bird was clearly a Buzzard which had strayed into Honey Buzzard breeding territory. Wing-quivering behaviour usually peaks during nest-building and egg-laying which here would be during May and early June, either during pair-courtship or to advertise territorial claims, but can be induced throughout the breeding season by intrusion of rival males or, as on this occasion, another closely related raptor species. Honey Buzzards are remarkable, mainly woodland birds, secretive in habit and with an unusually specialised insect diet, up to half of which may include the adults, larvae and pupae of wasps. That such a large raptor can catch adult wasps in flight seems barely credible but more often the bird follows them to their nests which are then excavated and broken open to access the contents. Other social insects are similarly predated, and the diet is varied to include caterpillars, grasshoppers, beetles, ants, frogs, lizards, mice, fledgling birds and fruit, a cuisine which entails the bird being on the ground or in trees for much of the time. To this end it walks like a crow even on tree branches and can run on the ground carrying its body in a horizontal posture. The bird's secretive nature extends even to continuously camouflaging its large stick nest with fresh green foliage, which renders it almost undetectable amongst the branches of the trees in which it is constructed.

With heightened expectation of what lay ahead I pressed on toward the snows, now abandoned by the Chamois. In those few minutes when my attention was elsewhere they must have detected my presence and retreated beyond the summit ridge. Now I was drawn to the purple-veined, pink pea-flowered clusters of a low-growing, pinnate-leaved shrubby plant, *Onobrychis montana* ssp. *scardica*, which was appearing amongst the grassland vegetation. Although not sufficiently confined to offer a dense splash of colour, this was still a very attractive plant and the subspecies has the distinction of being a Balkan endemic. Soon, however, the magnitude of what was in prospect began to emerge as I came to the first of the many solution hollows and sink-holes which pock-mark the final slopes leading to the summit, for here were the beginnings of what I had hoped for. The exceptionally deep snows augmented by heavy spring rains had been the catalyst for a floristic profusion which I had not witnessed during the previous five years and, as I was subsequently to learn would not see again in a further ten years of visits. For here was the zenith of what arctic-alpine snow-melt flora can create. Many of the species had been encountered sparingly during previous days but now most were present in tens of thousands, colouring the slopes for hundreds of metres up to the summit. Foremost of these were the prominent lavender-blue and lavender-pink goblets of *Crocus veluchensis* glowing in the intense midday sun as if the myriad stars of limitless constellations. Accompanying them in even greater density were the short sprays of *Scilla bifolia* imparting a purple-blue haze to the slopes, muted with the mauve-pink of *Corydalis densiflora* and pierced by the bright shining-yellow orbs of the buttercup *Ranunculus brevifolius*. On areas where screes had stabilised and compacted into a fine rubbly substrate, the blue-violet, lobed trumpets of *Edraianthus graminifolius* were again evident but here in numbers which I had never encountered elsewhere. In association and again in profusion was the yellow-flowered, densely tufted whitlow-grass *Draba lasiocarpa*. Most unexpected of all, as I had never seen it in flower here before, was that exquisite violet *Viola albanica*, the violet-purple spurred, lilac flowers of which had so captivated my attention on the screes of Krevvati the previous day. It was in similar abundance over much of the slopes with concentrations in the scree-lined sink-holes and hollows where, as on Krevvati, it was accompanied by the pure-white, yellow-eyed flowers of *Cardamine carnosa*, locally in dense patches. Meandering upward through this extraordinary floristic display and between the remnants of snow which infilled some of the deeper hollows, I made my way towards what I anticipated would be one of the most spectacular floral sights of the mountain. The swathes of dark cobalt-blue flowers had been unmistakable from some distance as those of *Gentiana verna* ssp. *balcanica* and when they combine in a ground-hugging density such as this they are an incomparable sight. I was nearing the summit now but deviated across to where there were conspicuous white-flowered clumps of Alpine Rock-cress, *Arabis alpina*, growing on rocks in semi-shade. Although unprepossessing in such flamboyant floral company, the species is a relict from glacial times, an arctic-alpine which invokes memories of finding it growing abundantly on bleak gravel-flats in Iceland and arctic Scandinavia. As if to emphasise another aspect of former environmental extremes on the mountain, I was surprised to find a single robust yellow-flowered spike of *Orchis pallens* growing within a hundred metres of the summit, yet another occurrence at high altitude of this orchid which signifies the probable former extent of woodland.

Emerging onto the largely snow-free summit, I allowed the grandeur of the distant views to assimilate gradually as I looked around for other anticipated additions to the flora. A leafy lousewort, *Pedicularis graeca*, was pushing up its yellow-beaked flowers from pinnate foliage, whilst on nearby rocks there were several large dome-shaped cushions of *Saxifraga marginata* rooted into crevices on near-vertical faces. The tiny, densely packed leaves secrete excess lime onto their surfaces, accentuating the rigidity of the structure, from which arise the numerous white-petalled flowers on short glandular stems. These flowers were in perfect condition unlike those seen the previous day on the cliffs of Kourtetsi. On the lip of an 800-metre plunge into the Aoos valley, which precipitously truncates Goura on the north-eastern side, some of the gully heads still retained remnants of snow and here, flowering through the very edge of the melting drifts, were the delicate thimble-sized, violet-blue frilly bells of *Soldanella pindicola*. Here also, the tiny white tubular flowers of *Valeriana crinii* ssp. *epirotica*, crowded into compact terminal heads, emerge on short stems from amongst a boulder scree. Both these plants are confined to a few mountains in this region of the Balkans and are probably remnants of populations which were more widespread in times of cooler climate.

With such an extensive panorama in view from the summit it was perhaps inevitable that I should turn eastwards to visually trace the ridge-top wedge of snow on which those Chamois had ventured, down and out across the forests of Laista and the valley of the Aoos, to cross the Pindos heights, out over Gravena and the Aliakmon River to the far Aegean shore. For there rising above all, glistening white on the furthest horizon was the great mass of Olympos, 130 kilometres distant. How many occupants of those ancient fortifications at Skamneli, I wondered, had toiled up here to survey the lands around and view the home of the Olympian gods. Perhaps even Pyrrhus had stood here in the spring of 274 BC to gauge his march into Macedonia where he was to confront and overwhelm the armies of Antigonas. But now I let my gaze wander from the village of Laista northwards along the valley of the Rascianitis River to its confluence with the Aoos and to the forested slopes of Smolikas which, mirroring those of Tymphi in extent, rise to occupy the immediate horizon, with the mountain's 2,637-metre high, snow-capped summit some fourteen kilometres to the north-east. A line of villages contours the lower slopes of Smolikas above the Aoos, with Elefthero, the most westerly just visible, and Paleosellio, Pades and Armata more clearly so, all linked by a rough road etched into the mountain side. I had travelled that ancient way, stone-paved in places, several years before, having passed through Samarina, the principal Arumani village of the region, on a route south down the valley of the Koumoumanitis River to Distrato and thence to Armata and further west. It had been an arduous journey through dark forests of Black Pine, *Pinus nigra*, in torrential late summer rain, necessitating crossing several swollen tributaries of the Koumoumanitis and the debris from recent landslides. Beyond Armata the rain eased and I recall gazing in awe at the massive cliffs marking the north-eastern limit of Tymphi, towering above great swathes of mist-shrouded forest sweeping down craggy slopes to the Aoos far below. It had at first sight seemed inconceivable that the villages of Iliochori and Vrisochori were somewhere in that apparently impenetrable wilderness.

Now those villages were far below me. Iliochori obscured by an intervening forested rise, but the red-tiled roofs of Vrisochori just visible at the lower end of a wooded and pastured valley leading north-north-east from the meadows of Magoula some 960 metres vertically below. Although both villages were accessible by a continuation of the road through Skamneli, the last twelve kilometres or so of this was a forest track, often blocked by snow for much of the winter and locally rutted and gullied during spring and summer. At the time of my first visit in 1987 there were no more than fifty inhabitants in either village, and few of those remained in residence during the winter. Since the completion of the tarmacked road in 1992, however, and the subsequent connection to Paleosellio across the Aoos, the fortunes of both villages have begun to revive, nurtured by the return of visiting expatriates or their descendants, for these are Arumani communities with a long history and strong cultural identity. Vrisochori, or Leshinitsa, as it was known to the Arumani, can trace its origins back to 1295 and in the early 1900s had a population of over 1,600, a reflection perhaps of the very extensive forested lands in village ownership. Iliochori originates from at least as early as the fourteenth century and, prior to 1926, was known by the Slavic name of Dobrinovo, which dates from the sixth to seventh centuries, although the village then was not necessarily on the same site as now. In 1431 it had 1,180 inhabitants and probably expanded to support an even larger population during the nineteenth century when, at the height of its prosperity, its merchant caravans and tradesmen were active throughout the Balkans.

Looking down on the continuous blanket of forest which now encloses the two villages and which extends almost unbroken in all directions, it is at first difficult to envisage how such isolated communities could have been established and to have thrived as they did. However, both their origin and subsequent history may not have been much different from that of many of the other Arumani villages scattered throughout the eastern part of Zagori and indeed throughout the Balkans. The Arumani, or Vlakhi as they are known to the Greeks, speak a Latin language similar to Romanian and were from earliest times a nomadic shepherding people who moved with their flocks between summer pasturage in the mountains and winter grazing in the lowlands, often in communal associations of many families under the patronage of a *Tshelniku*, the principal shepherd. Most mountain villages seem to have originated by the amalgamation of several of these *tshelnikadzi* whose summer-hut encampments were in proximity, the location of those camps and the names of the paramount families being part of the surviving folklore of many villages. Even after the foundation of permanent mountain villages, transhumance still continued, a few families staying throughout the winter to guard and maintain the village whilst most journeyed to the lowlands. Samarina, Smiksi, Avdhela and Perivoli, Arumani villages which occupy the heights east and south-east of Smolikas, still continued this tradition until recent times, but with a growing divergence between a steadily decreasing portion of the population concerned with shepherding and an expanding proportion pursuing other trades. Most would migrate to the plains of Thessaly and southern Macedonia for the winter, the shepherds and their flocks leaving around the time of St. Demetrius day, October 26th, and beginning the return sometime around St. George's day, April 23rd. The majority of the population, however, left the mountain villages during September and returned end of May, taking with them all that was necessary to continue their trades. During the latter half of the nineteenth century over 5,000 people from Samarina alone made that twice-yearly *dhiava*. Their mule trains, loaded with all that cobblers, metal-workers, carpenters, butchers and multifarious other tradesmen required, would, in their hundreds, have followed the well-trodden ways down to Grevena and on to Trikkala or Elassona and some further still to Larissa, 150 kilometres distant. The signature black or brown, and white, striped ridge-tents made from coarse woollen cloth and the similarly coloured saddle-clothes and blankets always marked their passing, the spindrift from the ebb and flow of a nomadic people. During that time the Samarina flocks numbered over 80,000 and Perivoli had so many sheep that hundreds of families remained in Thessaly permanently to shepherd them and to produce the kashkaval cheese then so prized in Italy, and to process the wool. Within two decades at the beginning of the twentieth century the Samarina flocks were reduced to less than a quarter of their previous number and the Arumani way of life embarked on a tumultuous era from which it was never to recover.

Of the thirteen Arumani villages within eastern Zagori, immediately west of the Aoos, most appear to have lost their reliance on shepherding quite early in their history, although still retaining it as a minor part of a much more diversified economy based on agriculture and trade. The red-tiled roofs of Vrisochori are widely spaced, each within a generous garden indicating a former self-sufficiency in home-grown produce and, although the forests have engulfed much of what must have been productive land, there are still indications of its former extent. Much of the three-kilometre-long valley which extends from above the village to the Magoula meadows directly below me was probably cultivated at times for growing wheat, barley and fodder crops, as was some of the land below the village down to the Aoos. Similarly for much of the land below Iliochori down to the Rascianitis River, perhaps in part cultivated for growing vines, as Dobrinovo gave its name to an acclaimed wine, Dobrovino. Despite the extent of these former cultivations and of the surrounding forests which would also have contributed to supporting the populace through the export of timber, both Leshinitsa and Dobrinovo are known to have relied heavily on trading activities throughout the Balkans for much of their income, especially from the fifteenth to nineteenth centuries when they benefited from the dispensations made available to the Zagori villages by the Ottomans. Subsequent economic decline was greatly exacerbated by the severance of those trading routes due to the imposition of frontiers and the numerous conflicts of the twentieth century, resulting in forced emigration for most of the villagers. Now they and their descendents return to a landscape largely reclothed by nature but still revealing a frame wrought from the wilderness by many generations of their forebears.

How many during those later troubled years must have looked to the hills and wished for the permanence and stability which the mountains evoke and yet little would they have known of the inappropriateness of their yearnings, for these are inconstant structures on a restless portion of the Earth's surface. That instability would not have been evident within the context of a lifetime apart from the frequency of landslips on the slopes of Smolikas and the seasonally muddied waters of the Aoos and Voidomatis steadily eroding the hinterlands of central Zagori. Nor is it adequately expressed in the environmental changes of historical times, eventful as these may have been with the advance and retreat of woodland and grassland during the millennia of human existence in the region. The glacial events and accompanying erosional episodes of the previous half million years were more profound in altering the landscape, but even these were only superficial sculptural modifications compared to that which determined the overall structure of this environment. That line of Arumani villages on the lower slopes of Smolikas is there because of events initiated 20-30 million years ago that determined the springline on which they were built. The Samariniot shepherd who curses the treacherous greasy black rocks, always underfoot, is railing against beginnings 170 million years before his time, and much of the floral splendour I have encountered on this and previous days is influenced by processes which have their origins some 70 million years ago. Plants depend upon the environmental conditions conducive to their existence and are here because geological processes have created the physical context for those conditions to develop. Without these limestones, at this altitude and latitude, little of this flora would exist, nor would much of the animal life which depends upon those plants for sustenance. All is interrelated and interdependent but also part of a dynamic system, ever changing, always in flux. Standing on the summit of Goura with much of north-west Greece in view, there can be no better reminder of this state of impermanence, for all that is encompassed in this scene has rotated at least 55 degrees clockwise within the last 30 million years and 25 degrees of that within the last 5 million years. The 1,000-metre plunge into the Aoos valley before me is the uplifted edge of a great slab of 55 to 90 million-year-old stratified limestone, a portion of ocean floor elevated and propelled eastwards, riding on the back of the Apulian continent. Pyrrhus would have appreciated the irony, for he had not long returned from Apulia and his Italian campaign, and was intent on fusing those territorial gains with Macedonia. Meanwhile, far beneath his feet, an Apulian continent drifting eastwards for millions of years was colliding with the western limits of a Pelagonian continent bearing Olympos and most of the lands he now prized. Gazing eastwards, he would, as I do now, have been looking at remnants of the ocean crustal floor which had separated those two continents, now thrust skyward to form the great bulk of Smolikas and the Pindos range south to Metsovo and beyond. The rocks those shepherds had cursed had once been magma from the Earth's deep mantle implanted in the ocean basement and since thrust eastwards as an immense sheet of which a small part, Smolikas, now rests upon the much younger rocks of the Aoos valley floor. It is from the contact zone between those rocks that the springs emerge to determine where the Arumani villages, strung along the slopes of Smolikas, would be built.

Whilst on the summit of Goura I had not been entirely oblivious to all but the distant views and preoccupied with the thoughts those scenes invoked. I had at various times been abruptly reminded of other presences when one or more of the Alpine Swifts, hawking high over the summits, came sufficiently close for the audible rush of air to startle momentarily. There were Alpine Accentors here too, appearing and disappearing mouse-like amongst the frost-shattered rocks of the saw-toothed edge which continued north-west from the summit. This serrated arête was all that remained of the corrie wall which had backed the ice-field at the head of the Goura and Tsepelovo glaciers, a rock barrier between the ice and a long drop into the Aoos valley beyond. Now the rock debris from that edge formed a massive mobile scree down to the corrie floor with the faint line of a path leading diagonally across and upward over the scree to the summit ridge above Krevvati, my route for the next day. There was snow obscuring the path in places although insufficient to be an obstacle but a far more generous cover to the corrie floor occupying perhaps half of the area, much of it drifted up against the huge rocks which gave it its name, *megala leethareeya*. This was where I was expecting to see what is perhaps the most emblematic of all the high altitude avian inhabitants of the mountain, as they nest high in the Goura and Krevvati cliffs and frequently feed in and around the corrie floor at this time of year. Snow Finches are extremely localized in Greece, found here and perhaps only two other mountains. So the sight, as now, of them flickering black and white over the snow and grassy sward far below never fails to excite. There would be an opportunity for a close encounter later in the day.

Although it was pleasantly cool at this altitude, the time I had spent at the summit had allowed the sun to pass its zenith as I embarked on a leisurely meandering descent in departing homage to this wondrous floristic display. A few weakly fluttering Apollo butterflies had made it to the heights to accompany the ubiquitous migratory Clouded Yellows, but apart from these and the ever watchful male Shore Larks there was little movement on the slopes. The descent also brought into focus a more southerly vista, that of the Selio valley below Skamneli and of the forested upper reaches of the Skamneliotikos, a region which in the vicinity of Kousta and Koziakas was as wild and wonderful a country as one could find anywhere. I had ventured several years before to find a route through the narrow densely wooded ravine which divides the two peaks and came away elated at finding the rare, carmine-flowered *Orchis spitzelii* growing there amidst the Black Pine. As there had been fresh prints of Brown Bear too, alongside the river, the orchid was more than adequate compensation for the reluctant decision not to persist with my original exploratory intention. The woods had, however, offered further restitution in an abundance of the tiny greenish-white, bell-flowered Nodding Wintergreen, *Orthilia secunda*, and of the green-flowered orchid *Neottia (Listera) ovata*, both commonly associated with more northerly climes and indicative of cooler times past. If I had for a moment perceived the forests as harbouring a potential ursine threat, that mood had perhaps been enhanced by the additional presence of that rather sinister orchid, *Limodorum abortivum*. The knee-high spikes of pale violet flowers on robust stems sheathed in violet leaves emerge from the pine-needle-carpeted forest floor as if surface manifestations of some alien subterranean existence, which in reality they are. That they shared the forest with tall, large-flowered sprays of the Greater Butterfly Orchid, *Platanthera chlorantha*, ghostly greenish-white in shafts of intruding light, accentuated the slight unease even further. It had been a welcome diversion to cross the river into one of the adjacent lush wet meadows and share the sun with stands of the magenta-flowered *Anacamptis (Orchis) palustris*, there too with a tantalizingly unidentifiable purple-flowered *Dactylorhiza* orchid and the reflexed-petalled, pale lilac flowers of *Geranium aristatum*, a Balkan mountain endemic. Further downstream, at the edge of a hazel coppice, the scarce *Orchis provincialis* added a liberal splash of yellow to the scene whilst nearby were the magnificent, half-metre-tall spikes of *Orchis purpurea*. Each of the hundred or more flowers is a purple and green bonneted figure in flamboyant white and purple skirt and blouse, hence the common name of Lady Orchid.

On being reunited with my pack, I sat for a while on the crest of the lower ridge to enjoy the afternoon sun, knowing that in the Goura valley I would be in shade during the walk to my intended overnight resting place near the Goura Spring. Here, where access to the higher slopes was narrowly confined, the well worn interlacing sheep tracks were a reminder that in a week or two the first flocks would arrive at the nearby *stanee* and would pass this way after the adjacent lower grasslands had been grazed. By then the floristic climax of the mountain would be over and the sheep on these and other heights would be nibbling the many *Festuca*, *Poa*, *Phleum*, *Bromus*, *Melica* and other grasses which rendered these pastures so desirable. Much else would be cropped too, and anything the sheep refrained from eating would be devoured by the goats which usually accompanied them. The combined effect of their grazing is inadvertently to suppress the incursion of forest trees and to maintain both the extent and characteristics of the grasslands and associated habitats without which the floristic wonders of the slopes above me would be no more. With that thought in mind, I shouldered my pack and, after regaining the track below, turned up the approach to the *stanee* and into the Goura valley.

I had been hoping to find Cretzschmar's Bunting here on the bare, stony terrain around the *stanee*, as the high invertebrate content of the well-manured ground is an attractive food source. Being habitual ground feeders, the birds are otherwise unobtrusive amidst the tussocky grass elsewhere on the slopes. After scanning the area for a while I was suitably rewarded. The plumage of this bird is sometimes described as 'immaculate' and here in the low-angled light of a summer afternoon a male in perfect breeding attire fully justifies that attribution. The rufous underparts were in this light a bright chestnut and only slightly less so on the back and wings, intricately patterned with bold, black markings. As it picked and pecked with a flesh-red bill around stones and stalks, the ash-grey head assumed a delicate pale blue, a perfect setting for the jewelled jet-black, cream-ringed eye. Perhaps their tame and confiding nature, for this bird was within only a few metres, is due to long habituation to the company of nomadic shepherds and their flocks, both a tribute to and a tribune of the Sarakatsani.

Without the noise and bustle of its occupants the *stanee* is a sparse and desolate place, a few crude structures around a water-trough amidst a dusty bare hollow. Here there are two circular brushwood enclosures used as milking pens, and two rectangular shelters constructed of short timber uprights supporting the remnants of a withe- and straw-thatched flat roof, providing daytime shade for the animals. To the

Sarakatsani a *stanee* was traditionally far more than the sheepfold; it was all that materially constituted a shepherding fraternity, an association of related families, with their combined flocks, grazing lands, sheepfolds and huts. The lowland winter *stanee* was the most substantial, as the work, which included lambing and the greater part of annual milk production, was more effectively undertaken by a larger gathering of families and their flocks. This ensured a combined milk production sufficient to meet the independent cheese-makers requirements. During that time families lived in permanent *konakia*, the traditional conical, timber and thatch huts. The summer *stanee*, in contrast, was often reduced to the personages and possessions of just a few or even a single family, especially after 1938 when they acquired the right to establish permanent homes in the village on whose lands they had traditionally grazed their animals. Now it is necessary for only one or two shepherds to remain with the flocks, assistance with the early morning and late afternoon milking being provided by family members who arrive from the village and return with the milk, which is either sold or processed for family consumption. During the intervening daytime the sheep rest in the shade, guarded by the dogs whilst the shepherd sleeps. Only after the late afternoon milking are the sheep led to their pasturage, to graze throughout the cool of the night when their appetite is strongest, under the watchful eyes of both shepherd and dogs. Under a cloudless, starlit night-sky or the silvery sheen of moonlight, the shadows amidst the fissured and gullied limestone hide dangers, both real and imaginary. Sheep can easily become trapped in deep grykes, and until recent times there was always the threat of thieves, wolves and bears, not so long ago as to be entirely out of mind even now. During a late summer storm or when dense mist descends, the landscape assumes a far greater menace, and to bring a flock of several hundred sheep safely through is both a challenge and a source of satisfaction for any shepherd however well he might know the mountain.

With the *stanee* behind me, it is only a short walk to the Goura Spring, flanked by the heights of Kourtetsi and the Kato Tsoeka ridge. There, after replenishing my water supply and collecting the fresh provisions which Fanis had left for me earlier in the day, I found a suitable resting place on the slopes below the Kourtetsi summit and settled down for the evening. It was a good vantage point from which to survey the cliffs and crags of Goura and the snow-pocked expanse of valley floor adjacent to the spring. Soon a small flock of Snow Finch which had taken flight on my approach returned to feed. They came in fast, on strong stiff down-beats, their black-tipped, white wings conspicuous against the snow and limestone screes, a single bird soon followed by five in unison. Alighting on the snow where they began searching for immobilized, wind-borne insects, they quickly hopped or flew to the water-saturated edges, attracted by the abundant fly larvae which live in the meltwater. The birds have young to feed and rely on the availability of insects and their larvae for most of their food during the breeding season, whilst resorting to seeds during autumn and winter. In observing their departing flight, seemingly prompted by a single harsh note from one bird, I was sure they were nesting in the cliffs of Krevvati as they disappeared in that direction behind the intervening summit of Kourtetsi. So having prepared my pitch for the night, I climbed the short distance to the summit from where there was a clear view of both the Krevvati and Goura cliffs and the broad amphitheatre between, intent on remaining until dusk. All but the pink-tinged summit of Goura was in shade and the scene was beginning that progression from pewter to indigo which the fading light of summer evenings often imparts to these rocks. Scanning the snow patches far below, I soon located more Snow Finches still feeding and after keeping them under observation for a while was rewarded to see most take flight and rise westwards, clearly heading for the uppermost cliffs and crags of Krevvati. There they will have bulky nests of grass, roots, moss and lichen lined with feathers, hair and wool, wedged into rock crevices and cavities. Watching them disappear into their unassailable rock fortress, I was reminded that it is one of the avian wonders of this mountain to see the massed flocks of juvenile and adult Snow Finches wheeling in the autumn sky and flickering like a snow-flurry across the parched grassy slopes.

After prolonging my vigil for as long as the failing light would allow I made my way down through the rocky slopes and prepared for a cold night. Thankfully the cloudless day appeared to presage a clear night sky, although little of it was visible from such an enclosed location. I did however have the compensatory satisfaction of welcoming sleep, to the accompaniment of the amphibian chorus emanating so joyfully from the springs nearby.

# Chapter 5

# Karteros and the Bear's cradle

I awoke to a cold dawn and the distant call of a Rock Partridge, a lone voice in the vastness enclosed by the walls of Krevvati and Goura, accompanied by intermittent murmurings from the nearby spring. Even with a cloudless sky it would be some time before the sun's warmth enveloped the valley floor, so I was soon ready to move on towards the summit ascent beyond the corrie. After replenishing my water supply at the spring I set off in the direction of the great scree slopes beneath the western buttresses of Goura, intent on seeing if the floral spectacle of the similarly oriented Krevvati screes was replicated. I was not disappointed, for the association of *Cardamine carnosa* and *Viola albanica*, although not in comparable abundance, was evident over much of the lower slopes. As I had not seen either species here in previous years, the importance of winter and early spring precipitation in determining growth and flowering could not be demonstrated more clearly. This was further emphasised by the wonderful scene unfolding before me as I meandered between the extensive snow patches down into the corrie basin, where the emerging snow-melt flora was colouring the newly exposed bare and bleached ground. Here the lavender and variously blue, violet and pink-tinted goblets of *Crocus veluchensis* dominated in their tens of thousands, so dense in places as to challenge the integrity of one's footfall, not wishing to tread on a single flower. Even in deep shadow they shone with an inner radiance aided by the glowing yellow and orange of anthers and style. Was it here that Krokos met the shepherdess Smilax and, having died of unrequited love, gave issue to the flower from his burial place amidst the *megala leethareeya*? There could be no more fitting floral effusion than this to commemorate his death and validate the myth.

Of the other floristic elements in this snow-melt-induced display all were familiar from previous encounters but no less impressive in their profusion and power to induce a sense of profound wonder. The disparity of form and colour displayed by the components of the floral assemblage should, we might imagine, produce a response of some dissatisfaction with the composition, and yet the association appears quite harmonious and in sympathy with the setting. Transfer the assemblage to the contrivance of a garden and it would appear most unsatisfactory but here, in these surroundings, it seems unquestionably compatible and aesthetically deeply satisfying. The myriad sprays of *Scilla bifolia* display their violet-blue splayed flowers on vinaceous stems, erect when freshly emerged but soon lax and wilting on a bed of glabrous, linear leaves, awash with meltwater. That such a disorderly canvas offers no incongruity in hosting the sculpted form of the crocus is a tribute to nature's artistic genius. Elsewhere the six-rayed white stars of *Ornithogalum oligophyllum* might predominate, the many-flowered clusters on finger-high scapes above linear leaves, forming a backcloth to the similarly proportioned but yellow flowers of *Gagea pusilla*. Some species however seem to demand, and nature obligingly provides, disassociation from others and none more so than *Gentiana verna* ssp. *balcanica* which even amidst this multitude of blooms, commands sole occupancy of much that it claims. The density of flowers, still closed from their overnight slumbers, emitted when open such an intense presence that an association with any other plant would appear incongruous.

Descending into the corrie, I rounded the northern limit of Kourtetsi on a deviation to the north-west facing slopes and crags, which I knew from previous visits to be of floristic interest. From there it would be an undemanding walk across the boulder-strewn *megala leethareeya* to the commencement of the ascent to the summit ridge above Krevvati. I had expected to encounter the Snow Finches again during this early morning sojourn but they were absent, perhaps preferring the higher sunblessed slopes where insect prey would be more evident. The only avian activity was from a male Wheatear induced by my presence into a frenzy of diversionary behaviour, indicating concern for a hidden brood. On arrival at the slopes beneath the Kourtetsi crags I was surprised to find *Viola albanica* again flowering in some abundance, for here the screes were sufficiently stabilised to support a thin soil and a generous vegetation, a habitat quite dissimilar from that which favoured the species elsewhere. Although still shaded, portions of the incline were a colourful patchwork of the white-flowered crucifer *Berteroa obliqua*, the yellow St. John's Wort, *Hypericum rumeliacum* ssp. *apollinis*, and in damp hollows luxuriant drifts of *Viola epirota*, all making a welcome reappearance. There were other less familiar species too. A wallflower, *Erysimum microstylum*, was in the early stages of adding bold bright yellow splashes of colour whilst locally, on patches of bare scree, dense glaucous-leaved mats of *Euphorbia herniariifolia* liberally covered in tiny golden-bronze floral cyathea provided attraction on a diminutive scale. Elsewhere the shade was abruptly pierced by the white woolly pinnate foliage of a knapweed, *Centaurea epirota*, which displayed exquisite pale pinkish-purple to lilac plumose flowers with conspicuous dark violet anthers. Here the flowers were on finger-length erect stems but in more exposed situations and on rock outcrops the plants are almost stemless, offering a most attractive visual composition. Elevated above all, and the prime objective of my deviation, were the luxuriously floriferous cushions of both *Saxifraga marginata* and *Minuartia pseudosaxifraga*, familiar from previous encounters but of inexhaustible delight, decorating the sheer-sided crags beneath the lip of Kourtetsi with galaxies of white stars amidst a rocky firmament. Leaving the slopes of Kourtetsi behind me, I was soon immersed in the sea of crocus and scilla which swirled around the islands of snow and rock across the corrie floor. The overwhelming impression was of life's profuse, but transient, emergence at the edge of the elemental world, a stark and sublime image of the impermanence of nature.

The thin line traversing the screes so clearly visible from the Goura heights is barely discernible when negotiating the route to the summit ridge, such is the instability of the slope. Remnants of snow mark the depression in places, sufficient to guide one's steps on the ascent which readily succumbs to a steady methodical pace. Soon the serrated crest, which seemed so distant from the corrie floor, loomed large and I emerged at a shallow col. This sloped away steadily to the north-west into a snow-filled gully bounded by a continuation of the main summit ridge forming its southern flank, and a secondary ridge, that of Tsouka Rossa, providing the northern limit and a vertiginous plunge into the Aoos valley. My route midday would be down through that snow-decked incline, but after reassurance that the snow – which was shaded for much of the day – would allow a safe and unimpeded descent, I turned to follow the main summit ridge leading to Krevvati and the peaks beyond. Although still thickly rimmed with snow cornices, the narrow ridge presented few challenges. I was, however, relieved to arrive at the broad knoll connecting Krevvati with the main summit ridge as here I could discard my pack and continue unencumbered. It remained cloudless, so despite the low air temperature it was already very warm in the early morning sun. Far below, the corrie floor remained partly shaded and the more distant Goura valley was still to benefit from the solar warmth impeded by the mass of Kato Tsoeka. With those scenes at my back, the continuing succession of peaks, Karteros, Gamila and Ploskos, which mark the northern termination of Tymphi's slopes at the great cliffs overlooking the Aoos valley, now beckoned.

Although much of the snow had gone from these heights, sufficient remained to sustain some of the now familiar snow-melt flora. Both *Crocus veluchensis* and *Scilla bifolia* were here, bordering the drifts, but it was the yellow-flowered twosome of the buttercup *Ranunculus brevifolius* and the tiny tufted whitlow-grass *Draba lasiocarpa* which predominated, brightly colouring the saturated stony ground. Here too, where the slopes steepened abruptly into the valley west of Krevvati, was a grassy sward thick with the burgeoning buds of *Gentiana verna* ssp. *bulgarica*. The flowers close during the evening or in cloudy, cold conditions and open rapidly in response to direct sunlight and rising temperatures. Within an hour this slope would be transformed into a cascade of dark cobalt-blue. Continuing on across the steep valley-head beneath an extensive infill of snow, I was able to climb back to the summit ridge to where I knew one of the mountain's rarest plants could be found. *Saxifraga oppositifolia* would have been familiar to those Palaeolithic hunters as dense purple-flowered mats, conspicuous on the gravel flats and bare rocky slopes, much as it appears today in the arctic. Now a few plants linger here and elsewhere on the Tymphaean summits, struggling to survive in an increasingly unsuitable environment. The flowers at my feet are a lovely warm reddish-purple, the five broad petals splaying outwards from a shallow cup, bearing dark blue anthers on long filaments. Exquisite as these finger-nail-sized flowers are, here they do not proliferate densely as in those magnificent purple or rosy-red cloaks which I have seen clothing rocks high in the Pyrenees or spread on Icelandic gravels. Rather, they grow uneasily, meagre-flowered on sprawling woody stems, the last of their kind in Greece and probably doomed to extinction with further climatic amelioration.

Further progress along the summit ridge led to one of the more prominent eminences, elevated no more than 100 metres above the adjacent terrain and sufficiently deprived of snow to reveal well-vegetated grassy slopes. Nestling low against the substrate were the silky-haired, yellowish-white pinnate leaves of a wormwood, *Artemisia eriantha*, which will soon emit tiny yellow composite flowers on short stems. Found on only three other mountains in Greece and always above 2000 metres, this is another survivor from glacial times and vulnerable to any further climatic change. It was accompanied by the distinctively yellow-beaked flowers of the lousewort *Pedicularis graeca*, previously encountered on Goura summit and well adapted to this similarly elevated and exposed aspect, with prostate, densely woolly-haired stems. Beyond, the ridge dips and undulates from crag to crag with deep infills of snow, an appropriate setting for the spectacular purple-flowered cushions and mats of *Aubrieta scardica* liberally scattered along the crest. At lower altitudes, the plants are often lax in form but here on the exposed heights the four-petalled, white-eyed flowers almost obscure the compact pale green foliage in a rosy-purple sheen. That such floristic exuberance as this can exist in so hostile an environment is always a source of wonder, however often I have encountered the scene. It was whilst accessing one of the more enticing of these ridge-top displays that an especially intriguing plant, clinging to an overhang above part of the sheer-walled, north-eastern face, caught my attention. Conspicuous plumes of feathery hairs protruding from what had been four large yellow flowers, with purplish calices above segmented foliage, were clearly visible through binoculars. This could only be a species of *Geum*, and, as I subsequently realised must have been *Geum reptans*, first discovered on the mountain three kilometres to the west in

1971. Found nowhere else in Greece this is another survivor from cooler times and more suitably established in the eastern Alps, Carpathian and Tatra mountains to which heights it has migrated as the climate has warmed.

As I was now approaching Karteros, a 2,453 metre-high peak and the limit of my intended excursion on the summit ridge, I circled below the still extensive snows on its slopes in a speculative search for other floristic surprises. There were dense cushions of *Astragalus sirinicus* with their pale cream, lilac-tinged pea-flowers tucked deep into fiercely spiny foliage and associated with them, the distinctive bi-coloured flowers of *Scutellaria alpina*. The compact terminal inflorescence is comprised of four opposing flowers, each a rosy-purple hooded canopy, over-arching a broad, white-flaired lip projecting from a white corolla tube, a structure which elicits the common name of skullcap for the genus. Nearby, sprays of the tiny four-petalled, purple-tinged, white flowers of *Thlaspi microphyllum* appeared abundantly in short turf. So easily dismissed with a passing glance and yet, closer inspection reveals each flower to have violet-tinged sepals and violet anthers flecked with yellow pollen, to produce an exquisite composition of form and colour. After regaining the ridge-top I crossed a snow infill leading to the summit, for a brief respite in the sun before commencing my return. Far below was the snow-filled gully which would be my route into the forested Aoos valley and to the meadows and woodland clearings which lapped against the base of the north-eastern cliffs of Tymphi, my destination for the next two days. Whilst the mass of Smolikas still occupied the horizon to the north, my present viewpoint provided a more extensive panorama to the north-west than had been available from the Goura summit. Now the great snowy massif of Gramos was just visible beyond the western slope of Smolikas, at the head of the bulk of Albania whose mountains shoulder Greece down to the Ionian shore and trace a thin white line across the far horizon. Whilst turning to scan the all-encompassing panorama my gaze settled for a while on the lone footprints in the snows below, steps as much a journey of discovery as if I were the first to have ever walked this way. In such places are we not all adventurers and it matters little whether we are the first or the millionth to have travelled this way, for it is our own personal odyssey and all that we encounter is newly discovered.

After retracing my steps along the summit ridge to Krevvati and retrieving my pack I returned to the col from where there was, after an initial steep plunge, a gradual descent through the snow-filled gully which led down into the Aoos valley. With the midday sun banishing all but the most inaccessible shade on these northern slopes, the snow was sufficiently yielding to allow safe and rapid progress, so it was not long before I was looking skyward towards the summits which had been beneath my feet only a few hours before. The cliffs beneath Karteros, and their continuation north-westwards below Gamila, overshadow snow-bound corries, beneath which a stepped succession of tree-lined crags and stabilised, vegetated screes falls steeply down to meet the termination of the gully I was following. There I turned north beside a rock-rimmed enclosure, an outpost of Kopana, the Sarakatsan *stanee* further down the valley, and then up through a break in the scattering of conifers which darkened the slopes before me. I paused for a while to admire these trees, for *Pinus heldreichii* is a veteran of its kind, a survivor from the Tertiary, long before the Tymphaean slopes where scoured by glaciers. It graces the heights of select mountains throughout the Balkans and Southern Italy with its up-curved branches of whorled and tufted needles, adopting a pyramidal form around a massive grey-barked fissured trunk. Now, in June, the terminal shoots are resplendent with their purple and orange-red floral excrescences and last years cobalt-blue cones, a startling contrast to the enclosing dark bottle-green foliage. Here there are many shrubby trees recolonizing the slopes, offspring of aged parents on the higher crags reclaiming what was lost to the Sarakatsan flocks. With the blanket snow-cover well behind me, familiar plants were colouring the grassy slopes amongst spiny cushions of *Astragalus sirinicus* and the ubiquitous foliage of *Eryngium amethystinum* and *Euphorbia myrsinites* threading their characteristic weft into the verdant weave. Yellow splashes of the wallflower, *Erysimum microstylum*, were present, amidst violet-tinged hollows of *Viola epirota* and those luminous purplish-red salvers of *Geranium cinereum* ssp. *subcaulescens*, everywhere shining brightly from between grassy tussocks. There were surprises too. A bristly leaved and stemmed hounds-tongue, *Cynoglottis barrelieri* ssp. *serpentinicola*, displayed its lingual sprays of bright sky-blue flowers on a stable grassy scree, accompanied by the compact, white, many-flowered heads of a yarrow, *Achillea fraasii*, much like the already familiar *Achillea abrotanoides*, but on almost leafless stems arising from tufts of grey, glossy-haired pinnate leaves. Beyond the trees I had a clear view of the cliffs which rise steadily south-eastwards towards the massive bastion of Tsouka Rossa and of my route towards the screes and steep meadows at its base. It was trammelled terrain ahead with several ravines and many more gullies to cross with intervening ridges to climb, much of it discontinuously forested with pine. I did not intend to linger much on the way as I knew what treasures lay ahead and was eager to be at my destination beyond Tsouka Rossa with sufficient time to explore the slopes above the Magoula meadows before evening.

    I knew this terrain well enough to tread with deliberation on these ravaged slopes of loose boulders and shifting rubble, as just one injudicious step in one of the many meltwater eroded ravines could be calamitous. There was little thought of what grew around me, even less of what birds were skyward.

That familiar scratchy refrain from a nearby Black Redstart might cause me to stop and watch for a while but it was only a temporary respite from the need to constantly navigate ahead and place one's feet carefully. We are remarkably adept at negotiating uneven ground but only with total concentration. Succumb to a distraction, however trivial, and all that proficiency is for nought. Even so, I did register the occasional occurrence of that lovely yellow-eyed, pinkish-lilac flowered crucifer, *Malcolmia orsiniana* ssp. *angulifolia*, which here seems to excel in brightening the most challenging boulder piles it can find. Its finger-length, needle-like seed pods are efficient sowers of its progeny, bursting vigorously and audibly in the summer heat. On cresting the penultimate ridge which allowed sight of the screes and meadows beneath the Tsouka Rossa cliffs, I could again broaden my horizons to that which was other than at my feet, and after a short descent began a long meandering climb across the lower stabilized screes towards a col where the distant ridge meets the cliff base. Snow still covered much of the higher slopes, littered with rock and pine debris from the crags and 500-metre-high walls which shaded all below for most of the day. Beyond the foot of the screes, stony meadows sloped steeply down to the upper limit of beech woodland and views out across the Aoos far below, to the forested and gullied slopes of Smolikas. A huddle of red-roofed houses halfway to the river revealed the Arumanian village of Vrisochori.

Floristic display on these northerly facing and well-shaded slopes was inevitably retarded but still sufficient to brighten the otherwise pewter-grey countenance of the limestone. Leafy clumps of *Geranium macrorrhizum* were exerting their natural exuberance with the promise of still more variously pink, red and purple blooms to come. Its relation, *Geranium cinereum* ssp. *subcaulescence*, was as expected, demonstrating its versatility in adapting to screes just as well as to the rough grasslands it so often frequents. The shortly branched rhizomes projected palmate leaves and those incomparable flowers from deep within the rocky pile, sometimes so deep that only the flowers were evident, as if a Molossian king had discarded a hoard of balas rubies in his wanderings. That ubiquitous pale-pink thrift, *Armeria canescens*, was also evident, protruding from the bedrock or where humus infiltrated the surface screes, as was the large yellow, crimson-tinged cups of *Hypericum rumeliacum* ssp. *apollinis* which made a generous display. Approaching the col and now onto rocky slopes with intervening grassy hollows, I was surprised to find a scattering of *Gentiana verna* ssp. *balcanica* with flowers fully open, welcoming the mid-afternoon sun. An outpost perhaps from the assemblage on the summit ridge above. The return to a familiar and cherished place is always preceded by its mental image but that never detracts from the joy of seeing it unfold once more to fill one's vision, and so it was with the scene beyond the crest of the col. The snowy hollows and wooded rocky terraces, which cascade down from the heights of Goura and its flanking serrated ridges to the lush meadows of Magoula, had provided my induction to the mountain several years before and, with the valley below down towards Vrisochori, has remained for me a delightful and enchanting place. Seeing it again brought back memories of the sight and scent of so many flowers I was then encountering for the first time, the joy of finding meadows alive with butterflies and the thrill of that first sight of the foot prints of a bear freshly imprinted in the soft streamside mud. Now I knew of so much more, as the valley had gradually revealed its secrets during the intervening years, in the shadow of the rock and snow-encrusted grandeur slung between the Goura and Tsouka Rossa peaks.

From this vantage point some 280 metres above the Magoula meadows it requires little imagination to envisage the four kilometre long glacier, which at the height of the Skamnellian glacial episode, some 450,000 years ago, scoured the valley and was to leave the flanking morainic ridges in its wake. Snow and ice fields feeding the glacier had gouged out the two kilometre wide embayment into the north-east face of the mountain now separating the Goura and Tsouka Rossa peaks, and it was within this depression 300,000 years later that permanent ice accumulated again, this time to erode several high-level corries occupying the uppermost 500 metres or so of the embayment. These and other Vlasian cold phase corries along the north-east cliffs, inaccessible to all but the most surefooted, provide a vital winter refuge for hibernating female bears which require several months of undisturbed solitude when nurturing their new-born cubs. The cubs are born during the darkest days of winter and will not emerge from their snow-bound den until May or June, still dependent on their mother's milk for many more months and vulnerable to many dangers; one in three will die in their first year. A densely wooded terrace, encrusted with an impenetrable thicket of *Pinus heldreichii* scrub, marks the lower limit of the bear's nursery, stretching as a broad dark band broken only by rock and snow-filled gullies, across the steep slopes, on a level with my ridge-top stance. Below, a great expanse of scree, intersected only by continuation of the gullies, extends down to fringe the meadows beneath, my next objective for the day.

Leaving the ridge-top and meandering downwards towards the boulder strewn edge of the screes, that innate sense of perceiving something different exerted itself again as I paused to look more closely at some harebells growing amongst the rocks. These were a darker blue than the ubiquitous Common Harebell, *Campanula rotundifolia*, variable as that is in colour and form, and were a deep violet-blue on ankle-high leafy stems. This was *Campanula spatulata* ssp. *spatulata*, a plant usually encountered in high altitude shaded hollows where snow lingers late into the summer. Whilst this was flourishing near its lowermost altitudinal limit, nearby were a few plants of the fragrant Lily-of-the-valley, *Convallaria majalis*, uncharacteristically distant from its more usual lowland woodland environment. Those sprays of delicate porcellaneous white bells were strikingly incongruous amidst the tumble of intimidating rocks. Further on and seemingly more at home on the screes were leafy clumps of a skullcap, *Scutellaria rupestris* ssp. *adenotricha*, liberally covered in spikes of variously pinkish-purple to pale purple-tinged, double-lipped flowers. Lower still, and approaching a copse of willow scrub from which a party of Long-tailed Tits, erupted in a spray of undulating streamers, I headed for a long-remembered place near the scree base. It was here that I had first encountered that exquisite violet, *Viola albanica*, several years before, although then I had been uncertain what I had found, and here it was again, just a few plants on stony ground. Alongside was another of those earlier discoveries which had induced similar adulation at the time and no less so now, for *Campanula hawkinsiana* is a delightful plant when generously flowered and in a sympathetic setting. The deep bluish-violet bells at the tips of slender leafy stems look skyward with a distinctive white eye, each flower a portrait, together a harmonious composition.

Now the cloudless sky I had been accustomed to was streaked with high level cirrus and the breeze had shifted noticeably to the west, a portent of change, so with the lower slopes my intended preoccupation for the remainder of the day I headed for the south-eastern limit of the valley and for the ridge which was to be my overnight-resting place. There I would leave my pack before setting off across the scree to the lowermost crags and gullies. Although I had cumulatively spent many weeks in this valley and knew the terrain and its flora and fauna well, there were always surprises to supplement the joys of reacquaintance. Returning to that with which one is familiar in nature never seems to have any of the disadvantages of repetition, perhaps because nothing in the natural world is ever static. All is in flux, dynamic and ever-changing, however subtle and seemingly timeless some of those changes may be.

After hoisting my remaining provisions into a tree well away from my intended resting place and stowing my pack amidst a rock-pile, I retraced my route down, and across to where a ridge of stable scree and bedrock provided an inviting ascent. My arrival was promptly noted by a male Black Redstart, presumably with a nest in the vicinity as my presence was clearly causing much anxiety. Pausing to watch his distraction ploys for a while, I became aware of a commotion high on the Tsouka Rossa cliffs, signalled by a chorus of harsh, scolding calls from what I assumed was a flock of Choughs. Suddenly a portion of the flock aggregated into a tight bunch and plunged down the cliff face to vanish out of sight, presumably Alpine Chough, the high-pitched whistling alarm-calls of which would be inaudible from this distance, as simultaneously the cause of this confusion came into view. The rapid and deep wingbeats of a Peregrine Falcon on hunting patrol are unmistakable when combined with that sharp-winged, bull-headed silhouette and characteristic black-moustached white face. If intent on a kill it had clearly disregarded the Chough and Alpine Chough, but then momentarily dipped violently sideways and downwards with closed wings towards a flock of Rock Dove which had exploded out of the cliff face in a dash for safety. With equal alacrity it resumed its onward flight. Although capable of extraordinary speed during a stoop, the Peregrine had accepted the doves' advantage, as they have a remarkable manoeuvrability when evading an attack. As they sped away with flashing white underwings, one could only wonder how in such tight formation they accomplish their synchronised aerial gyrations. They must instinctively accede to a hierarchy with the dominant bird setting the course and all others subservient to it. In contrast, a flock of feral doves, though descendants of the

Rock Dove, will scatter in confusion when threatened by a falcon. As the Peregrine passed overhead, the heavily black-barred undersides with a rufous tinge to the chest and belly were clearly visible, this a male bird presumably intent on returning with a meal for chicks, secreted on a remote ledge somewhere along this cliff or in the Vikos Canyon. The Mediterranean race of the Peregrine, *brookei*, is a rare resident in Greece and this is one of the few places where it breeds successfully.

Resuming my ascent, it was pleasing to be welcomed by familiar floral faces of which the yellow countenance of *Helianthemum nummularium*, a rockrose, was everywhere its trailing stems could find a stable stony home. Billowing leafy masses of that gloriously flowered denizen of boulder piles, *Geranium macrorrhizum*, were present too, and again accompanied by its incomparable relative *Geranium cinereum* ssp. *subcaulescens* gracing the more stable adjacent screes. The many and variable roseate and purpuraceous hues which this pair impart to the mountain are a never-failing wonder and so seductive in their visual appeal that other more discrete and retiring presences can be easily overlooked. Nestling in a rocky hollow with its trailing stems of grey-green, fleshy leaves was a catchfly, bearing tiny off-white, pale pink and reddish-tinged flowers above a green-veined calyx, somewhat diminished in stature compared with the norm for *Silene caesia* but no less enticing as an example of its kind. It is more at home much higher on the mountain where it flowers a month later. On a comparable, diminished scale were the likewise lemon-yellow, mop-headed inflorescences of an onion, *Allium flavum* ssp. *flavum*, on finger length stems, emerging into flower. Further up the slope towards a remnant infill of snow, two of the now familiar contributors to the snow-melt assemblage of higher altitudes were also making an appearance, the shining butter-yellow cups of *Ranunculus brevifolius* and the similarly bright yellow floral clusters of the diminutively tufted whitlow-grass, *Draba lasiocarpa* ssp. *lasiocarpa*. On reaching the lowermost crags, the fleshy-leaved rosettes of *Saxifraga porophylla* ssp. *federici-augusti*, with their slender nodding dark reddish flower spikes, were conspicuously protruding from many of the rock crevices as were tufts of the silky-haired, linear foliage of a cudweed, *Gnaphalium roeseri* ssp. *pichleri*, soon to decorate the rocks with its tiny composite flowers, each like a short-haired artist's paintbrush.

Working my way cautiously out across the slopes required frequent dips down into shallow gullies and scrambles over intervening divides, the ground ever-changing underfoot. Loose mobile scree, rocky outcrops, boulder piles and gravel banks were interlaced, all with their attendant vegetation, some ephemeral as demanded by the impermanence of substrate, others established, often with deep taproots or long, rhizomatous stems. Remarkable amongst these more persistant occupants is one which is sometimes found growing in the dry bed of these meltwater gullies where it evidently flourishes despite the erosional onslaught unleashed by the mountain every year. *Centranthus longiflorus* ssp. *junceus* sends up many, sometimes waist-high, woody-based, narrow-leaved stems, which terminate in clusters of tiny tubular, rose pink, long-spurred flowers, unprepossessing perhaps in visual entirety but entrancing in constituent detail and confined to just a few mountains in Greece. Isolated and infrequent as these plants appear to be, they are on the regular feeding trail of a remarkable member of the lepidopteran fraternity, for there, rendered almost invisible by its rapidly vibrating wings, was a Humming-bird Hawk-moth probing the long pink floral spurs for nectar as it hovered and darted from flower to flower. These moths are great wanderers, able to navigate from one nectar source to another with such precision that they often arrive at each plant on their lengthy circuit at exactly the same time each day. Their speed of flight defies the ability of the human eye to follow, but watch them carefully when hovering and you discern the hindwing flickering as if an orange-yellow flame flanking the chequered margin of a broad, black tail-fan. The grey-brown, darkly streaked forewings provide a reminder of how selective our perception of the natural world is, for to other insects of its kind those wings appear brilliantly patterned in violet, purple, green and yellow, a vision denied to us. Perhaps it is this additional visual dimension which assists these moths in their ability to navigate in rain or shine, at dawn or dusk and in the darkest of nights, an extraordinary adaptive facility for such a seemingly delicate creature. It is one of my earliest childhood memories, watching enthralled as these mystical beings hovered in an English country garden and, unknowingly, set me on the wandering path I continue to follow. After the moth vanished I emerged from the gully in time to disturb an Alpine Accentor which took flight with a clear rippling call from the rocks amongst which it had presumably been foraging for insects and seeds, and disappeared up and over the crags above me. As is so often the case when this bird is alarmed, the call was oddly disembodied, as if emitted from elsewhere, a remarkable natural stratagem for distraction. It was not a bird I had anticipated seeing at this low level and, in following its undulating flight, my thoughts accompanied it into the realm of the bears, for this was the time of day when any mother with new-born cubs would emerge to catch the last few hours of sun before the shadow of Tsouka Rossa enveloped the slopes. Being at the foot of the crags, I was far too close to see the upper corrie where the bears usually appear. That can only be observed from the lower end of the Magoula meadows, but I was content with just the thought of sharing the last of the day's sun with such creatures and amidst such grandeur.

During early June of the previous year when on the summits I had seen many recently overturned boulders, a sure sign of a bear foraging for food, and had found tracks in the snow indicating the ascent of a lone adult out of the corrie above Magoula. This and the absence of any daytime sightings in the vicinity at that time suggested that if the den in the upper corrie had been occupied it was most likely to have been by a lone female. That would allow the possibility of the den now being occupied by a mother with one or more newly born cubs and it would be only now, four months or so after birth, that the family would be making its first tentative excursions onto the nearby slopes. The mother would still be reliant on the store of body fat acquired the previous autumn for the energy neccessary to feed her young and would only be able to extend her own foraging range when the cubs were strong enough to accompany her. That would begin soon and would increase significantly during the summer culminating in the autumn peak, an essential pre-requisite for the winter hibernation. The family would over-winter together and emerge to begin what would be an intensive spring and summer territorial familiarization for the yearling cubs when they are weaned and finally driven away to fend for themselves.

Continuing my progression across the base of the crags to where I knew other floristic delights lay in store, I was amply rewarded, for there on a crumbling rock-face were the lilac pompons of *Globularia cordifolia* in their hundreds, amongst thick mats of dark green foliage wedged tightly into the crevices. Although having enjoyed the sight of this plant throughout the mountains of central and southern Europe, the reacquaintance is never dimmed by familiarity as it varies much in form and colour and never ceases to surprise in the variety of its setting. Here the excessively dark, tiny, compact leaves often have a thin, white edge which accentuates their outline and provides a sympathetic backcloth for the globular flower heads, lilac when freshly open and often fading to a lilac-tinged silvery white. Each of the twenty or so flowers in the composite head has a pronounced lower lip divided into three linear lobes, collectively imparting a frilly, tufted countenance to each inflorescence. Not content with clinging to the rock-face, there were other plants too, with woody stems firmly anchored into the more stable screes and bedrock elsewhere on the slopes, each creating its unique configuration molded on whatever rock form it encountered. Nearby were some densely floriferous cushions of *Aubrieta scardica* providing a startlingly bright purple contrast to the restrained composition of their neighbour but never an unwelcomed combination, just another contribution to nature's artistry. The canvas provided by a pavement of well-compacted scree was a further illustration of that, with its liberal covering of the now familiar violet-blue bells of *Edraianthus graminifolius* interspersed with the tiny five-rayed, red-tinged, white stars of *Sedum atratum* borne on compact sprays. This is another plant more usually encountered at high altitude on the mountain but which periodically appears at these lower levels.

My route across the screes, although in part exploratory and speculative, was planned to include places which I knew from previous visits harboured particularly elusive plants, and that was especially so for my next objective, a rare plant of the north-east facing slopes. *Linum flavum* ssp. *albanicum* is a flax which at its finest can present a mass of bright yellow, five-petalled flowers which would surely arrest the passage of any wanderer across this stony wilderness, however urgent their travels. The many ankle-high flowering stems arise from a woody stock buried in the rubble, but despite the plant's apparent ability to flourish in this and a considerable variety of other situations, both challenging and benign, it is rarely prolific, often choosing a solitary and isolated existence. Finding it is to meet a kindred spirit. Here it does, however, keep very commendable company, for nearby were sprays of the yellow-eyed, pink-petalled flowers of *Malcolmia graeca* ssp. *bicolor* spreading low from clumps of foliage, startlingly colourful against the white limestone scree. There were other more familiar floral faces too, including the radiant yellow discs of the leopard's bane, *Doronicum orientale*, a lowland cousin of the previously encountered *D. columnae*, here secreted amongst shaded rocks, and the tall wands of *Asyneuma limonifolium* with their lovely pale-blue to lilac, five-rayed flowers. Of much greater surprise were two robust spikes of the yellow-flowered orchid, *Orchis pallens*, growing in one of the boulder-strewn meltwater gullies, about as far removed as possible, both in altitude and habitat, from the summit grasslands where it had been previously encountered.

With shadows lengthening, I began my descent towards the meadows but not without further interest presenting itself in the form of some richly flowered clumps of the deadnettle, *Lamium garganicum* ssp. *laevigatum*. Hooded in pinkish-purple and with purple-striped frilly-lips, a fertile imagination could see a crowd of cowled mythical beings amidst the serrated foliage. Amongst the now familiar Tymphaean floral fraternity were the purple-veined, bright pink pea-flowers of *Onobrychis montana* ssp. *scardica* and the red-stained buds of yellow-flowered *Hypericum rumeliacum* ssp. *apollinis*, especially evident against the white scree. The pale lemon-yellow flowers of a vetch, *Anthyllis vulneraria* ssp. *alpestris*, were also an arresting sight, as in this form of an otherwise widespread and highly variable species, the plant is a dwarfed and prostrate perennial, spread very attractively over the rocks. On arrival at the base of the screes I set off to replenish my water supply from the spring which emerged at the lower end of the uppermost meadows and initiates the stream occupying the valley down to Vrisochori and beyond. The high cirrus had by now deferred to a uniform cloud cover from the west and the landscape was assuming a different countenance to that I had become accustomed to under a relentless sun. Pausing to glance back, cloud was already shouldering the Tsouka Rossa heights, and the pines scattered over the slopes up towards Goura were etched in black upon the snowy crags. In this light and from this aspect I was struck by the enormity and seeming inviolability of that rocky domain, much of it perhaps never sullied by human presence, as rock-climbers would see little of challenge beyond the sheer walls of Tsouka Rossa and there was even less to tempt, and much to deter, other possible human intruders. That realm of the bear is perhaps known only to these creatures and so it should remain, for a mother with cubs is acutely sensitive to human intrusion and the consequent displacement would disrupt the territorial acclimatization essential for the cubs' survival.

My route to the spring passed through meadows and woodland clearings to which any family of bears resident in the corrie above would descend as soon as the cubs were strong enough to do so. New born cubs might perhaps make the descent within the next few weeks but yearling cubs would already have done so and the family would probably now be utilising temporary dens elsewhere as part of their territorial familiarization. Whilst meandering through the meadows I was therfore prompted to look for signs of foraging and especially in places where there were boulders, rotting logs, tree-stumps and forest ants' nests. Female Brown Bears are partial to ants, especially during the spring, when bees, wasps and any other ground-nesting insects are also sought, a behavioural adaptation which derives benefit from the high protein and essential amino acids they provide, hence a propensity for turning over rocks, breaking open rotten logs and tree-stumps, and thorough dismemberment of ant nests. Other invertebrates and indeed any lizards, snakes and small mammals thus revealed are also consumed, supplemented by bulbs, corms and tubers for their sugars and starch. Springtime is when plant food is at its most nutritious, so grasses and herbaceous flowering plants are eaten too, in large quantities. All that was evident were a few boulders which had been dislodged or overturned but none recently so.

During these wanderings I had as always been careful to survey the ground ahead with binoculars and it was whilst doing so in the woodland clearings close to the spring that I detected a slight movement of an as yet indeterminate form amidst the adjacent trees. Backing myself against a tree, I waited motionless and after a while thought I could discern the characteristically heart-shaped pale rump of a Roe Deer presumably browsing foliage from the low branches amongst which it was partly concealed. Fortunately it was not down wind and was clearly unaware of my presence, so I waited in the hope it would emerge into the open. After a while it moved further into the trees and in the hope that its attention would be elsewhere, I moved closer to a place where I could squat down to wait. Although the light was fading, there was sufficient for the white-flowered composite heads of *Tordylium apulum*, tall amidst the meadow grasses, to shine like phosphorescence on a gently rolling sea. I knew the place well and of the options available to the animal, that is downstream to the lowermost meadows or up the track to terraced meadows a few hundred metres further east where it would be downwind of my scent. In the past I had been within five metres of a Roe Deer in a woodland clearing in the Welsh Marches simply by remaining motionless amidst branches, as the animal appeared unable to discern a static outline but could detect an eye-blink from fifty metres. Its sense of smell, hearing and vibration from footfall are, however, acute, so the challenge of achieving proximity is great. The reward is incomparable, as the Roe is so elegantly proportioned and delicate in features, and when you have looked into those large dark eyes you have experienced something truly profound in your relationship with the natural world.

Momentarily lost in preoccupation with my surroundings and such recollections of past encounters, I was suddenly alerted by the sonorous outburst of a Nightingale proclaiming his presence from the streamside vegetation just below the spring. The unpaired males are most likely to broadcast during late evening at this time of year, although a paired male can be provoked into doing so in response to the vocalization of a neighbour or an unpaired intruder, and this is the time and circumstance when the full vocal splendour of this bird is often revealed. It reserves its full repertoire of several hundred different phrases and its maximum ability to project its calls to evening and dawn performances, considerably surpassing the more selective daytime renditions in both variety and duration. Here, with the rippling flow of spring water as accompaniment, the clarity and tonal purity of song seems as if from another world, as from a mystical place. Listen intently and an extraordinary variety and richness of composition is revealed, of phrasing flowing and liquid, often sad in tone, but then suddenly bubbling as if chuckling with mirth, sometimes whistling or piping with great musicality then harshly toneless, but ever briefly so. It was whilst immersed in that characteristic high-pitched crescendo of fluting tones which the bird is so justifiably fond of repeating that the Roe Deer reappeared, moving cautiously out into the meadow edge, head erect with his black muzzled and moustachioed nostrils testing the air. This was a yearling buck with only the smallest indications of the three tines to his antlers, flanked by those huge pointed and white fur-lined ears now straining to discern the sounds of the forest. Seemingly reassured he came forward a few paces and bent to nip the head of some choice plant amongst the many. Roe are epicureans of their kind, selecting only the most nutritious parts of carefully chosen foodplants and then only in small quantities, constantly moving from place to place throughout a strongly defended territory. Their world is permeated by aroma as they leave a continuous scent trail from glands between the hindfoot digits signalling their age, sex, dominance and individuality, and also demarcate their territory with scent from a pre-orbital gland, which males supplement with other secretions especially those from head glands. This youngster is probably trespassing and will move on if the scent of a dominant male is detected or will be ejected if an encounter ensues. Suddenly his head was up and alert and with a flash of sandy-brown flanks turned back into the trees with his pale rump patch expanded in instinctive response to a perceived threat. Perhaps a momentary shift in the air had carried my scent to his nostrils. Whatever the cause there was a sharp warning bark as he moved away into the forest.

With the Nightingale still in full voice as accompaniment, I filled my water-bottle at the spring and in the rapidly fading light began my return through the woodland clearings to the upper Magoula meadows. Passing several huge rectangular rocks looming dark and isolated on the edge of a clearing, I was reminded of the glacial events which had brought them there and created these extensive meadow flats. The rocks were eratics carried on the glacier surface and stranded when the ice ceased to flow. The meadow flats were outwash gravel and lake sediment deposited by glacial meltwater. Now the rocks were a useful landmark as I turned towards my destination for the night and across the uppermost meadows beyond the forest limits. By the time I was reunited with my pack on the south-eastern ridge it was dusk but with the sky clearing from the west I was hopeful of yet another starry canopy over my head. The faint churring of a Nightjar was just discernible from somewhere out across the meadows and a Scops Owl had begun its persistent metronomic call from the heights towards Goura, a fitting duo to herald the approaching night. Soon a bright gibbous moon emerged from the retreating cloud with Venus and Jupiter some ten degrees beneath and shortly to disappear below the black mass of Tsouka Rossa. I had positioned myself to have a clear view out over the upper meadows, which even in the lunar half-light, should reveal any animal movement during the hour or so before the moon followed the planets down below the summit ridge, and settled down to my vigil. Above the meadows the screes appeared ridged and furrowed in shade and light, and long white shafts of gully-bound snow pierced the cragbound rim. In the realm of the bear the corrie snow glistened and shone bright, beyond the Black Pines, and the summit edge gleamed sharp against the darkening sky.

After scanning the meadows periodically for some time, I glimpsed the white underwing of an owl as it flapped and then glided out from the forest edge across the open grassland. Wingbeats were languid and few between the long straight glides but then sinuous as it circled close to a bush, hovering briefly before continuing on in a methodical quartering of its chosen ground. Suddenly it dipped and disappeared before rising a minute or so later, its broad wings and generous bulk suggestive of a Tawny Owl as it flapped back to the trees. A sharp *ke-wick* contact-call from the forest a few minutes later confirmed its identity and the delivery of a meal for its well-fledged chicks. With the moon soon to dip below the summit ridge and lunar light seeping out of the landscape, it was time to settle down for the night. The splendour of the Milky Way was now rising from beyond Smolikas and the north-east horizon, but as I lay waiting for the onset of sleep, it was the figure of the Great Bear high above the mountains of Albania which was the last to fade from sight and my mind.

# Chapter 6

# The Forest of Ghiol

The summit cliffs and crags of Goura were already bronzed and bright when I awoke to a clear sky and the promise of another fine day. This most easterly portion of the great escarpment, which delimits the northern edge of the Tymphaean massif, has an orientation which benefits most from the morning sun as the cliffs swing south-eastwards beneath Goura and on to Tsoumako. Hence, when I descended from my ridge-top refuge I could anticipate a rapid dissolution of the shadows now incised into the lower slopes and flooding the valley floor to the south-east. I intended to return here for a second night such that the steep rocky descent which immediately confronted me would be made easier without the burden of a pack. Here at 1,600 metres altitude, I was above the apron of stunted *Pinus heldreichii* which clothed the lower crags and scree slopes, forming an impenetrable barrier, breached only by the rock and snow-filled gullies which cut through the dense coniferous scrub. I knew of a way through directly below however and so was soon traversing the valley-head, towards the far ridge and the col which would lead to the valley of Ghiol and beyond.

Beneath the pines' steep screes held firm in the grip of entrenched vegetation were beginning to unfold their flowery mantle to the radiance of the early morning sun. Most of the floral constituents bore the welcoming countenance of re-acquaintance but of the few which were unfamiliar a variant of the ubiquitous milkwort, *Polygala nicaeensis* ssp. *mediterranea*, succeeded in delaying my progress. The trailing leafy stems terminating in dense sprays of bright pink, large-winged flowers blushed brightly on the pallid limestone. Whilst this plant was greatly limited in stature and encountered almost underfoot, others more robust and visible in form elicited deviations and none more rewarding than that of *Rosa villosa* shyly peeping from amidst a shady rock-pile. The shell-pink, broadly-ovate petals surrounding a mass of bright yellow anthers form flowers so perfectly complemented by the glaucous foliage that the occurrence in such a harsh rocky setting is rendered so much more memorable by its situation. It was here too that I found one of the rarer plants of the mountain, *Ranunculus platanifolius*, a tall white-flowered buttercup with red-tinted sepals and large segmented basal leaves, a plant more usually associated with the shade of forest margins elsewhere in Europe. I would search for others during my return through the woodland and meadows below. For now I was intent on maintaining a height that would minimise the climb to the ridge ahead and which necessitated crossing an extensive steeply inclined sheet of compact snow. As there were drifts of the brightly yellow-flowered buttercup *Ranunculus sartorianus*, newly emergent in adjacent saturated ground, I felt duly compensated for having to contend with the icy obstacle but then doubly rewarded on discovering a scattering of *Soldanella pindicola*, a plant previously only seen on the summits. There are few flowers exhibiting such apparent fragility as this, their thimble-sized, frilly violet-blue bells delicately suspended from finger-length, slender stems, so often at the margin of retreating snow or protruding through it. Much of life exists at the very edge of sustainability but to ally that with such beauty and transience of form permits these snow-bells a special place in the floral pantheon and in the hearts of those who wander the mountains of Europe.

Resting for a while on the ridge-top above the Ghiol valley, I watched the sun seep into the burgeoning landscape, the beech forest still in vernal greenery, shining bright amidst the encircling pine and fir. A Jay called harshly from the wooded slopes below as I scanned the nearby forest margins and more distant canopy, momentarily glimpsing what I thought was a buzzard dipping back into the trees. Re-emerging, the bird began to circle higher with brief deep wingbeats and longer glides on outstretched wings. An abrupt turn betrayed the outline of a long tail and the characteristic wing shape and proportions of a Goshawk, apparently female, as the male is appreciably smaller. Watching it circle ever higher soon revealed the heavily barred underwings and tail before it moved away on a long straight glide towards the cliffs beyond Tsouka Rossa. Perhaps it was this unerring trajectory which elevated the bird in the eyes of the ancients to be 'the swift messenger of Apollo'. The female will not leave her young unattended until they are fully fledged, relying upon the male to supply food which is transferred to her some way from the nest, so strong are the maternal instincts which drive her guardianship that even he must keep his distance. Now the juvenile birds will be perched quietly amongst the boughs of a large tree, adjacent to their birth-place deep in the forest, awaiting a meal perhaps of a hapless chough, a hare or some forest bird. As the Goshawk faded from view, what had been a soundless episode abruptly ended with that far-carrying and unworldly cry, emblematic of European arboreal wilderness, the call of the Black Woodpecker. Of the considerable repertoire, this penetrating banshee wail, always emitted when the bird is static on a tree, is so alien that most succumb to an involuntary spinal shiver.on hearing it for the first time. Perhaps the bird was prompted by the passage of the raptor or glimpse of me, a surveillance I anticipated would be maintained throughout the day as I knew the woodpecker to be resident here and extremely wary of human intrusion.

From the ridge it was a steep rocky descent in part through woodland to the valley floor, an area much confined by the encroachment of scree, forest and flanking slopes, and partly flooded by meltwater from the still considerable snow accumulations beneath the Goura cliffs and crags towering above. A forest road which would form part of my return route later in the day emerges on the far side of this expanse, but my immediate intention was to continue south-eastwards to the wooded slopes beneath Tsoumako and above the place known as Yiftokambos.

The forest road was built in part to aid scree extraction for use in construction, as the deep excavations into the slopes testify, and yet the quantity removed is proportionately such a small part of the rock debris accumulated along the length of these cliffs that it serves as testimony to the effectiveness of the erosive forces prevailing during glacial times. The cliffs must have receded by many tens of metres to have produced such a volume of scree.

Beyond the road, where the forest meets the open slopes, a few leafy stems of a tall Dame's Violet, *Hesperis dinarica*, were holding their heads of large four-petalled, snow-white flowers aloft as if conscious of their infrequency amongst Greek mountains. Nearby, the delicately purplish-pink, tessellated bells of *Fritillaria thessala* ssp. *ionica* made a much less assertive appearance as they blend unobtrusively into the enclosing vegetation and yet are far too handsome to justify such introversion. Their occurrence is a further reminder of the former extent of woodland on the southern slopes of the mountain where the plant was seen in the compensating shade of a rock face well above Tsepelovo. Also here are densely branched low shrubs of a rose with softly white-haired, finely proportioned dark foliage and the most exquisite pale shell-pink flowers. The broad, wavy-edged petals have delicate darker veining and encircle a crown of yellow anthers around a central boss of gold, as richly scented as one could wish any rose to be. As to an appellation, that of the highly variable *Rosa pulverulenta* seemed most appropriate. Away from the woodland, the rocky slopes are in places fragrant with the sweet-scented, creamy-white flowers of the evergreen shrub, *Daphne oleoides*, which here present especially dense floral clusters amidst the blue-green tufted foliage. Also making a reappearance were numerous spiny cushions of that strangely structured relict from pre-glacial times, *Drypis spinosa*, with its rectangular associations of tiny white or pale pink flowers which are so attractive to butterflies. Although too early in the day for much to be on the wing, the red-gold of a Small Copper flashed momentarily in flight above the richly marbled and silvered underwings of a Pearl-bordered Fritillary engrossed in imbibing nectar.

Whilst traversing some of the bouldery terrain at the foot of the slopes I became aware that my presence had recently been preceded by another, as several of the larger rocks were overturned and now had yellowing foliage beneath. A male bear had perhaps been this way on his solitary wanderings, a journey which would lead through the territories of many females and for a considerable distance ranging far and wide in servitude to his procreational instincts. A fully grown male would have required little effort to move aside these sack-sized obstacles to access any morsel scented beneath. His Herculean passage was clearly marked just above the forest edge towards the ridge and the wooded slopes beyond. My inferiorly heroic route was up the screes to the crags above and then onward to the same slopes and their *Pinus heldreichii* woods. An immediate impression of the screes ahead is of the familiar luxuriant growth of *Geranium macrorrhizum* coupled with the more discretely placed, but equally dazzling, blooms of *Geranium cinereum* ssp. *subcaulescence*, vividly colouring the slopes. Only belatedly do the robust stems of an asphodel impinge on consciousness, as these, having rather inconspicuous terminal spikes of white flowers above dense linear foliage, are not easily differentiated amongst the limestone. This is *Asphodeline taurica*, previously only known within Greece from Smolikas and two mountains on the northern borders. Far more conspicuous were several brightly yellow-flowered clumps of that beautiful flax, *Linum flavum* ssp. *albanicum*, seen growing equally sparingly on the screes above the Magoula meadows, the previous day. There were other familiar plants here too of which the lemon-yellow flower-heads of the onion, *Allium flavum* ssp. *flavum* and the pale pink thrift, *Armeria canescens*, were especially abundant, with a few large wreath-like clumps of the skullcap, *Scutellaria rupestris* ssp. *adenotricha* amongst them. Nearby and apparently well adapted to the rocky environment were extensive drifts of a white-flowered bittercress, *Cardamine glauca*, which has distinctly notched petals and, although not quite comparable floristically with those wonderful displays of *Cardamine carnosa* seen at higher altitudes, is still a splendid sight. For a plant rarely found on limestone it clearly thrives here.

Although I had seen elsewhere most of the floristic inhabitants of crags and cliffs usually found in flower on the mountain at this time of year, the pleasure of reaquaintance is not diminished by yet further encounters. Even before reaching the lowermost crags, the richly purple-flowered mats of *Aubrieta scardica* had been evident, vying for attention alongside many dense cushions of *Saxifraga marginata* which still retained some of the splendour they had doubtless exhibited a week or so before. In contrast, the similarly white-flowered sprays of *Saxifraga paniculata* were assuming the peak of sartorial splendour, the ivory-white, almost cream-coloured petals minutely spotted in red, elevated above mats of lime-encrusted leaf rosettes. There was another, far less exuberantly flowered saxifrage as well, one which normally appears locally at high altitudes but which had been elusive during the previous days. At 1,600 metres altitude this is a rare low-level occurrence for *Saxifraga rotundifolia* ssp. *taygetea*, which displays up to a dozen white-petalled, purple-spotted flowers, above rounded, shallowly lobed basal leaves. Whilst moving further along the base of the crags there were reminders of other, now familiar inhabitants of these rocky environments growing both on ledges and on the nearby slopes. Both of the yarrows, white-flowered *Achillea abrotanoides* and pale yellow-flowered *A. holosericea* were here in abundance, whilst the white-flowered shrubby candytuft, *Iberis sempervirens*, grew conspicuously on a rocky ridge. Dominating all however were robust stands of *Iris germanica* on some of the ledges, with huge variously blue, purple and violet tinged flowers glowing magnificently in the early morning sunlight. These are exotic plants in any context but none more so than in such a wild and majestic mountain setting, and therein lies a mystery for the flowers are often sterile and so can only reproduce by displaced fragments of rhizome, a problematical means of dispersal in any location. It has been cultivated since ancient times for its floral beauty and both perfumary and medicinal purposes, so it is widespread in Europe and Asia in a naturalised state, but there are very few occurrences which appear to be truly indigenous. This is one of perhaps only eleven such places in Greece, three of them on Tymphi, including that already seen on the cliffs above Tsepelovo, the third in the Vikos Canyon. Pyrrhus and his contempories would have been familiar with the plant as an unguent from *orris* root was famed throughout Macedonia from at least as early as the fourth century BC, for use in treating wounds, and of the three *Iris* contenders, *germanica* is the most likely candidate from that time. Perhaps these and the few other plants on Tymphi are all that remain of those gathered for such purposes.

On cresting the rise I paused for a while to assess the way ahead as it was some two kilometres to the destination I had in mind, albeit far less challenging than the ravaged terrain faced the previous day. There were a few gullies and ridges to contend with but deviations down-slope, through open woodland and clearings, would circumvent these obstacles. Momentarily diverted by the sight of a few white-flowered *Narcissus poeticus* ssp. *radiiflorus* offering their golden, flame-tipped coronas to the sun, I was suddenly alerted by a loud ringing bird-call from the crags above. The phrases, each of a few short pure notes, were repeated several times with long intervening pauses but imbued with a plaintive and melancholic quality which instantly transported me back to where I had, as a youth, first heard this sound, echoing from the walls of Cwm Idwal in Snowdonia. Then it had been the more exuberant and melodious refrains of early spring. Now it was the constrained and contemplative utterances of maturity as the Ring Ouzel was nearing the seasonal end of his song repertoire. As I was too close in to the crags to see the bird I dropped down to where the trees would provide a screen for a more advantageous view. The slim and rakish thrush-like form was readily visible on a rock pinnacle, with the distinctive white crescentic chest-band on an otherwise all black plumage, unmistakable in the sunlight. Although too distant to see the detail, this *alpestris* race has white and grey fringes to most of the body feathers which imparts a strikingly scaly or zigzag patterning that appears greyish in flight. After a while, obligingly the bird plummeted down on flickering wings to alight with tail cocked, on a lower prominence, where it briefly resumed its oratory before disappearing in rapid and direct flight into a gully. As this is a rare bird in Greece, it was reassuring to know that it was still present.

Yiftokambos, 'Gypsy Fields', is a grazing area, formerly under the aegis of Nouka, a small settlement incorporated into

Skamneli in the seventeenth century and has since become the focus of an annual gathering of the Sarakatsani on the first weekend in August. The slopes above, and extending to the crags and cliffs of Tsoumako, are of open woodland with some venerable and majestic *Pinus heldreichii* above a stony grassland, an environment created and maintained by centuries of grazing and associated pastoral activities. On approaching the area, an increasing floristic diversity becomes evident, as the familiar robust yellow-flowered spikes of *Asphodeline lutea* make an appearance and the many deep reddish-purple flower-heads of *Dianthus cruentus* begin to colour the scene. On the lower slopes, *Anacamptis* (*Orchis*) *morio*, the Green-winged Orchid, also makes a welcome return, not in the profusion seen below Tsepelovo but plentiful enough to impart a violet tinge to the hillside. Searching amidst the throng, a few plants of rosy-sepalled *Ophrys scolopax* ssp. *cornuta* seductively induce inspection on bended knee of their intricately patterned and sculpted flowers, whilst nearby majestic spikes of a lizard orchid similar to those seen in the Vikos Canyon and attributable to either *Himantoglossum caprinum* or *H. calcaratum* invoke similarly reverential attention. It was whilst engrossed in examining the latter that a sharp and penetrating *kik kik* call averted my attention and with repetition led to the location of a black and white woodpecker in the canopy of one of the nearby pines. As I knew from previous observations that Greater Spotted Woodpecker, a local and infrequent bird in Greece, occurred here, I continued to watch in the hope of confirming the identification. A black facial band continuous to the nape and a bright crimson, not pink, vent are sufficient to differentiate it from the Syrian Woodpecker, a species more commonly found at lower altitude and in diverse habitat. After tolerating my attentions sufficiently long for a positive determination, the bird disappeared in characteristic undulating flight as it alternated between rapid wingflaps and complete wing closure in a bounding trajectory towards more distant trees. As winters in these mountains can be severe and food sources consequently limited, I surmised that these woodpeckers might rely, at least in part, on the seeds of *Pinus heldreichii* for sustenance during that time just as the birds have a similar dependency in more northerly climes.

As I moved further up the grassy slopes, the familiar rockrose *Helianthemum nummularium* became increasingly evident, colouring the more stony areas with its bright yellow flowers on trailing leafy stems, whilst elsewhere the deep pink, clustered and white-spotted flowers of *Dianthus viscidus* were liberally scattered on short upright stems amongst the verdure. Its tiny white-flowered cousin, *Dianthus integer* ssp. *minutiflorus*, familiar from more elevated occurrence on the mountain and from a propensity for stable screes, was also present, demonstrating its adaptability to a range of habitats. A seemingly disparate association of small birds took flight in ones and twos from where they had presumably been foraging on the slopes into nearby pines. The flickering exposure of white wing bars and outer tail feathers was sufficient to indicate they were female and juvenile Chaffinch with a few of the more colourful male birds in tow. Characteristic *chink* calls confirmed their identity. It was not long after that a more distant signature call came drifting in from the woodland canopy and alerted me to locate the direction in the hope of finding the source of this, the distinctive metallic and far-carrying *chüpchüp* flight call of a Crossbill. I had encountered these birds on a previous visit and had been intrigued by apparent disparities in colour and form compared with those elsewhere, so an opportunity to obtain further and hopefully closer observation was very welcome. Working my way cautiously through the trees towards where I estimated they might have alighted, I soon identified their characteristic communal feeding call and was fortunate, as they are extremely wary, to get a clear view of the flock in the canopy of some adjacent pines. Several, which I assumed to be males, were in full sunlight almost plum coloured, a purplish-pink rather than the more usual orange-red of northern races. Others with an olive green plumage appeared to be adult females and none displayed the wing-quivering usually exhibited by juveniles waiting to be fed. The stout build and stubby forked tail were typical, but the large crossed bill was distinctively bulkier than the norm, a possible adaptation to feeding on the seeds of *Pinus heldreichii*. They are characterful birds appearing and behaving like small parrots, sidling and jumping along branches, clambering and hanging upside down and always busily gregarious, accompanied by their homely *chuk chuk* feeding call. As befits such restless birds, they were all airborne in an instance and were off over the tree-tops propelled by bursts of powerful wingbeats in fast undulating flight. Whether some at least had young to feed one could only surmise as they breed at variable times in response to the availability of conifer seeds.

Resuming my upward progression and through an area a little further to the south-east than I had previously explored, I was rewarded with sight and scent of a shrub not recorded from Tymphi before. The bright pinkish-purple, four-petalled flowers with long corolla tubes, densely clustered at the tips of woody stems, are the unmistakable characteristics of *Daphne mezereum*, accompanied on this occasion by the lanceolate leaves which often appear later. Although this plant was of rather limited stature, it was wonderfully floriferous and fragrant, its discovery a serendipitous consequence of the deviation in pursuit of the Crossbills. Regaining my intended route brought me to more rocky open slopes where the now familiar knapweed *Centaurea epirota* was abundant, its densely white-woolly basal foliage a fitting backdrop to those lovely pinkish-purple radiating flower heads speckled with dark violet and steely-blue anthers. Here at the lower limit of its altitudinal range most flowers were on ankle-high stems but a few, on rocky outcrops, were almost stemless. It was here too, forming small densely leaved cushions amongst the rocks, that the strongly scented *Dianthus sylvestris* made a welcome reappearance, its frilly-edged, pink-petalled flowers usually held singly on tall stems, an irresistible lure to the day-flying moths it attracts. A little further on I disturbed a small flock of Serin which, having been feeding amidst the ground vegetation, erupted in bouncing, dancing flight and communal metallic twittering towards the nearest pines. At this time of year juveniles were on the wing and the adult males still distinctively yellow-fronted. A few pairs of adult Goldfinch were also foraging, their gold-barred black wings and bright red, white and black head plumage brilliant in the morning sunlight.

It was warming up now, sufficient for a perceptible hum of insect activity to emanate from the slopes and for a few butterflies to contribute, usually fleetingly, to the scene. I was heading for screes where I knew there was a liberal covering of *Drypis spinosa*, that strangely flowered shrub often favoured by butterflies and day-flying moths, in the hope of some lepidopteran surprises. Even from a distance it was evident I would not be disappointed as a quick binocular scan highlighted the unmistakable form and alternating fluttering-gliding flight of a Scarce Swallowtail. Although this flew purposefully onward there were other butterflies less itinerant. A bright fulvous brown fritillary was patrolling rapidly back and forth across the slopes, and it was only when it alighted briefly to feed on one of the flowering shrubs, that the splendour of this, the *cleodoxa* form of the High Brown Fritillary was fully apparent. With wings obligingly only half closed, the complex pattern of black spots, lunules and irregular markings on the upperwing surfaces contrasted with the pale buff and yellowish undersides, that of the hindwing with a row of four prominent red-ringed white-eyed spots. From its modest proportions and assertive exploratory flight I assumed this to be a male. There were Burnet Moths too, quietly imbibing nectar, the crimson hindwings and smoky-grey, iridescent steely-blue five-spot forewings bright against the pale pink *Drypis spinosa*. Elsewhere on the slopes were several Painted Lady butterflies which, like that seen on the Kourtetsi plateau, were in such pristine condition as to suggest recent emergence locally rather than migration from North Africa.

As I was at the limit of my morning's deviation and it was time to head back towards the Ghiol valley, an exploratory ramble across the lower slopes of Tsoumako and then down into the woodland to rejoin my outward route seemed appealing. I had not gone far when I came across a giant of the bedstraw genus *Galium* draped over an outcrop and unlike any I had encountered before, although perhaps closest to species *pisoderium* previously unknown from the mountain. With myriads of tiny white, four-petalled flowers amassed along metre-long, slender branches crowded with bright green, elongate, whorled leaves, this was a most imposing sight. The hefty woody rootstock suggested a plant of considerable antiquity. Further on, as I was approaching the woodland, a small flock of thrushes took flight with harsh chattering calls, rising swiftly to the safety of some tall pines where they alighted with anxiously flicking wings and tail. They were clearly a group of adult and characteristically much paler juvenile Mistle Thrushes, an uncommon bird in Greece, emphasising their wariness by retreating further with powerful bursts of wingbeats above and away over the trees as I approached. That they had good reason to be wary was made evident not long after, when a male Sparrowhawk appeared momentarily, dashing through the trees on what would be a regular hunting route. Fleeting as the encounter was, it was sufficient to gauge the smaller, sleeker frame and rapid wingbeats which differentiate it from a male Goshawk, the other contender for the thrushes' fears.

After negotiating the rocky slope down into the head of the Ghiol valley, I was looking forward to the shade of the forest as a relief from the heat and humidity of this windless hollow. The meltwater pool at the forest margin offered a brief diversion to see Yellow-bellied Toad and Alpine Newt, both of which congregate here to breed, on this occasion in such profusion that the shallows rippled and glistened red and yellow with colourful underbellies. A nearby stand of *Veratrum album* added further justification for the minor deviation, the waist high, leafy stems supporting dense spikes of yellowish-green, six-rayed flowers, unlike the white, green-veined flowers usual throughout most of its European range. A Speckled Wood butterfly floated lazily by on almost motionless wings, fluttering to a brief stall before continuing down the forest road to which I also turned in the wake of the butterflies' patrol. The beech forests extend from here for many kilometres down-slope and are dissected by numerous fast-flowing streams, and gentler, often well-vegetated tributaries devoid of dense canopy. Much of the forest floor resembles that of beech woodland anywhere, largely bereft of plantlife due to lack of direct sunlight and with a surfit of leaflitter. What is inhospitable to many is however accommodating to a few, so a plunge into some of the darkest and densest parts of the woodland soon revealed the two plants most commonly associated with this environment. *Neottia nidus-avis*, the Bird's Nest Orchid, is sometimes abundant, as it was on this occasion, but is somewhat sporadic in its appearance either due to dormancy or the plant's ability to flower underground. Now it was evident in clusters or isolated spikes scattered liberally in almost every direction, protruding in various stages of growth from the dense brown carpet of the last autumnal leaf fall. Being destitute of chlorophyll, the orchid is a sickly yellowish-brown in all parts, but with a form which would attract adulation if it was of a more appealing hue. Each of the many flowers, condensed into a columnar spike, is a hood of sepals and petals, shielding a nectar-producing cup above a large, bilobed pendant lip. Although a viscous nectar is produced the instance a fly comes in contact with the pollinia, thus ensuring transference of pollen to the next flower visited by the insect, the flowers are frequently self-pollinated, a preferential stratagem which apparently functions also when the plant flowers underground. The other plant of interest is far less frequent here but shares some of the orchid's characteristics in also being devoid of chlorophyll. *Monotropa hypopitys* unfurls a cluster of drooping yellowish flowers atop a stout, fleshy, scaly-leaved stem with a waxy yellowish sheen. Its other-worldly appearance reflects an absence of affinity to any other plants as it is another survivor from Tertiary times, with an ancestry long pre-dating the glacial episodes.

As it was difficult to tread noiselessly on the deep crisp leaf-litter of the mature beech stands and even more challenging to negotiate the dense coppices, I returned to the forest road which at least offered the option of unimpeded progress and access to a varied marginal flora. The road is a corridor for butterflies too, as was evident from the procession of Orange Tip, Speckled Wood and Wood White patrolling the borders, and is favourable to most woodland birdlife. Chiffchaffs were fluttering like humming-birds, picking insect prey from the roadside foliage but more often heard during monotonous repetition of their eponymous call whilst foraging unseen amongst the dense canopy. A Blackbird was singing somewhere ahead, with all the joyous and uplifting fervour of which those wonderful songsters can muster. Such male vocalizations during a hot June day are often intermittent and subject to interruptions for other preoccupations, but the characteristic inventive phrasing and unique timbre are always recognisable. Throughout life these birds continuously assimilate much of the phraseology their rivals invent, so creating a local and evolving dialect to which are added snatches of mimicry to produce an often distinctive regional repertoire. This bird was still engaged in full-throated performance as I drew nearer and, as I stood quietly, listening, gradually altered his delivery into a rambling medley of phrases, part phrases and quite uncharacteristic sounds. These infrequently heard interludes are times when the bird resurrects and reviews little used portions of its vocal store. Within a few minutes it had gradually reverted to its normal phraseology which was promptly curtailed, perhaps on detecting my presence, as with swift and agile flight it descended from its lofty song-perch into the dense forest understorey. This Balkan race, *aterrimus*, appears to lack the glossy blackness of more northerly birds and is a very shy and skulking occupant of these forests, of which I was reminded as the bird emitted a paroxysm of alarm rattles during its panic-stricken departure.

The Blackbird had been proclaiming territorial rights at the margin of a roadside clearing, which had been rutted and furrowed by logging activities and was now being reclaimed by the encroaching forest. Here were the distinctive dark-violet-leaved spikes of an orchid which I had encountered quite frequently in this and adjacent valleys in previous years but not being in flower had always defied identification. Now I could see a few newly opened buds which though unprepossessing in appearance, were intriguing for being unlike any species of helleborine I knew. These were not the dark wine-red flowers of *Epipactis atrorubens* I had expected but were tinted pale violet and pink, and crowded in a pendulous row along one side of the terminal third of the tall dark arching stems. Only later did I establish that this was *Epipactis subclausa*, a newly recognised species described only three years previously from Mount Olympos, and confined to northern Greece where it is rare and local. Also here, glowing bright pink amidst the rampant vegetation, were the large, five-petalled flowers of a catchfly, *Lychnis coronaria*, held high on tall, white-haired stems. Whilst these had been the subjects of a pleasant interlude and occasioned by little more than a temporary clearance, it was the more open wayside woodlands further down the valley which beckoned as I knew they harboured the greatest floristic prizes. So, taking advantage of a route which would exclude a lengthy circuitous portion of forest road, I ventured once more into the forest. There was no path for guidance, just the certainty that the road would be intercepted somewhere below. The forests here do not aspire to the grandeur of those of more northerly climes but what they lack in stature is compensated by an air of antiquity and permanence. There have been forests of beech in the vicinity of these mountains for thousands of years. Here woodland continuity has been interrupted repeatedly by cutting and coppicing, perhaps for a millennium or more, but being locally confined and periodic has allowed the integrity of the forest community to prevail. Although most clearly manifest in the floral diversity, this continuity is evident also in aspects of the fauna. Thus the beech woodland is a vital source of food for the bears during autumn, a time when they must accumulate adipose tissue in preparation for hibernation by consuming quantities of beech mast to supplement that of acorns, chestnuts and hazelnuts. Without sufficient energy reserves a female bear cannot sustain her cubs through their first spring. Wild Boar has a similar dependency on this autumnal food source, an association which has a particular resonance since it seems that their ancestors survived in the forests of Greece throughout the last glaciation and it is from here alone they colonised the rest of Europe as the climate ameliorated. The animals which emerge at dusk to root and snuffle the forest floor can claim rights of pannage here spanning at least 30,000 years.

Following a trail of dappled sunlight beneath the least dense canopy soon brought me into the company of other forest floral associates. Clusters of the large, four-petalled, lilac flowers of *Cardamine bulbifera* atop sparsely leaved stems locally coloured the forest floor. The visual assertiveness of these flowers belies their propensity to produce infertile seed or none at all, hence a reliance in part on propagation by subterranean rhizomes. On closer scrutiny, however, there are tiny, dark purple bulbils in the leaf axils, compact buds of fleshy scale-leaves, which will fall to earth and in three or four years time produce the aerial shoots of new plants. One of nature's many manifestations of reproductive ingenuity. Here also, and widely scattered wherever there is sufficient light, are the variously pale to dark pink-flowered spikes of the orchid *Cephalanthera rubra*. Although often borne on tall spindly stems, a plant with a dozen or more large salmon-pink, hooded and winged flowers above dark green, violet-veined leaves is a glorious sight amidst the coppery leaf-litter. The pause necessary to admire these plants provided an interlude uninterrupted by the crunch of boots on dry leaves, a silence broken only by a vigorous tapping from amongst the nearby trees. A momentary fluttering of wings soon revealed a tiny black-crowned form frenetically hammering its bill at a bark crevice and tearing away fragments of dislodged lichen. In a spasm of flitting, bouncing flight it alighted amidst branches only a few metres distant and disclosed its identity with a loud explosive *pit-choo* and a harsh scold, for this was a Marsh Tit. The similarly plumaged Willow Tit, equally infrequent, appears to favour the coniferous forests here. After briefly inspecting the intruder it disappeared into the trees to resume its search for insects and spiders, doubtless to be ferried to nestlings within a tree-hole nest. As beech mast constitutes part of its diet during autumn and winter, this is another dependent on the continuance of these woodlands.

After observing that the forest road was not too distant I cut across-slope with the intention of intercepting one of the small spring-fed streams which I knew intersected the forest at intervals. This would provide a break in the canopy and conditions which favoured some of the other flora I anticipated. The rivulet I encountered was too insignificant to have restrained the overhead tree cover but it appeared promising so I waded through some clumps of an aromatic fern, *Dryopteris villarii*, which fringed its bouldery source, savouring the lemon scent of the sticky fronds as I followed the water's course downstream. After a few discontinuous breaks in the canopy this opened to allow a sunlit descent alongside a burgeoning flow. Here were the tall, branching, many-flowered stems of *Saxifraga rotundifolia* ssp. *rotundifolia*, the forest form of the high altitude subspecies *taygetea* which had been encountered on rocks earlier that day. This is a much more robust plant, often with a knee-high spray of fifty or more white-petalled flowers with small reddish-purple, sometimes yellow, spots in mid-petal. In places where the rosettes of basal leaves crowd together adjacent to the stream, the air above appears turbulent with clouds of their white stars oscillating in the breeze. Also vying for waterside space and effortlessly winning the attention of any discriminating eye were the dark bluish-violet, nodding flowers of *Aquilegia nigricans*, combining the extraordinary architectural form typical of the genus with the rich colouration of the species. Although locally abundant in these woods, it was discovered only recently, being previously unknown from anywhere in Greece. To a disinterested wanderer there are probably few flowers which would warrant a second look, but one which would certainly command attention came into view even whilst in semi-shade and some distance ahead. The fist-sized, bright scarlet blooms of *Lilium chalcedonicum* are always an arresting sight, sometimes amassed in a cluster, with the tightly up-curved petals above prominent pendulous scarlet anthers. Some approached a metre in height on their robust leafy stems. Perhaps less visually enticing but certainly of interest, the stream sides were also host to the insectivorous *Pinguicula crystallina* ssp. *hirtiflora*, the yellowish fleshy-leaved rosettes of which crowded the banks and rocks wherever saturated or water-sprayed. It is the upper surface of the sticky leaves which exude an insect-digesting enzyme. The flowers, on finger-length stems, are five-lobed and of a delicate pale pink or lilac, surrounding a yellow throat, a most attractive contrast to the gruesome scene beneath.

Further downstream, whilst preoccupied with convincing myself that a knee-high, leafy stemmed stand of orchids, some with sixty or more tiny violet-tinted, green-winged, pendent flowers, was indeed that of *Epipactis helleborine*, I was abruptly alerted by the call of a Green Woodpecker from nearby amidst the trees. Heard at close quarters, the volume of their utterances is astonishing and the abruptness of the seemingly sardonic outburst quite disconcerting especially to anyone unacquainted with the sound and unaware of its origins. As the bird is also inclined to remain concealed, the absence of an obvious source compounds the unease. I was inclined to listen more intently in the hope of differentiating this call from that of the much less common Grey-headed Woodpecker which lacks the full-throated rendition of its cousin, but to no avail as it appears not to have invaded this far south. Returning to the immediate surroundings, there were other less conspicuous orchids here too. These had superficially similar flowers to those of their more robust neighbours in being violet-washed and green-sepalled but were fewer and in a one-sided pendant array on grey-green, velvety-haired stems bearing similarly coloured leaves. This was *Epipactis microphylla*, which disregards being both vanilla scented and nectar producing, in favour of self-pollination.

In the mid-afternoon heat any lethargy I felt from the day's exertion was compounded by the humidity of the close-bound forest, so with a cooling stream at hand the temptation of a rest was irresistible. A solitary Speckled Wood occupied my attention for a while having settled obligingly as they often do with wings flat and open, sufficient to display the intricacy of its markings and reminding me of how handsome is this *tircis* race of the butterfly. The contrast provided by the rich cream fenestrations amidst a chocolate-brown background only serves to accentuate the dark-ringed ocelli even more than is usual for the species. If my rest had been rewarded with this alone I would have been more than content but as so often happens when you sit and watch, nature comes to you. On this occasion it was a male Cleopatra which filled my cup, alighting briefly to feed on a sunlit knapweed, with closed wings glowing a translucent pea-green, and the forewing flaring a bright orange-red in the moment of departure. That is all one will ever glimpse of the upperside of a Cleopatra wing in life, as only in flight are they opened.

After regaining the forest road it was time to return to the valley-head but with time enough to linger whenever the waysides or woodland inhabitants beckoned. The marginal shade was a welcome relief for much of the way and served to nurture tall sinuous leafy stems of the orchid *Cephalanthera damasonium*. Most were still in bud, but a few were spreading their ivory wings, which is as much as these shy flowers venture, preferring to remain closed and inviolate since they also favour self-pollination. The forest remained voiceless apart from the familiar short metallic calls and ringing trills of Nuthatch and the occasional rasping screech of Jay from the darker depths. As the road was seldom used and there were no tyre tracks in what remained of former muddy pools, I had nurtured the hope of finding evidence of former travellers on the route, so I was not too surprised when I came across the unmistakable footprints of a bear. The animal appeared to have come out of the forest and, as the trail indicated, ambled along the remaining few hundred metres of road to the valley-head. As the few complete imprints were slightly abraded and the claw marks obscured, I equated these to the same animal which had been upending boulders above the treeline perhaps two weeks before. The twenty-centimetre span of my spread hand just encompassed the sole of the most complete fore-foot imprint of what must have been a fully grown male. It is both exhilarating and sobering when gazing down on these huge impressions to recall that the same feet which will excavate a choice bulb or corm can disembowel a Chamois or Roe Deer at a stroke. What we might foolishly perceive as a lumbering hulk is able to outpace even these nimble creatures in an explosive burst of speed, a capability I am graphically reminded of from personal experience. Whilst tracking a Brown Bear through the Djindjiritsa forest of Bulgaria I realised too late the imminent danger when, on kneeling down to examine some fresh faeces, I saw blades of grass rising from where feet had only recently been impressed. Although having been in many comparable situations, this was the only time when the hackles on my neck rose in instinctive and emphatic warning, a second before the bear crashed out of the adjacent shrubbery a bodylength to my right and with a low grunt bounded away into the forest. At the same instance a Red Deer barked to my left and sped away with two companions. Coming between a bear and its intended prey is almost as unwise as occupying the space between a mother bear and her cubs.

On nearing the upper limit of the road, I turned down into a forest clearing which, being immediately beneath the meltwater pool at the valley-head, was well watered and luxuriant, with the appearance of having been maintained as a hay meadow. Here the prominent pinkish-purple flower heads of *Dianthus giganteus* were swaying gently above the dense verdure, thick with the similarly coloured and clustered heads of *Dianthus viscidus*, both familiar floral faces from elsewhere on the mountain. Less obtrusive were the dark lilac-purple flowers of *Geranium reflexum* with its oddly deflexed petals and the nodding blue bells of *Campanula rotundifolia*. A near relative, that of *Campanula foliosa*, with a terminal cluster of violet-blue bells on stout leafy stems, was also here just protruding from the grasses, whilst yet another, *Campanula trachelium* ssp. *athos*, extended its taller spikes of similarly coloured flowers well aloft. To complete a quartet of bellflowers there were a few stems of *Campanula versicolor* amidst the rocky margins but yet to reveal their dark-eyed, five-lobed, violet stars in full array.

Leaving the meadow, intent on following a forest track from which I could regain access to the valley-head west of Ghiol and thence to my overnight camp, I re-entered the forest. The initial climb through a dense intergrowth of the fir *Abies borisii-regis* and Black Pine, *Pinus nigra*, laced with beech and other deciduous intruders, provided only meagre wayside vegetation. My senses were however directed elsewhere as I had seen a few indistinct but possibly recent bear prints on the approach where forestry vehicles had the previous year churned subsoil into a morass. The enhanced alertness served me well as an otherwise barely discernible purring trill betrayed the presence of a Crested Tit feeding in the adjacent conifers. Frenetic foragers, ceaselessly searching for insects and spiders amidst foliage and fissured bark, they are as agile when inverted, hanging from beneath branch tips, as when probing and prodding the cracks and crevices of a scaly pine. The brief calls elicited a raising of the salt and pepper tufted crown above a handsome black bibbed and collared face as the bird hopped and jumped along a thin branch before bouncily flitting to another to resume its search. Watching it picking delicately from the underside of tufts of pine needles, it seemed barely credible that the same tiny bill could excavate or enlarge an existing hole for nesting within a living tree. The bird also relies on conifer seeds for food during the harsh winters, a challenge which its numbers suggest it is adapted to quite successfully.

A little further on and warily conscious of the visual limitations provided by the all encompassing forest, I was momentarily surprised by a large dark brown butterfly which swept purposefully down into the corridor before me and disappeared into a dense fir. After a brief search and prompted by movement amongst a tangle of branches, there in a close huddle were revealed five of its kind, with closed wings hiding all but the variegated underside of the scalloped-edged hindwings. Irregular bands of brown, shading from dark chocolate to pale buff, all minutely stippled and scaled, created the illusion of tree bark, an immaculate camouflage. With the newcomer still unsettled, a jostling of wings briefly revealed a yellowish-buff suffusion with two black-ringed, white-eyed spots on the underside forewing. These were Southern Grayling butterflies of the *senthes* race, settling in for an overnight roost. Although I had moved quietly and stealthily, senses more acute than mine had it seemed detected my presence, as a frenzied chittering from an adjacent pine disclosed a Red Squirrel flicking its tail before disappearing rapidly into the canopy. This animal appeared to be a uniform dark chocolate brown with pale whitish undersides and whether through their natural shyness or scarcity remained one of the very few I have ever seen in these woods.

On attaining the ridge-top, the track digs into the hillside beside a rocky exposure. Here it provides an invitation to linger a while amidst the enclosing trees. *Abies borisii-regis*, the predominant indigenous fir in these forests, is thought to be a natural hybrid of the Greek Fir, *Abies cephalonica*, and the Silver Fir, *Abies alba*, both of which clothed parts of the mountain for thousands of years before disappearing some two millennia ago probably due to felling for timber. The builders of Greek warships favoured these trees above all others and by the fourth century BC were importing the timber from far beyond their own shores having exhausted most local sources. To gaze now over the great swathes of forest down to the Aoos is to invoke images of the firs which once clothed these slopes, transformed into the keels, masts, spars and oars of the sleek-hulled triremes which devastated the Persian ships at Salamis. Perhaps even Pyrrhus himself called upon his native Tymphaean firs for construction of the fleet and of the great septireme which carried him to Italy in 280 BC. If these imaginings had dulled my senses it was not for long. A sudden rush of air followed by a piercing demonic cry heralded the arrival of a Black Woodpecker on a pine trunk only a few metres distant. Without the usual flight-call the bird must have launched itself from the forest-floor above the rocks which obscured my presence. Now it clung flat against the pine, glossy black with huge clawed feet splayed either side, and the scarlet-crowned, ivory-billed head, turned to fix me with a staring yellow-rimmed eye. Time stands still in moments like this: neither participant is inclined even to blink, fear and flight tugging at one, intense and timeless awareness overwhelming the other. Perhaps it was precautionary instinct which prevailed, as the bird took flight without alarm and vanished through the trees in a low, undulating departure on irregular wingbeats. Cumulatively I have spent weeks stalking these wary and elusive birds in forests from Cantabria to the Carpathians, rarely with success but often with compensatory reward, and yet it is still the serendipitous encounter which impresses one the deepest. It requires effort and determination to create the opportunity for such events, and so much greater is the reward when it comes freely from nature. However briefly, we are returned at such times to the great wilderness from which we came.

Abandoning the track, I began to follow the sheep trails which lead down through the woodland to the meadows beneath the Goura crags, pausing for a while at a grassy clearing which had recently been disturbed by foraging Wild Boar. What had commanded their attention was not evident but the few snout impressions and freshly bitten roots indicated a productive excavation. From here the snow-filled corrie beneath the Goura summit appeared clearly through the break in the trees, with lengthening shadows darkening its smooth white flanks. After a prolonged binocular aided search of the corrie and surrounding rocks for any sign of life, I was just about to continue when a line of Chamois, five adults and two young, appeared, running across the broad expanse of the basin floor towards the adjacent pine-covered crags. Sight or scent of a bear would certainly elicit such response but just as they reached the rocks I caught sight of the aerial threat they had clearly seen. For there gliding in fast from the direction of the Tsouka Rossa cliffs, with intermittent deep and powerful wingbeats, was what I assumed to be a Golden Eagle. At this distance it was indistinguishable from an Imperial Eagle, but having seen the former regularly patrolling these cliffs in previous years, the assumption was well founded. Obligingly it turned towards me with wingtips raised and soared back over the corrie revealing the characteristic form and the elegance and mastery of flight sufficient to dispel any remaining uncertainty as to its identity. The Chamois had good reason to be wary as a youngster exposed on the snowy slopes would have little chance of evading the five-centimetre-long talons with which it would be impaled and hoisted aloft, although hare, Rock Partridge and tortoise are the more usual victims. As the bird rose to follow the line of summits westwards, I was reminded of seeing a juvenile here in June three years before, an indication of local breeding success for which the Vikos Canyon is the most likely location of the several rock-ledge eyries which they require.

After descending the remaining slope and emerging from the trees, the steep rocky climb back to my overnight camp lay directly ahead through the lowermost limit of the *Pinus heldreichii* scrub I had negotiated on the outward route. There was little to detain me when crossing the stony meadow which led to the base of the screes, so I continued, with the intention of spending the remainder of the evening returning to the spring below the Magoula meadows. Whilst climbing beneath some of the more substantial pines on the slope I became aware of a familiar repetitive trill, so high-pitched as to be barely audible and without a readily discernible direction. A few minutes observation however served to locate the source as the restless form of a Goldcrest moving mouse-like through the uppermost branches. In the evening light it flashed a yellow and orange crown above a white-rimmed eye, as it picked and pried amidst the black-needled tufts. Weighing little more than a two-pence coin, these tiny birds live at the very edge of existence. Their perpetual motion amidst the foliage and branches is a sequence of tiny hops with constant lateral wingflicks too fast for human vision to differentiate, a behavioural imperative, as the bird must consume an insect or spider every two or three seconds throughout most daylight hours to survive. Such is the necessity to feed that it even continues to forage whilst singing. With whirring wings it was gone in an erratically jinking flight, into the nearby forest and to a cobweb-bound nest of moss, lichen, hair and down, with a feather-rimmed entrance. As few as one-fifth of the adults may survive from one summer to the next, so, to compensate for loss, two broods each of ten or more offspring are often raised in adjacent nests, the female incubating the second brood whilst the male feeds the first. Although only half the young may survive, the balance between procreation and mortality is thus maintained.

It had been a tiring day, so my ridge-top camp provided welcome relief in the warm glow of evening. After a suitable rest and having consumed most of my remaining provisions I set off down into the Magoula meadows following the upper limits of the woodland. There were dense clumps of Herb Paris, *Paris quadrifolia*, here, with its characteristic elliptic whorled leaves and somewhat undistinguished terminal four-rayed greenish flowers. The occasional *chink* of a Chaffinch unseen amidst the trees was all that intruded on my silent passage. It had been a cloudless day and as the westerly view from my ridge-top had thankfully not disclosed a cloudbank comparable to that of the previous evening, I was confident of a moonlit return. These upper meadows, fast becoming a scattering of grassy clearings amidst an encroaching forest, must have been much more extensive in times when the people of Vrisochori relied upon the land for pasturage. Now, if there is any utilization of the meadows for anything other than the annual village festivities, it appears insufficient to stem the arboreal tide. Without human intervention these flower-rich grasslands and the diversity of fauna they support will soon disappear.

Whilst still some distance from my destination I was heartened to hear that the Nightingale was already proclaiming his existence to the world. That led me to ensure a silent approach by way of the clearings leading down to the spring and leaving the stony forest road I had been following. There I settled down against a tree to listen and await whatever nature might reveal. Effusions of cold, clear, life-giving water from subterranean sources are places of reverence in many cultures and are often imbued with great mystery and symbolism. I shall never forget the increasing and eventually overwhelming terror with which a Garhwali villager led me to a spring-fed shrine in the Himalayas, nothing more than a place of considerable natural beauty in my eyes but for him a realm of such power and significance that he was shaking and physically unable to approach or even look fully on the scene. Those Molossian shepherds may not have had quite as extreme a view of such places, after all they and their animals needed the water, but would certainly have considered many springs sacrosanct, as portals to the other world and as the domain of mystical beings. A spring not far to the west is known to this day as the Nereid's Spring, so what apparitions might this place reveal, I wondered. That I should have a Nightingale, the mythical Philomela, as an orphean accompaniment seemed most appropriate. However often the evening song of a male Nightingale is heard, the performance is unique as the bird's ability to extemporize from several hundred phrase types, each constructed of a few components chosen from many more hundreds of sound units ensures a singular composition. Add to that the propensity to adopt aspects of the song repertoire of rival males and to mimic many other species in a continuous evolution of vocalization throughout life and the immense diversity of rendition becomes apparent. Listen in the knowledge that this performance will never be repeated in its totality.

Perhaps it was the darkening shadows which prompted an interruption to my reverie as the bird was still in full-throated song when I decided it was time to begin my return through the approaching dusk. If any other being had entered the scene during my protracted vigil they had done so unnoticed or had sensed my presence and quietly withdrawn. I filled my water bottle and set off along the track. An argentine lunar light was already slowly permeating the landscape as I approached the glacial erratics now looming disproportionately large and ghostly pale in the darkening meadow. A heady perfume drifting on the evening air invoked images of *Lilium martagon* somewhere near. Alerted by what appeared to be an indistinct movement at the distant forest edge I paused at the nearest rock for a precautionary binocular-aided scan. There, barely visible against the dark woodland, were the distinctive compact forms of several Wild Boar moving slowly in a close-knit group along the meadow margin. I counted six adults, possibly sows, with piglets too small to be seen with certainty in this light and at this distance. As I watched them fade from view into the trees I was unsure if the shiver I felt was due to the cooling evening air or a preternatural response to the proximity of these archetypal denizens of the forest. They are the descendents of the few animals which in Greece alone survived the last glaciation and then spread north and westwards to colonize the great 'Wild Wood' of Europe.

As I made my way towards the woodland edge leading up to my ridge-top destination, a Nightjar began its pulsating churr from the confines of a lone island of trees nearby. With the moon beyond and low above the summit ridge, I hoped for an opportunity of seeing it silhouetted against the sky if the bird flew, so I moved closer and sat on a convenient rock to watch and wait. There are few sounds as mesmeric as this extraordinary vocalization with its incessant rhythmic modulation and nowhere more appropriate than the mythylogically imbued landscape of Greece in which to experience it. Without prior knowledge, an avian attribution would seem improbable, leaving the imagination free to conjure all manner of origins, both spiritual and temporal. As the bird is usually silent in flight, its protracted rendition with only a few abrupt but brief pauses suggested my wait might be lengthy. However, after a longer than usual silence I assumed it must have slipped from its perch. A flash of white – for the male bird has conspicuous white patches on the undersides of both tail and wing extremities – was all that was necessary to locate its presence low over the meadow. With deep wingbeats between floating bouyant glides its intermittently silvery form was just discernible in the lunar light, the white flashes accompanying abrupt dips or turns in pursuit of insect prey. After losing sight of its progress, beyond the immediate confines of the meadow, my remaining return passed in deep contentment with the events of the day, and it was not long before I was gazing at a blazing Arcturus directly overhead as once more the tolling of a Scops Owl aided the onset of sleep.

# Chapter 7

# The Meadows of Magoula

A bird which reserves its most brilliant vocal artistry to daybreak could not have been accompanied by a finer dawn, as a golden glow flowed over the Ghiol ridge towards the Blackbird's forested dominion. Alone amongst the avian chorus his soliloquy rose to command the air in all too brief a rendition. He would have a family to help feed, so proclamation of territorial rights demanded brevity. What his performance lacked in duration was redressed by composition and delivery, for this is the time when every superlative phrase is embellished with an extended coda and there is barely a pause in the stream of inventiveness; a time when timbre is most refined and ethereal gliding tones most indulged. As I lay listening and waiting for the sun's warmth, his song alone filled my every moment.

By the time I was ready to move on, the light of a clear sky was already pervading the more prominent aspects of the cliffs and crags, still incised by those darker recesses where shadow lingered. Following the bouldery edge of the screes, I disturbed a Black Redstart from his quest for insect prey, although as the necessity for food overcame fear, he continued foraging between brief hops onto boulder tops, where wing flicks to expose a bright chestnut rump disclosed apparent unease at my presence. Tufted clumps of the Common Male Fern, *Dryopteris filix-mas*, were liberally scattered throughout the screes, an occurrence contrary to the association with shade and humidity of forest and woodland more usual in the northern hemisphere. Now the large-fronded tufts appeared as if dark eruptions from beneath the pewter-grey limestone. Stunted shrubs of *Rhamnus fallax*, a large-leaved buckthorn of gullies and rocky defiles almost to the summits, were here anchored deep into the substrate beneath the screes. The sprays of tiny four-rayed, yellowish-green-sepalled flowers disguised minute reddish-brown petals. Leaves peppered with tiny holes betrayed the green caterpillars of Cleopatra butterflies concealed and feeding beneath.

Being intent on a parting homage to the two floristic deities, *Campanula hawkinsiana* and *Viola albanica*, I made my way across to the willow thicket adjacent to their location. As the Long-tailed Tits were however in possession and disinclined to leave, I took the opportunity to watch their delightful antics as these are such endearing birds with their over-long tails and unceasing energetic behaviour. This was a family flock, the dozen or so darker and shorter-tailed juveniles constantly emitting a short, thin contact call, whilst accompanied by three equally voluble adults. I concluded that the third adult was a helper as these birds have a commendable community spirit. The males of pairs which have lost a nest, as many do due to predation by jays and squirrels, often help raise the young of their brothers by assisting with feeding, an altruism which doubles the survival rate of the offspring. A feeling of admiration seemed appropriate as I watched the little band disappear in a stream of undulating tails and whirring wings across the meadow. After paying due regard to the violet and harebell I wandered a little further along the base of the screes and stood for a while contemplating the grandeur and absorbing the essence of this place, as close a sentiment I surmise to that of the appreciation of *genius* of place expressed by the ancients. If at any time I had walked in the footsteps of those Molossian shepherds perhaps it was at times such as this.

Crag Martins were wheeling high against the cliffs of Tsouka Rossa flickering brightly against the bronze walls before fading mysteriously into the shadows. I turned and began my departure towards the meadows below.

Although somewhat preoccupied with thoughts of how best to apportion my time in the valley, I was sufficiently alert to hear a thin, sharp *tzit* call and turned just in time to see the distinctive form of a male Rock Bunting rise from some grassy tussocks to alight on a nearby boulder amidst stony ground. With its bold black-barred crown and facial markings, and bright buff-chestnut underparts, this is a strikingly attractive bird. As it had not flown far and had flicked wings and tail on landing to expose a rufous rump and white outer tail feathers in sign of agitation, I assumed there was a nest or family nearby. The female would remain unmoved and if there were young they would have vacated the nest within a few days of hatching and be huddled in dense vegetation. Not wishing to prolong the bird's disquiet; I continued on. As I was content to linger a while in these upper meadows until the sun had shortened the shadows I headed for the sunnier side where life would be free from the torpor of overnight chill. Amongst the more familiar flowers there were a few new faces. A tall, slender-branched flax, *Linum tenuifolium*, was beginning to unfurl its many large pale-pink flowers above tufts of blue-grey linear leaves, sharing the arena with another of the genus, *Linum hologynum*. The lovely broad-petalled violet flowers, delicately veined in a darker violet, open into large wavy-edged salvers held aloft on delicate stems. When this duo combine in profusion, to bestow their fragility and restrained palette on select portions of meadow, they impart a refined visual quality to the scene. Being suddenly reminded of the scent I had encountered the previous evening, I went in search of the anticipated source. *Lilium martagon* is a desirable companion in any garden, but no amount of acquisitive pleasure can match the delight of encountering it in its natural setting. Here the large pendent flowers displayed long, darkly spotted petals of variously pale to dark vermilion, strongly recurved above golden, pollen-dusted anthers suspended on long, white filaments. These generously clustered, aloft metre-high leafy stems, justly maintained their status amongst the floristic aristocracy of the forest.

All ways return to the vicinity of the spring to where the valley floor narrows. The lilting phrases of the Nightingale which had been distantly audible for much of the early morning, were now at the forefront of my attention. The early morning song is equally voluble to that of the late evening and at dawn has many of the same qualities but, as the day progresses, the frequency of song declines, the phraseology becomes less variable and those beautiful whistling tones are only sparingly voiced. Like matinee performances, the daytime renditions are for interaction with an audience, of rivals, whilst at night time the oration proclaims supremacy on the stage for as far as the sound will carry. With the first shafts of sunlight now piercing the surrounding trees to brighten the springside clearing, the Nightingale's contribution left little scope for enhancement. I did, however, find a few robust spikes of the scarce orchid *Anacamptis* (*Orchis*) *coriophora* amidst the lush growth of a wet flush. Yet to open fully, the compact heads of dark burgundy-red flowers were just visible above the grasses, on stout stems. Look closely and each flower appears as a sharply peaked cowl above a thick, fleshy, three-lobed lip, pale centred and red spotted. Whilst this structure in other orchids invites allusion to petticoated and bonetted ladies, here the appearance is less flattering and the flowers emit an unpleasant odour. What this plant lacked in form however, was more than compensated for by another in the meadow, as the waist-high elegance of *Thalictrum aquilegifolium* appeared with its dense clouds of tiny cream flowers above sprays of delicate celadon-coloured foliage. With Chiffchaff calling incessantly in the canopy overhead I lodged my pack in the branches of a tree from where I would recover it later in the day.

After its journey from the snow and ice-bound corries below Goura and Tsouka Rossa, through the glacial gravels flooring the Magoula meadows, the springwater emerges cold and clear into a boulder and fern-fringed flow, immediately contained within woodland and bordered by rank vegetation. Billowing white-flowery masses of the now familiar *Saxifraga rotundifolia* ssp. *rotundifolia* brighten the sunnier waterside locations, but it is the large orange-red flowers of *Geum coccineum* which more immediately command attention when glimpsed amongst the greenery. Further into the shady recesses of the woodland amongst wet streamside rocks are the delicate fronds of the Brittle Bladder Fern, *Cystopteris fragilis*, which for all its apparent vulnerability survives in mountains from the high Arctic to the Chilean Andes. The Nightingale had ceased to sing, perhaps having detected my presence, but maybe more so from habit as the morning performance is rarely prolonged, whether delivered by an unpaired or paired male. If there was a nest in the vicinity it would be slung low amidst the densest streamside scrub, a bulky, sometimes domed cup of leaves and grass lined with finer material and feathers, and there would be young to feed. Now the medley of rippling water and the ubiquitous calls of Chiffchaff and Chaffinch contrived to occupy the auditory space.

A trackway on the eastern slopes would lead me down to the lower meadows, but with time to spare I was happy to poke and pry into the adjacent woodland and wayside vegetation wherever interest beckoned. A large-leaved maple, closest to the highly variable *Acer opalus*, invited admiration from amongst the wayside trees, its handsome, shallowly five-lobed leaves interwoven in a shining spring-green and straw-yellow, translucent canopy beneath a bright blue sky. The delightfully vernal Hop Hornbeam, *Ostrya carpinifolia*, was here too, some resplendent with a heavy crop of their hop-like pendulous fruits already turning from springtime yellow to summer white. A solitary Speckled Wood floated down to settle on the white-flowered spray of a red-stemmed thicket of the Dogwood, *Cornus sanguinea*, whilst nearby a close relative, *Cornus mas*, the Cornelian Cherry, displayed promise of its autumn harvest of scarlet fruit amidst matt-green, oval leaves. Whilst this foliate panoply appeared sufficiently replete to satisfy the most demanding admirer, nature had contrived otherwise, adding two floristic embellishments. The pink-flushed, yellow-flowered clusters of a honeysuckle, *Lonicera caprifolium*, were perhaps most sympathetic to the colour scheme, draped over shrubs and low branches alike, each cluster presented within a cup of dark green-fused leaves. In contrast, the huge, purple-keeled, rosy-purple pea-flowers of *Lathyrus grandiflorus* were a startlingly bright addition to the shrubbery wherever the rambling leafy branches could climb. Energetically hopping, jumping and fluttering, a Blue Tit came to enliven the scene, persistently flicking its wings and tail whilst it foraged to the accompaniment of soft, sibilant calls. Often idiosyncratic, its habit of seeming to feign short-sightedness when focusing on prey is always endearing. A harsh churring scold on recognising my presence preceded a rapid departure on whirring wings.

Beyond the woodland a mosaic of terraced meadows and encroaching peripheral vegetation adjacent to the stream comes into view, a reminder of the former extent to which the lower valley was cultivated until quite recent times. Reversion to nature is rapid as even the track I am following reveals. Here any freshly exposed ground is soon covered with the Wild Strawberry, *Fragaria vesca*, newly white-flowered, and the variously violet, white and yellow-streaked flowers of *Viola tricolor* ssp. *macedonica*. Of the other invaders, the spiny pink, lilac and blue-flowered towers of *Echium italicum* and the similarly colourful and imposing *Salvia sclarea* are familiar from earlier encounters. It is a newcomer, though, which overshadows all in the generously floriferous form of *Salvia nemerosa* with its many tall dense spikes of richly violet-purple flowers, a commanding sight in any setting. Realising I was not alone in appraising the vegetation, I paused for a while to watch the progress of a tortoise which, seemingly oblivious of my presence, was crossing the track. The orangy-brown unscathed carapace of almost symmetrical proportions indicated a relatively youthful Hermann's Tortoise, a species which is quite abundant here near the upper limit of its altitudinal range. Seeing an invitation to leave the track myself, I followed a break in the trees to the scrub- and tussock-covered slopes beneath the eastern ridge-top limit of the valley. There were magnificent specimens of a lizard orchid here, again closest to *Himantoglossum caprinum* or *H. calcaratum* as seen elsewhere. Although a metre tall and endowed with flowers strikingly decorated in royal purple and extravagant in form, surprisingly they are not readily discernible from the enclosing vegetation. Much more evident on the slopes are the low shrubs of *Chamaecytisus austriacus*, bright with their terminal clusters of yellow pea-flowers above dense, trifoliate-leaved branches. Such floral assertion is however further countered by the secretive habit of a memorable orchid often obscured within the densest shrubbery. The compact terminal head of as many as fifty flowers appears white when in bud but opens from the apex downwards to reveal another remarkably structured floral design, a violet-streaked pale hood above a deeply divided lip likened to the form of a long-limbed gibbon, hence the common name Monkey Orchid. The four filiform limbs of the lip are reddish-lilac when they first appear but soon transpose into dark violet and unfold from a slender, violet-spotted, white body. Although abundant in this valley, *Orchis simia* is infrequent throughout much of its widespread distribution. Another floristic surprise obscured amidst the thickets was a scattering of the Bee Orchid, *Ophrys apifera*, each flower a dark velvety, chocolate-brown, inflated lip, intricately decorated and borne on rosy-sepalled wings.

Viewed from near the ridge-top, the former extent of forest clearance in the valley and on adjacent slopes is subtly revealed. When wandering through woodland clearings and in the vicinity of the meadows it is only the remnant of terrace wall or the incongruous rock-pile amongst the trees which indicates a previously greater expanse of pasture and cultivated land. But seen from a more elevated stance, the contrast in colour and density clearly reveals the border between older mature forest and recent regeneration. The many scattered and now unconnected clearings are also disposed in ways which suggest former coalescence, and the valley-floor meadows appear under siege from encircling ranks of advancing shrubbery and spinney. For much of the 700 years since Vrisochori was founded, this valley would have echoed the resonant ringing of the woodman's axe and whispered the rasping tones of the harvest sickle. Now nature's chorus performs alone. With timely concurrence, the mewing call of a lone Buzzard signalled its broad-winged gliding passage over Vrisochori, out across the Aoos valley towards the dark forests of Smolikas.

After rejoining the track, I continued down to where it provides access to one of the lower meadows adjacent to the stream. Several female Large White were patrolling the space in rapid and undulating flight, alighting only briefly to feed before resuming their aerial exertions. Their bold, coal-black markings appeared especially prominent as these were newly emerged second-brood butterflies of a pristine pure white. Being habitual migrants, they were amongst the earlier active participants of the day imbibing nectar sufficient for their onward journey. Perhaps I was prompted by memories of the former profusion of these and other 'whites' in the idylls of my youth, for as I waded into the flowery verdure, it was with thoughts of long lost summer meadows and of how quickly those edens of childhood pleasure had vanished from so much of the English countryside. Here much of the flora is alien but there were sufficient others in common to reinforce the association. Seating myself for a while on a remnant of terrace wall, it was those links to the past which now seemed most evident in this pastoral effusion of life's myriad forms. The pea-flowered sprays of the Tufted Vetch, *Vicia cracca*, which I recall had always appeared lost amidst the abundance of its own foliage were here gathered in a luxuriance of the most vibrant violet-blue, a colour shared by an accompanying profusion of the Spreading Bellflower, *Campanula patula*. The bells when fully open would soon adorn the meadow with a multitude of five-rayed stars. A Meadow Brown undulated lazily by to enhance the association, but it was the dense-flowered spikes of the Fragrant Orchid, *Gymnadenia conopsea*, tall above the grasses further into the meadow which stirred deeper recollections, for those long-spurred, intensely pink flowers, so precise and uniform in structure, had so often filled the evening air of home with an intoxicating perfume. More distant, on the far fringes, a few Marbled White dipped and danced, whilst almost at my feet a Small Skipper rested in delta-winged pose, its tawny-fringed, black-margined, bright russet wings poised for explosive flight.

There were other evocations of those flower-filled fields of the past, apparent when I resumed my wanderings through the grassy tide. A yellow rattle, *Rhinanthus pindicus*, assumed a similar profusion to that of the meadows of my youthful memories, here accompanied by a St. John's wort, *Hypericum perfoliatum*. The densely whorled, prominently beaked flowers of the rattle consorted with terminal clusters of the five-petalled wort in a suffusion of yellow. Meadow buttercups would have completed the scene at home in England but here their place was taken by an impressive variant of the Sulphur Cinquefoil,

*Potentilla detommasii*, its large yellow flowers in crowded clusters above silky-haired digitate leaves. Assisted, no doubt, by this bout of self-indulgent recollection, the sight of abundant azure-blue, floretted flowers of Chicory, *Cichorium intybus*, in part of the meadow, prompted thoughts of possible former cultivation here. Not only were the roots of this plant used, when dried and powdered, as an additive but the young leaves, and the shoots, when forced and blanched, also had their culinary purposes. Elsewhere the presence of Tassel Hyacinth, *Muscari comosum*, indicated cultivation for the edible bulbs, and of the vetch, *Coronilla varia*, as a fodder crop for livestock. The compact heads of delicately pink-flushed flowers above voluminous pinnate foliage were a pleasing addition to the flora, regardless of any function as former animal feed. My intrusion into this flowery field had disturbed a few resting Glanville Fritillary which in short low flight disclosed darkly marked, fulvous uppersides, instantly extinguished on resettling to reveal the wondrous complexities of the hind underwing. Those pale luminous windows, beset with black spots and lunules, trembled gently as the sun suffused their black-veined tracery with its warmth. Soon the butterflies would be sufficiently enlivened to join the mounting aerial throng.

The mesmeric sound of running water is perhaps even more potent in a hot and seasonally desiccated terrain than elsewhere, as the stream worked its siren attraction to good effect in drawing me towards its course. There a staccato outburst from a waterside thicket signalled the presence of a Cetti's Warbler, the proximity to such a volume being momentarily perturbing. There will be a nest slung low in dense vegetation amidst the tangled scrub, within the bounds of a streamside territory volubly defended by the patrolling male. As the bird is skulking in habit, the nearby flora seemed more worthy of immediate attention, especially as there were conspicuous stands of orchids in sight. The bright pink, almost magenta floral columns of *Dactylorhiza saccifera* were standing proud of the surrounding vegetation on slender stems sheathed in lanceolate, darkly-blotched leaves. Although the fifty or more flowers on each spike are densely disposed, the capacious cylindrical spurs which justify the specific name are an especially prominent component of otherwise frilly structures. Only the three-lobed lip is decorated, this with an attractive marbling of dark magenta on a white or pale pink centre. They were keeping good company as both the pale-lilac-flowered *Geranium aristatum* and the much darker purple-lilac *Geranium reflexum* offered a welcome re-acquaintance in the adjacent shade. Also amidst the dense fringing vegetation was the familiar fiery-flowered *Geum coccineum*, encountered further upstream and elevated in profusion on long branching stems above large serrate, dark-veined leaves. The five orangy-red, notched petals surround a crown of golden anthers, flaring brilliantly in sunlight filtered through adjacent shrubbery. Elsewhere the dark bluish-violet pendent flowers of *Aquilegia nigricans* also made a re-appearance, each an exquisite construction of long-necked spurs and sepaloid wings, so like the confluence of five spread-winged swans that even the downwardly projecting black-anthered stamens conspire to appear as an association of extended web-footed limbs. It is no injustice to the supreme elegance of the bird to equate it to that of the flower. Although circumstantial, it seemed appropriate that the similarly elegant form of a Scarce Swallowtail should come winging in to flutter at the flowers of a nearby *Prunus*. Contrary to the scarcity implied by its name, the butterfly is of frequent occurrence here but such is its beauty that familiarity does not lessen the command it exercises one's attention. It was, however, momentarily challenged by another butterfly flying swiftly around the tree tops and, although not alighting, displaying the form and orangy-brown tones of a Large Tortoiseshell. These reveal their winged beauty for only a few days prior to a long hibernation until the following spring, so as I watched its rapid departure I was hopeful of other encounters as the butterfly emerges in abundance in the valley during this brief interlude.

It seemed my progress had not gone unnoticed as a strident *kekekek* call betrayed the presence of an observant and alarmed Middle-spotted Woodpecker hidden within a nearby stand of trees. There is a mildly mocking tone to this chattering call, seemingly consistent with some of the bird's idiosyncratic characteristics. It will remain rigidly immobile for a while with red crest raised but when sufficiently reassured will resume its usual restless and often acrobatic search for insects amongst the upper branches. Whilst active, the predominantly black and white plumage effectively counters our perception of outline, rendering the bird's progress almost impossible to follow through the dappled shade of a tree canopy. Flashes of a rose-pink vent and scarlet crown may assist in periodic location of movement, but for now I had to be content with a bird heard and not seen. Re-engagement with the stream-side vegetation, however, provided ample compensation, for here almost obscured by surrounding herbage were spikes of the strangely flowered *Rhynchocorys elephas*. The bright yellow blooms project a long thin beak above a large spreading pendulous lower lip, blotched chocolate brown in the throat of the corolla tube from which the other floral components arise. Crowded into the leafy terminations of tall erect stems, the flowers provide a vivid island of colour amidst the greenery. Perhaps prompted by the woodpecker's warning call, there was a further note of alarm as I continued, that strange frog-like utterance of a Nightingale from deep in a dense waterside thicket. As this location was some way below that of the early morning songster, there was, it seemed, at least one other pair in the valley.

In making my way back towards the valley-side track, the meadows were again generous in revealing more of their floral opulence, many welcome re-acquaintances but some newly revealed. A few densely magenta-flowered spikes of an orchid appeared from the greenery on dark red stems above rosettes of lanceolate leaves, each flower a broad, pendant, four-lobed lip beneath a projecting hood, erect sepals and a long, cylindrical spur. A variously distributed white suffusion provided the background for dark magenta spots in the centre of the lip. This was one of the *Orchis mascula* group of orchids, perhaps close to subspecies *pinetorum*. Much more abundant were the compact inflorescences of the Pyramidal Orchid, *Anacamptis pyramidalis*, bearing many tiny pink flowers which, with a deeply incised, three-lobed lip, lateral sepals and dorsal hood, present the appearance of a six-pointed star. An elongate, filiform spur completes the structure and being a rich repository of nectar attracts those butterflies and moths with a proboscis long enough to reach it. Such visitors inadvertently reciprocate as agents of pollination. Appropriately, a Red Admiral arrived to patrol the scene, its vigorous flight a reminder of the migratory tendencies which propel its kind in great numbers into more northerly climes every spring. It is a butterfly which habitually investigates an intruder's threat potential, flying ever closer and sometimes making contact if you remain motionless, before resuming its activities reassured. Alighting briefly with wings splayed, the striking array of white and scarlet on dark chocolate and black appeared uniquely bright in this revelatory Grecian light. In such circumstances recollection of its original name, The Admirable butterfly, seemed most appropriate.

The remaining walk to the track's end, at its junction with the dusty road down to Vrisochori did not take long. After fording the stream I followed a route which meandered westwards into the welcoming shade of the coniferous woodland. Here nurtured in the mossy carpet beneath the trees, the diminutive Creeping Lady's Tresses Orchid, *Goodyera repens*, projected its slender, pale-stemmed spikes of hooded, white flowers towards the forest-filtered light. It is not alone in being a southern refugee from colder climatic times and more appropriate in northern temperate and boreal forests, for there are others here of kindred temperament. All of evergreen creeping disposition, four of the Wintergreen family were scattered throughout the forest, hiding their lovely pale bells from all but the most persistently searching eyes. The one-sided, greenish-flowered sprays of *Orthilia secunda*, the Nodding Wintergreen, were familiar from a previous encounter in the woods above Skamneli, but its compatriots appeared new to me, at least in Greece. Of these, the porcellaneous white cups of *Pyrola rotundifolia* were the most surprising as I had previously made its acquaintance in the Pirin Mountain forests of Bulgaria and had not expected to meet it further south. Its near relative *Pyrola chlorantha*, with spikes of yellowish-green, globular bells, was also present as was *Moneses uniflora*, its solitary nodding flowers opening into a five-rayed, white star beset with a golden corona of anthers encircling a prominent bright green stigma. One must at least kneel if not prostrate oneself to appreciate these tiny gems, a not inappropriate deportment for mankind in the presence of such natural wonders.

After retracing my steps I turned towards the mountain along the old forest road following the western flank of the valley, leading back to the spring and the Magoula meadows. In the humid cauldron of midday the air throbbed with the stridulation of grasshoppers and crickets, a cacophony which seemingly grew to dominate all else when allowed into the forefront of awareness. The wailing call of a Black Woodpecker from far up the valley, at first barely audible, gained in clarity and volume as my mind focused on the primeval sound, a subtle reminder that we are still habituated to the selective hearing which our survival in the wilderness once demanded. As I set off coincidentally in the direction of the woodpecker, a small but very long-tailed lizard crossed the track in a puff of dust. Searching the matted vegetation in which it was temporarily obscured, I could discern a dark reddish-brown colouration to the body and, as the lizard raised its head, a brilliant blue throat, indicative of a male Dalmatian Algyroides, *Algyroides nigropunctatus*. Thankfully my route had been neglected by forestry vehicles and still retained the floral variety I expected, so it was pleasing to be greeted by a quartet of yellow-flowered leguminous shrubs. *Chamaecytisus austriacus* previously encountered on the opposite slopes was accompanied by the pale-yellow, pea-flowered sprays of *Coronilla emerus*, the Scorpion Senna, elegantly complemented by its delicately refined foliage. Overarching these were several shrubs of Bladder Senna, *Colutea arborescens*, some still flaunting their sprays of large, bright yellow blooms, others with grotesquely inflated pendulous pea pods. Regardless of the various merits of this floral competition, it was the sulphurous cloud of *Lembotropis nigricans* that dominated the assemblage. What this slender-stemmed shrub lacks in stature and subtlety of form is well compensated for by its exuberance.

Whilst pleasantly preoccupied with this display I became aware of two tiny dark butterflies spiralling skyward and then parting, only to resume their mutual aerial pursuit for a few more minutes before separating and settling on the foliage of adjacent shrubs, seemingly disappearing from sight. Such are the wiles of the Green Hairstreak which always close their wings on alighting to hide the dark brown uppers in favour of the superbly camouflaged emerald green undersides. They enhance this artifice by orienting their closed wings to avoid creating a shadow, simultaneously reducing heat absorption. The two were males disputing the right to a preferred resting place and territory. Observed closely, there is wonderful intricacy to these butterflies, with finely black and white banded legs and antennae and prominently white-rimmed compound eyes. Alter your angle of view and the emerald green assumes a turquoise hue, or an apple-green with a metallic sheen, framed within a fulvous white-fringed border. If this experience had sharpened my visual acuity the enhanced perception was put to good use as I had not gone much further before recognising the characteristic frenetic flight of a skipper butterfly buzzing erratically above a trackside swathe of Wild Strawberry. Although difficult to follow in flight, a few brief interludes of rest revealed the sharply defined white on black markings and chequered wing margins of a Grizzled Skipper.

As the track paralleled the stream at a level which provided an uninterrupted view of the valley and of the meadows below, it invited a leisurely progression generously punctuated by pauses to assimilate the scene. With the magnificent backcloth of the Tymphaean crags and cliffs beyond, the presence of the place is such as to become indelibly imprinted on the psyche, as I found even during my first brief visit. Now I ponder what thoughts and feelings those descendants of Vrisochorian exiles might experience when they walk this way during the annual Panigyri of Saints Pandelis and Paraskevi, to the gathering in the Magoula meadows. It seems inconceivable that the *daimon* (*genius*) of place would not impinge on the celebratory mood and invoke a sharing of the loss which expatriation visited on their forebears. Perhaps the *daimon* has a compensatory generosity of spirit, imparting something of itself, a solace which accompanies them to wherever they return in the world. As the plaintive tones of the Nightingale broke through the heat of the day, I resumed my journey. The bird was calling quietly in the desultory conversational phrasing reserved for a mate.

The wayside shrubbery now relented from its earlier monochromatic floral theme with a welcome display of the lovely white-flowered *Cistus salvifolius*, each bloom an intimate interlacing of five wavy-edged, delicate milk-white petals around a disc of bright yellow anthers. There were orchids too, with the familiar dark arching stems of *Epipactis subclausa* making a reappearance, although outshone floristically by a compatriot, *Epipactis palustris*. A streamside gathering of this Marsh Helleborine was flaunting its provocatively flaired, white-lipped and purple-flushed flowers in full sunlight. With the intervening slopes brightened by a shock of the densely yellow-flowered loosestrife, *Lysimachia punctata*, and violet spikes of the shrubby *Salvia amplexicaulis*, the arrival of a Large Tortoiseshell seemingly intent on alighting from its habitually intense flight routine could not have enhanced the scene more. Settling on the loosestrife, the butterfly's contrasting boldly marked orangy-brown brightness was fittingly framed in cream and black-bordered, elegantly scalloped wings. Despite preoccupation with feeding, a natural wariness prevailed and, as I tried to move closer, it was away and above the streamside trees in rapid irregular flight.

Towards the spring the woodland closed in on my approach and, to an accompaniment of water cascading over rocky rims, masked sight and sound of my deliberate progress. There are trees favoured by the Black Woodpecker here and stealth, as now, sometimes repays with generous reward. An intermittent rain of wood dust and fine bark chips with some coarser fragments was falling through the foliage of a huge fir, but I was too close for a binocular view of the source, so retreated to where I could watch and listen from the cover of both bank and shrubbery. A dagger-length bill would be expected to generate clearly audible results, but surprisingly the dull thuds from angled chiselling into rotting wood often escape human hearing, and bark or fresh wood splinters are frequently levered rather than struck. A crow-sized bird can be remarkably silent and remain motionless for a long time at even the slightest suspicion of something awry in its surroundings, as this one appeared to be from the minutes of inactivity which ticked by. Eventually a slight movement from behind the leafless apex of a dead stump protruding above the fir revealed the bird's shoulder followed by the scarlet-crowned head with that piercing, unblinking, yellow-rimmed eye. A quick sideways and downward shuffle and it was obscured by the enveloping foliage of the tree. I walked quietly on and to the spring. Crossing the broad, shallow flush, I was momentarily diverted towards a cloud of 'blues' which had been imbibing mineral salts from the saturated ground before I realised there were superior presences in attendance. For there, drifting on outstretched and then briefly fluttered wings, was the magnificent bright fulvous form of a Silver-washed Fritillary floating mesmerically above the tree-canopied waters. There were others too, all males, at the water's edge, with wings closed, flashing the lovely silvery sheen and subtle mauve and green tints of the hindwings as they jostled for advantage at the richest mineral-fed source. I emulated them in drinking from the cold refreshing flow before moving on further up the track and into the coolness of the forest.

Here, away from the sounds of running water and the stridency of excessive insect life was a different soundscape, which, apart from the crunch of leaf-litter underfoot and the intermittent rippling of breeze through the canopy, was that of a select ensemble amidst the gentler hum of existence. The ringing trills and metallic calls of Nuthatch were never far removed and that ever-watchful sentinel of the forest, the Jay, was always a portent of one's passing with its rasping screech. Other voices were more surprising being unexpected in this setting, the scolding *tic tic* of a Robin, here a skulking and elusive bird seemingly both out of place and of character compared to its more sociable British counterpart. The repetition of a sharp alarm call I would normally associate with a Blackbird prompted me to pause to survey the vicinity of the sound's origin, just in time to glimpse the variegated black and white form of a woodpecker rise from near the ground and disappear through the trees. Was the bird slightly larger than a Greater Spotted Woodpecker and did I see continuous white barring across the wings, or did I in those few seconds subconsciously add those details to satisfy wishful thoughts? The *lilfordi* race of the White-backed Woodpecker is of rare occurrence in Greece and lacks the white rump of more northern birds, so requires closer scrutiny and better light than this encounter allowed to confirm identity. There was a substantial and well excavated rotten tree-stump near where the bird had risen but it showed none of the deep conical holes which I had seen made by the *leucotos* race of the same species in Romania. So the encounter remained unresolved. There were, however, compensations, for where the sunlight illuminated the forest floor it kindled the insipid clusters of *Neottia nidus-avis*, the Bird's Nest Orchid, into a glowing yellow-gold and the tall spikes of *Cephalanthera damasonium* a candescent white.

Wandering on towards the light of more open forest and faintly heard phrases of distant bird song, the flora already familiar from the previous days' encounters began to make an anticipated reappearance. Of these, the orchid *Cephalanthera rubra* assumed ascendancy in several clearings where the slender spikes bore their variously pale pink to deep crimson-pink-winged and hooded flowers tall above the lesser incumbents. It was here too, resting on the sunlit remains of a fallen tree-trunk that I encountered that wonder of the beetle fraternity, *Rosalia alpina*, a majestic 'long-horn' in powder-blue attire, meticulously decorated in black. The huge antennae which bear conspicuous tufts of black hair at intervals along their length were slowly inscribing the air as the creature moved ponderously forward. Its long narrow elytra, too, were patterned with three bold black patches on each, created by a coat of very fine hairs which impart a velvety texture to the decoration. Gazing at this magnificent beetle, which was once widespread throughout the 'Wild Wood' of Europe, is to witness yet another emblem of the decline of that ancient heritage. In the absence of any other contender for my attentions it was a while before I succumbed to the curiosity elicited by the bird song which, although intermittent and poorly discernible, had seemed to precede my progress for some time. Whilst trying to locate the source I was sure it must be either from a Treecreeper or Short-toed Treecreeper as the snatches of high-pitched, sibilant and at times tremulous refrains were what I associated with these birds. Differentiation on the basis of song is impossible however, as each can imitate the other precisely, so I abandoned the search and retraced my route back to the spring.

After reclaiming my pack I relaxed for a while in the shade, musing on the idyllic scene which surrounds that life-giving source and thankful for the physical relief which temporary inertia brings to an otherwise energetic existence. A couple of Silver-washed Fritillaries were still drifting lazily above the water, flickering dark and bright from shade to light beneath the trees bordering the spring. The relentless hum of life and mesmeric murmurings of water on stone contrived to induce a torpor which I was happy to embrace for a while. I would meet Theofanis in Vrisochori that evening so would while away the afternoon in these upper meadows content to wait for the *genius* of place to reveal whatever might transpire. For many the wild is both unpredictable and unfathomable, but a lifetime shared with the natural world allows some privilege of insight into the natural order which prevails. That familiarity provides some reassurance of the reliability of habituation in nature, as I anticipated the afternoon would confirm.

When sufficiently rested I moved a little way further up the valley to a place where I had an unobstructed view across the meadows to the crags and snow-fields between the great cliffs of Tsouka Rossa south-eastwards to the Goura summit and settled down beneath the trees to watch and wait. The elegantly sculpted wings of a Comma butterfly, slowly opening and closing in the sunlight, drew my attention to the exceptional brightness of the fulvous colouration which this, a first-brood insect, displays. The lightness of tone, unlike that of the much darker later brood, greatly enhances the complex pattern of black wedges and lunules. With wings closed, the butterfly was indiscernible amidst the dead leaf-litter, except for the conspicuous silver crescent on its hindwing. If I had invaded the territory of a male I would have both company and entertainment, for it is another of those butterflies which intercepts all others straying into its vicinity. Obligingly a Woodland Ringlet fluttered weakly onto the scene, invoking a vigorous chase by the Comma. Across the meadow a gentle ebb and flow of the taller grasses acknowledged periodic cool down-draughts from the snowy slopes which I scanned from time to time for any indications of life. Much of nature is quiescent when the sun is at its highest and, except for the occasional screech of a forest Jay and repetitive *chink* of the Chaffinch, there was little to embroider the monotonous hum of insect life. I thought how welcome it would be to hear the music and voices of the Panigyri drifting across the meadow. A contemplative 'pentasimos' perhaps, danced 'Zagorisios' to the idiosyncratic rhythm of the touberieki drum and halting clarinet; and on the breeze the lilting refrains of 'Viryinadha' unfolding its symbolic vision of a women seated in the shade of a courtyard tree knitting a golden cord. For the music of Zagori is as much born of the soil and rock of the mountains as are the flowers and wildlife.

A single adult Chamois had moved out onto the snows beneath Goura and was soon followed by four others and two youngsters, seemingly not concerned as two promptly lay down whilst others dispersed, apparently searching for anything edible amongst the debris on the surface. They clearly derive some benefit as this is a regular routine in hot weather. A few Clouded Yellows were now appearing and crossing the meadow northwards, having flown up and over the summit ridge during the morning, although many others will have maintained height until well over and beyond the Aoos valley, driven onward by their migratory instinct. Soon the shadow of Tsouka Rossa would begin to encroach on the adjacent snows and crags even though still only mid-afternoon. If my anticipation was to be realized it would not be long now. Whilst carefully scanning at regular intervals all of the mountain terrain before me, it was a snow-filled gully opening onto extensive snow-clad slopes above the main wooded terrace which commanded my attention. For that seemingly inhospitable defile was where a bear occupying its over-wintering den would emerge. I did not have to wait long as the power of habituation imposes a predictable timeframe on these events. The mother appeared first, striding purposefully out from the gully followed by a single cub moving uneasily in the snow. Backward glances during short pauses by the adult indicated concern and reassurance, especially when the youngster slipped on the steep slope and lay with limbs splayed. After a brief scramble the cub was soon upright. Although the surface would have softened during the day, at that altitude and with a northerly aspect the snow could still be icy beneath. When out in the centre of the snow-field, the mother stopped and fussed around the cub for a few minutes before climbing directly upslope, a task the youngster had difficulty in emulating but eventually accomplished, followed after a short pause by a steep descent. Watching the repetition of this procedure for fully thirty minutes or so, the evident relationship of parent to offspring, of tutor to pupil, diminishes the gulf between wild beast and human, between the wilderness and the tamed. We see something of ourselves in the other being and acknowledge an affinity.

In time the pair disappeared from the snowfield into adjacent rocks which obscured them from view but reappeared soon after on the lip of a vegetated terrace. There, side by side on the brightly sunlit grassy rim, bronzed and haloed in the receding light, they sat as if surveying their great domain. There was no need to forage for food as the cub still relied upon its mother's milk. How long they remained there I do not know as in deference to what seemed an appropriate time for farewell I began my return along the forest edge, back towards the spring. A solitary Scarce Swallowtail glided and fluttered in accompanyment across the rippling meadow, my winged guide back toward the Ithacan shore at journey's end.

# Chronology of climatic and associated changes on Tymphi

**Years BP**
(before present)

(Adapted from Tzedakis 1994, Willis 1992 & Hughes *et al.* 2006)

**850 – 4,250** Formation of Klithi Terrace in Vikos Canyon. Montaine grassland predominates until rapid invasion of pine forest around 1990BP and return to grassland after 1170BP.

**4,250 – 6,200** Decline in extent of woodland commences as grassland increases. Increasing influence of human settlement in adjacent lowland regions. Predominance of mixed deciduous and coniferous woodland on Tymphaean slopes.

**6,200 – 7,000** Dense forest of the hornbeams *Carpinus orientalis* and *Ostrya carpinifolia*. Forest of *Abies alba* (Silver Fir) and *Abies cephalonica* (Greek Fir).

**7,000 – 10,400** Deciduous highly diverse woodland with predominance of oak.

**10,400 – 13,000** Return to colder climate with grassland and alpine vegetation predominant. Warmer climate with spread of woodland to higher Tymphaean slopes.

**13,000 – 16,500** Prolonged cold period with grassland and alpine vegetation on slopes, and seasonal human occupation of rock-shelters in Vikos Canyon.

**16,500 – 24,000** Period of severely cold climate (Tymphaean Glacial Phase) with permanent ice in high corries on Tymphi, and sparse vegetation on slopes.

**24,000 – 28,000** Period of severely cold climate with formation of Aristi Terrace and massive screes in Vikos Canyon. At 25000BP earliest known human seasonal occupation of lower Vikos Canyon.

**28,000 – 140,000** 112,000 year-long period of variously forested, sparsely-wooded and grassland terrain with corresponding climatic change.

**140,000 – 160,000** Period of severely cold climate (Vlasian Glacial Phase) with maximum extent of glaciers around 150,000BP. Formation of Kipi Terrace in Vikos Canyon. Tymphaean slopes with treeless arctic/steppe vegetation.

**160,000 – 370,000** 210,000 year-long period of alternating cooler and warmer climate with corresponding changes on Tymphi between forest and grassland.

**370,000 – 423,000** Dodoni Forest Period with predominance of *Abies alba* (Silver Fir) and *Abies cephalonica* (Greek Fir) alternating with various associations of deciduous tree species.

**450,000** Peak of Skamnellian Glacial Phase with maximum extent of glaciers on Tymphi.

# Principal Sources

Amanatidou, D. (2005). *Analysis and Evaluation of a Traditional Cultural Landscape as a basis for its Conservation Management. A case study in Vikos-Aoos National Park – Greece*, Albert-Ludwigs Universität, Freiburg im Breisgau. Dissertation.

Bailey, G. ed. (1997). *Klithi: Palaeolithic Settlement and Quaternary Landscapes in North-west Greece*. 2 vols. McDonald Institute for Arcchaeological Research, Univ. of Cambridge.

Buxton, R. (1994). *Imaginary Greece. The contexts of mythology*. Cambridge Univ. Press.

Campbell, J. K. (1964) *Honour, Family, and Patronage. A Study of Institutions and Moral Values in a Greek Mountain Community*. Oxford Univ. Press.

Cross, G. N. (1971) *Epirus: A Study in Greek Constitutional Development*. Bouma's Boekhuis Groningen. Reprint of Cambridge Univ. Press edition 1932.

Foss, A. (1978) *Epirus*. Faber & Faber.

Gage, N. (1987) *Hellas: A Portrait of Greece*. Collins Harvill, London.

Garoufalias, Petros E. (1979) *Pyrrhus, King of Epirus*. Stacey Intl., London. First English ed.

Hedges, R. E. M. *et. al.* (1990) Radiocarbon Dates from the Oxford AMS System: Archaeometry datelist 11 *Archaeometry* 32 (2): 211-237.

Hughes, P. D., Gibbard, P. L. & Woodward, J. C. (2006) Middle Pleistocene glacial behaviour in the Mediterranean: sedimentological evidence from the Pindus Mountains, Greece. *Journal of The Geological Society, London*, 163: 857-867.

Lawson, J. C. (1910) *Modern Greek Folklore and Ancient Greek Religion: A Study in Survivals*. Cambridge Univ. Press.

Salmon, T. (1995) *The Unwritten Places*. Lycabettus Press, Athens.

Stamatopoulou, C. (1988) *Greek Traditional Architecture: Zagori*. Melissa Pbl. House, Athens.

Strid, A. (1986) *Mountain Flora of Greece*. Vol 1 Oxford Univ. Press.

Strid, A. & Tan, K. (1991) *Mountain Flora of Greece*. Vol 2. Edinburgh Univ. Press.

Tzedakis, P. C. (1994) Vegetation Change through Glacial-Interglacial Cycles: A Long Pollen Sequence Perspective. *Phil. Trans. Royal Soc. London B* **345**: 403-432.

Wace, A. & Thompson, M. (1914) *The Nomads of the Balkans. An Account of Life and Customs among the Vlachs of Northern Pindus*. Methuen & Co.,London.

Willis, K. J. (1992) The Late Quaternary Vegetational History of Northwest Greece II. Rezina Marsh. *The New Phytologist.* **121**: 119-138.

Woodward, J. C., Macklin, M. G. & Smith, G. R. (2004) Pleistocene glaciation in the mountains of Greece In: *Quaternary Glaciations – Extent and Chronology*. Ehlers, J. & Gibbard, P. L. eds. Part 1: Europe. Elsevier B.V.

Woodward, J. C.,Lewin, J. & MacKlin, M. G. (1992) Alluvial sediment sources in a glaciated catchment: the Voidomatis basin, Northwest Greece. *Earth Surface, Processes and Landforms* **16**, 205-216.

Woodward, J. C., Lewin, J. & MacKlin, M. G. (1995) Glaciation, river behaviour and the Palaeolithic settlement of upland northwest Greece. In: *Mediterranean Quaternary River Environments*. Lewin, J. *et al.* eds, Rotterdam: Balkema, 115-129.

# Combined Index and Species List

Entries in [ ] indicate nomenclature additional to that within the text.

*Abies alba* (Silver Fir) 24, 71, 72, 93, 194, 225, 226
*Abies borisii-regis* 193, 194
*Abies cephalonica* (Greek Fir) 24, 71, 72, 93, 194, 225, 226
*Acanthus balcanicus* 60
[*Accipeter gentilis*] Goshawk 173, 184
[*Accipeter nisus*] Sparrowhawk 183
*Acer opalus* 206
*Achillea abrotanoides* 42, 105, 154, 177
*Achillea fraasii* 154
*Achillea holosericea* 42, 120, 177
Achilles 9
*Acinos alpinus* (Alpine Calamint) 42, 91
*Acinos alpinus* ssp. *meridionalis* 91
*Actaea spicata* (Baneberry) 104
Adonis Blue [*Polyommatus bellargus*] 39
[*Aegithalos caudatus*] Long-tailed Tit 158, 203
Aeschylus 90
Agia Paraskevi (monastery) Skamneli 25
Agios Nikolaos (church) Tsepelovo 26
Agios Nikolaos (monastery) 25
[*Alauda arvensis*] Skylark 107, 122
Albania 9, 17, 42, 52, 84, 98, 99, 103, 152, 170, 229
[*Alectoris graeca*] Rock Partridge 46, 106, 114, 115, 121, 146, 196
Aleppo Pine (*Pinus halepensis*) 10
Alexis Gouris 26--28, 95

Aliakmon (river) 133
*Algyroides nigropunctatus* (Dalmatian Algyroides) 216
*Allium flavum* ssp. *flavum* 160, 176
*Alnus* 73
Alpine Accentor (*subalpina* race) [*Prunella collaris*] 109, 139, 162
Alpine Calamint (*Acinos alpinus*) 42
Alpine Chough [*Pyrrhocorax graculus*] 40, 41, 94, 159
Alpine Newt [*Triturus alpestris*] 184
Alpine Rock-cress (*Arabis alpina*) 132
Alpine Swift [*Apus melba*] 84, 139
Altar 114
*Alyssum montanum* ssp. *repens* 91
Amanda's Blue [*Polyommatus amandus*] 65, 66
Ambracia 82
[*Ammotragus lervia*] Aoudad 127
*Anacamptis* (*Orchis*) *coriophora* 205
*Anacamptis* (*Orchis*) *morio* (Green-winged Orchid) 19, 20, 64, 179
*Anacamptis* (*Orchis*) *palustris* 20, 141
*Anacamptis pyramidalis* (Pyramidal Orchid) 64, 214
Antares 114
[*Anthocharis cardamines*] Orange Tip 57, 185
[*Anthocharis damone*] Eastern Orange Tip 57
*Anthyllis vulneraria* (Kidney Vetch) 69
*Anthyllis vulneraria* ssp. *alpestris* 165
*Anthyllis vulneraria* ssp. *bulgarica* 69
*Anthyllis vulneraria* ssp. *pulchella* 98
Antigonas 133
Aoos 10, 11, 17, 23, 36, 37, 70, 84, 89, 98, 114, 127, 132-134, 136-139, 149, 150, 152, 153, 155, 195, 201, 223
Aoudad [*Ammotragus lervia*] 127
Apollo butterfly [*Parnassius apollo*] 57, 140
[*Aporia crataegi*] Black-veined White 19
Apulian continent 138
[*Apus melba*] Alpine Swift 84, 139

Aquila 114
[*Aquila chrysaetos*] Golden Eagle 196
[*Aquila heliaca*] Imperial Eagle 10, 33, 34, 46, 51, 112, 196
*Aquilegia nigricans* 189, 212
*Arabis alpina* (Alpine Rock-cress) 132
Arcturus 49, 201
[*Argynnis adippe*] Fritillary, High Brown (*cleodoxa* form) 182
[*Argynnis paphia*] Fritillary, Silver-washed 219, 221
Aristi (river terrace) 76, 79, 226
Armata 133
*Armeria canescens* 95, 106, 120, 156, 176
Arta (song of the bridge of) 17
*Artemisia eriantha* 151
[*Artogeia ergane*] Mountain Small White 57
Arumani (see Vlakhi) 10, 133-136, 138, 139, 155
*Arum petteri* 60
*Asphodeline lutea* 40, 179
*Asphodeline taurica* 176
*Asplenium fissum* 104
*Asplenium trichomanes ss.p inexpectans* 104
*Asplenium viride* 104
[*Astacus astacus*] Noble Crayfish 15
*Astragalus creticus* ssp. *rumelicus* 31
*Astragalus sirinicus* 121, 152, 154
Astraka 55, 59, 74, 86, 88, 93, 101, 112, 113
*Asyneuma limonifolium* 96, 120, 165
[*Athene noctua*] Little Owl 113, 128, 129
*Aubrieta scardica* 35, 56, 100, 151, 164, 176
Aurochs [*Bos primigenius*] 79, 81
[*Autographa gamma*] Silver-Y moth 31
Avdhela 135

[*Barbus peloponnesius, Pachychilon pictum*] Cyprinid fish 15
Balkan Marbled White [*Melanargia larissa*] 63

Balkan War 25
Balkan Whip Snake [*Coluber gemonensis*] 62
Baneberry (*Actaea spicata*) 100
Beaver [*Castor fiber*] 80
Beech (*Fagus sylvatica*) 155, 173, 184, 185, 187, 188, 193
Bee Orchid (*Ophrys apifera*) 208
*Bellis perennis* (Daisy) 28
*Berteroa obliqua* 97, 148
Bharal [*Pseudois nayaur*] 127
Bird's Nest Orchid (*Neottia nidus-avis*) 184, 220
Blackbird (*aterrimus* race) [*Turdus merula*] 186
Black Kite [*Milvus migrans*] 123
Black Pine (*Pinus nigra*) 10, 133, 140
Black Redstart [*Phoenicurus ochruros*] 105, 122, 155, 159, 202
Black Stork [*Ciconia nigra*] 83
Black-veined White [*Aporia crataegi*] 19
Black Woodpecker [*Dryocopus martius*] 173, 195, 215, 218
Bladder Senna (*Colutea arborescens*) 218
Blue Rock Thrush [*Monticola solitarius*] 86, 87, 97
Blue Tit [*Parus caeruleus*] 207
[*Bombina variegata*] Yellow-bellied Toad 13, 111, 184
[*Boloria euphrosyne*] Fritillary, Pearl-bordered 175
[*Bos primigenius*] Aurochs 79, 81
Brittle Bladder Fern (*Cystopteris fragilis*) 206
Brown Bear [*Ursus arctos*] 140, 166, 192
Brown Hare [*Lepus europaeus*] 46
Brown Trout [*Salmo trutta*] 15, 68
[*Bubo bubo*] Eagle Owl 85
Burnt-tip Orchid (*Orchis ustulata*) 53
[*Buteo buteo*] Buzzard 129, 209
*Buxus* 73
Buzzard [*Buteo buteo*] 129, 209

Callimachus 60

[*Callophrys rubi*] Green Hairstreak 216
Camberwell Beauty [*Nymphalis antiopa*] 63
*Campanula foliosa* 193
*Campanula hawkinsiana* 158, 203
*Campanula patula* (Spreading Bellflower) 19, 210
*Campanula ramosissima* 38
*Campanula rotundifolia* (Common Harebell) 95, 157, 193
*Campanula spatulata* ssp. *spatulata* 157
*Campanula trachelium* ssp. *athos* 193
*Campanula versicolor* 193
[*Canis lupus*] Wolf 11, 126
[*Capra falconeri*] Markhor 127
[*Capra ibex*] Ibex 77-80, 88, 127
[*Capreolus capreolus*] Roe Deer 114, 167, 168, 192
[*Capricornis sumatraensis*] Serow 127
[*Caprimulgus europaeus*] Nightjar 48, 50, 53, 169, 200
*Cardamine bulbifera* 188
*Cardamine carnosa* 97, 131, 146, 176
*Cardamine glauca* 176
[*Carduelis carduelis*] Goldfinch 182
*Carpinus betulus* (Hornbeam) 72
*Carpinus orientalis* (Eastern Hornbeam) 61, 93
[*Castor fiber*] Beaver 80
[*Celastrina argiolus*] Holly Blue 63
*Celtis australis* (Southern Nettle Tree) 66
*Centaurea epirota* 148, 181
*Centaurea pawlowskii* 42
*Centranthus longiflorus* ssp. *junceus* 161
*Cephalanthera damasonium* 191, 220
*Cephalanthera rubra* 188, 220
*Cerastium decalvans* 99
[*Certhia brachydactyla*] Short-toed Treecreeper 221
[*Certhia familiaris*] Treecreeper 221
[*Cervus elaphus*] Red Deer 79-82, 192

[*Cettia cetti*] Cetti's Warbler 211
Cetti's Warbler [*Cettia cetti*] 211
Chaffinch [*Fringilla coelebs*] 180, 98, 26, 220
*Chamaecytisus austriacus* 208, 216
Chamois [*Rupicapra rupicapra*] 77-80, 88, 114, 126-128, 130, 133, 192, 196, 222
Chaonia 75
Chequered Blue [*Scolitantides orion*] 66
Chicory (*Cichorium intybus*) 211
Chiffchaff [*Phylloscopus collybita*] 185, 205, 206
Chough [*Pyrrhocorax pyrrhocorax*] 41, 159
*Cichorium intybus* (Chicory) 211
[*Ciconia nigra*] Black Stork 83
[*Cinclus cinclus*] Dipper 14, 37, 234
[*Circaetus gallicus*] Short-toed Eagle 45
*Cistus salvifolius* 218
Civil War 25
Cleopatra butterfly [*Gonepteryx cleopatra*] 34, 191, 203
Clouded Apollo [*Parnassius mnemosyne*] 39
Clouded Yellow [*Colias croceus*] 19, 39, 57, 99, 140, 223
[*Coenonympha arcania*] Pearly Heath 64
[*Coenonympha pamphilus*] Small Heath 64
[*Colias croceus*] Clouded Yellow 19, 39, 57, 99, 140, 223
[*Coluber caspius*] Large Whip Snake, western form 23, 62
[*Coluber gemonensis*] Balkan Whip Snake 62
[*Columba livia*] Rock Dove 159, 160
*Colutea arborescens* (Bladder Senna) 216
Comma [*Polygonia c-album*] 222
Common Harebell (*Campanula rotundifolia*) 157
Common Male Fern (*Dryopteris filix-mas*) 202
*Convallaria majalis* (Lily-of-the-valley) 158
Corfu (Kerkyra) 82
Cornelian Cherry (*Cornus mas*) 207
*Cornus mas* (Cornelian Cherry) 207

*Cornus sanguinea* (Dogwood) 207
*Coronilla emerus* (Scorpion Senna) 216
*Coronilla varia* 211
[*Corvus corax*] Raven 90
*Corydalis densiflora* 39, 90, 131
*Corylus* 73
*Corylus avellana* (Hazel) 21
crab, freshwater [*Potoman fluviatile*] 15
Crag Martin [*Ptyonoprogne rupestris*] 59, 204
Creeping Lady's Tresses Orchid (*Goodyera repens*) 215
Crested Tit [*Parus cristatus*] 193
Cretzschmar's Bunting [*Emberiza caesia*] 116, 142
*Crocus veluchensis* 90, 99, 110, 131, 146, 150
[*Crocuta crocuta*] Spotted Hyaena 81
Crossbill [*Loxia curvirostra*] 180, 181
*Cruciata laevipes* 28
[*Cyaniris semiargus*] Mazarine Blue 39
Cygnus 114
*Cynoglottis barrelieri* ssp. *serpentinicola* 154
Cyprinid fish [*Pachychilon pictum, Barbus peloponnesius*] 15
*Cystopteris fragilis* (Brittle Bladder Fern) 206

*Dactylorhiza saccifera* 212
*Dactylorhiza sambucina* 52
Daimon 5, 6, 217
Daisy (*Bellis perennis*) 28
Dalmatian Algyroides (*Algyroides nigropunctatus*) 216
*Daphne mezereum* 181
*Daphne oleoides* 31, 120, 175
[*Delichon urbica*] House Martin 54
[*Dendrocopos leucotos*] White-backed Woodpecker (*leucotos* race)/(*lilfordi* race) 220
  [*Dendrocopos major*] Greater Spotted Woodpecker 179, 220
[*Dendrocopos medius*] Middle-spotted Woodpecker 213

[*Dendrocopos minor*] Lesser Spotted Woodpecker 51
[*Dendrocopos syriacus*] Syrian Woodpecker 179
Deneb 114
Dhiava 136
*Dianthus cruentus* 18, 179
*Dianthus giganteus* 18, 192
*Dianthus haematocalyx* ssp. *pindicola* 52
*Dianthus integer* ssp. *minutiflorus* 96, 105, 180
*Dianthus sylvestris* 95, 182
*Dianthus viscidus* 180, 193
Dice Snake [*Natrix tessellata*] 15, 68
Dipper [*Cinclus cinclus*] 14, 37, 234
Distrato 133
Dobrinovo (= Iliochori) 134, 137
Dobrovino (wine) 137
Dodona 9, 23, 45
Dodoni Forest Period 73, 226
Dogwood (*Cornus sanguinea*) 207
*Doronicum columnae* (Leopard's Bane) 54, 100, 128, 165
*Doronicum orientale* 165
Dove's-foot Crane's-bill, form of (*Geranium molle* ssp. *brutium*) 28
Downy Oak (*Quercus pubescens*) 61
*Draba lasiocarpa* 93, 131, 150
*Draba lasiocarpa* ssp. *lasiocarpa* 161
Dryad 45
[*Dryocopus martius*] Black Woodpecker 173, 195, 215, 218
*Dryopteris filix-mas* (Common Male Fern) 202
*Dryopteris villarii* 189
*Drypis spinosa* 33, 38, 175, 182, 183

Eagle Owl [*Bubo bubo*] 85
Early Spider Orchid (*Ophrys sphegodes* ssp. *epirotica*) 21
Eastern Hornbeam (*Carpinus orientales*) 61, 93
Eastern Orange Tip [*Anthocharis damone*] 57

*Echium italicum* 18, 207
Echo (the nymph) 88
*Edraianthus graminifolius* 95, 131, 164
Egyptian Vulture [*Neophron percnopterus*] 74, 123
Elassona 136
Elefthero 133
[*Emberiza caesia*] Cretzschmar's Bunting 116, 142
[*Emberiza cia*] Rock Bunting 204
[*Emberiza hortulana*] Ortolan Bunting 111, 116
Ephyra 23
*Epipactis atrorubens* 186
*Epipactis helleborine* 190
*Epipactis microphylla* 190
*Epipactis palustris* (Marsh Helleborine) 218
*Epipactis subclausa* 186, 218
Epirus 17, 23, 118
[*Equus hydruntinus*] European Wild Ass 81
[*Erebia medusa*] Woodland Ringlet 222
Erhard's Wall Lizard [*Podarcis erhardii*] 40
[*Erithacus rubecula*] Robin 219
*Eryngium amethystinum* 4, 43, 154
*Erysimum microstylum* 148, 154
Escher's Blue (ssp. *dalmaticus*) [*Polyommatus escheri*] 65
*Euphorbia herniariifolia* 148
*Euphorbia myrsinites* 43, 154
European Wild Ass [*Equus hydruntinus*] 81

[*Falco peregrinus*] Peregrine Falcon (*brookei* race) 160
[*Falco tinnunculus*] Kestrel 36, 112
Feast of St. George (April 23rd) 124, 135
Fire Salamander [*Salamandra salamandra*] 13
Five-spot moth [*Zygaena trifoli*] 183
*Fragaria vesca* (Wild Strawberry) 207, 217
Fragrant Orchid (*Gymnadenia conopsea*) 210

[*Fringilla coelebs*] Chaffinch 180, 198, 206, 222
*Fritillaria thessala* ssp. *ionica* 100, 174
Fritillary, Glanville [*Melitaea cinxia*] 211
Fritillary, Heath [*Melitaea athalia*] 19, 39
Fritillary, High Brown (*cleodoxa* form) [*Argynnis adippe*] 182
Fritillary, Knapweed [*Melitaea phoebe*] 39
Fritillary, Pearl-bordered [*Boloria euphrosyne*] 175
Fritillary, Queen of Spain [*Issoria lathonia*] 36
Fritillary, Silver-washed [*Argynnis paphia*] 219, 221
Fritillary, Spotted [*Melitaea didyma*] 39, 66
Fritillary, Spotted (ssp. *meridionalis*) [*Melitaea didyma*] 66

*Gagea pusilla* 90, 147
*Galium pisoderium* 183
Gamila 55, 150, 153
[*Garrulus glandarius*] Jay 173, 191, 203, 219, 222
Genitsari 24, 45, 67, 75, 76, 117
Genius 3, 4, 17, 23, 24, 123, 127, 203, 217, 221
*Gentiana verna* ssp. *balcanica* 131, 147, 150, 156
*Geranium aristatum* 141, 212
*Geranium cinereum* ssp. *subcaulescens* 95, 128, 154, 155, 160, 176
*Geranium macrorrhizum* 54, 56, 96, 155 160, 175
*Geranium macrostylum* 28
*Geranium molle* ssp. *brutium* (Dove's-foot Crane's-bill, a form of) 28
*Geranium reflexum* 193, 212
*Geum coccineum* 206, 212
*Geum reptans* 151
Ghiol 1, 171, 173, 183, 184, 193, 202
*Globularia cordifolia* 163
*Gnaphalium roeseri* ssp. *pichleri* 161
Goldcrest [*Regulus regulus*] 197
Golden Eagle [*Aquila chrysaetos*] 196
Goldfinch [*Carduelis carduelis*] 182
[*Gonepteryx cleopatra*] Cleopatra butterfly 34, 191, 203

*Goodyera repens* (Creeping Lady's Tresses Orchid) 215
Goral [*Nemorhaedus goral*] 127
Goshawk [*Accipeter gentilis*] 173, 184
Goura 37, 97, 99, 100, 102, 108, 109, 111, 112, 115, 116, 122-128, 132, 138-142, 144, 146, 149, 151, 152, 156, 157, 166, 169, 171, 174, 196, 206, 222
Goura glacier 101, 102, 139
Goura Spring 27, 102, 109, 111, 113, 141, 144
Gramos 152
Greater Butterfly Orchid (*Platanthera chlorantha*) 141
Greater Spotted Woodpecker [*Dendrocopos major*] 179, 220
Greek Fir (*Abies cephalonica*) 24. 25, 93, 194, 225, 226
Green Hairstreak [*Callophrys rubi*] 216
Greek Stream Frog [*Rana graeca*]15
Green Toad [*Pseudepidalea viridis*] 111
Green-winged Orchid (*Anacamptis* [*Orchis*] *morio*) 19, 21, 64, 179
Green Woodpecker [*Picus viridis*] 190
Grey-headed Woodpecker [*Picus canus*] 190
Grey Wagtail [*Motacilla cinerea*] 20
Griffon Vulture [*Gyps fulvus*] 83
Grizzled Skipper [*Pyrgus malvae*] 217
Gulf of Arta 120
*Gymnadenia conopsea* (Fragrant Orchid) 210
[*Gypaetus barbatus*] Lammergeier 10, 89, 127
[*Gyps fulvus*] Griffon Vulture 83

Hart's Tongue Fern (*Phyllitis scolopendrium*) 104
Hazel (*Corylus avellana*) 21, 71
*Helianthemum nummularium* 22, 35, 160, 180
*Helleborus cyclophyllus* 40
[*Hemitragus jemlahicus*] Himalayan Tahr 127
Herb Paris (*Paris quadrifolia*) 198
Hermann's Tortoise [*Testudo hermanni*] 69, 208
*Hesperis dinarica* 174

High Atlas (Morocco) 109, 127
Himalayan Tahr [*Hemitragus jemlahicus*] 127
*Himantoglossum calcaratum* 60, 179, 208
*Himantoglossum caprinum* 60, 179, 208
[*Hipparchia aristaeus*] Southern Grayling (*senthes* race) 194
[*Hirundo daurica*] Red-rumped Swallow 27
Holly Blue [*Celastrina argiolus*] 63
Holly Fern (*Polystichum lonchitis*) 104
Honey Buzzard [*Pernis apivorus*] 129, 130
Hoopoe [*Upupa epops*] 53
Hop Hornbeam (*Ostrya carpinifolia*) 93, 206
Horned Ophrys (*Ophrys scolopax* ssp. *cornuta*) 62
House Martin [*Delichon urbica*] 54
Humming-bird Hawk-moth [*Macroglossum stellatarum*] 161
*Hypericum perfoliatum* 210
*Hypericum rumeliacum* ssp. *apollinis* (St John's Wort) 4, 35, 148, 156, 165

*Iberis sempervirens* 108, 120, 177
Ibex [*Capra ibex*] 77-80, 88, 127
Idas Blue (ssp. *magnagraeca*) [*Plebejus idas*] 39, 65
Ilex Hairstreak [*Satyrium ilicis*] 63
Iliochori (= Dobrinovo) 134, 137
Illyria 23
Illyrians 20
Imperial Eagle [*Aquila heliaca*] 10, 33, 34, 46, 51, 112, 196
Ioannina 9, 57
[*Iphiclides podalirius*] Scarce Swallowtail 34, 182, 212, 224
*Iris germanica* 43, 177
[*Issoria lathonia*] Fritillary, Queen of Spain 36

Jay [*Garrulus glandarius*] 173, 191, 203, 219, 222
*Juglans regia* (Walnut) 31
*Juniperus* 30, 73

*Juniperus foetidissima* 30
Jupiter 48, 85, 113, 170
[*Jynx torquilla*] Wryneck 31-33, 53

Kalamas (river) 71, 82
Karteros 55, 146, 150, 152, 153
Kashkaval (cheese) 136
Kastritsa (cave) 82
Kato Tsoeka 37, 108, 115, 116, 144, 150
Kazarma 86
Kepesovo 10, 27, 118, 119
Kerkyra (Corfu) 82
Kermes Oak (*Quercus coccifera*) 21, 61, 63
Kestrel [*Falco tinnunculus*] 36, 112
Kestrini 75
Kidney Vetch (*Anthyllis vulneraria*) 69
Kioproulides (stone masons) 16
Kipi (river terrace) 70, 226
Kipoi 11, 59
Kipseli 17
Klithi (river terrace) 60, 70, 76, 225
Klithi (rock-shelter) 80, 93
Kokkorou or Noutsos (bridge) 14, 16, 59, 70, 74
Konakia 143
Konitsa 17
Kopana 153
Kotili 17
Koumoumanitis (river) 133
Kourtetsi 30, 36, 99-101, 104, 105, 111, 115, 128, 132, 144, 148, 149, 183
Kousta 10, 37, 47, 140
Koziakas 140, 37, 47, 140
Krevvati 30, 36, 37, 49, 86, 89, 93, 95, 96, 98, 101, 102, 108, 112, 116, 128, 131, 139, 140, 144-146, 148-150, 153

Krokos 147

*Lactuca intricata* 108
Lady Orchid (*Orchis purpurea*) 141
Laista 11, 133
*Lamium garganicum* ssp. *laevigatum* 56, 165
Lammergeier [*Gypaetus barbatus*] 10, 89, 127
[*Lanius collurio*] Red-backed Shrike 50
Large Tortoiseshell [*Nymphalis polychloros*] 212, 218
Large Whip Snake, western form [*Coluber caspius*] 23, 62
Large White butterfly [*Pieris brassicae*] 209
Larissa 136
*Lathyrus grandiflorus* 207
*Lembotropis nigricans* 216
Leopard's Bane (*Doronicum columnae*) 128, 165
[*Leptidea sinapis*] Wood White 185
[*Lepus europaeus*] Brown Hare 46
Leshinitsa (=Vrisochori) 134, 137
Lesser Spotted Woodpecker [*Dendrocopos minor*] 51
*Lilium candidum* (Madonna Lily) 43, 60
*Lilium chalcedonicum* 189
*Lilium martagon* 199, 204
Lily-of-the-valley (*Convallaria majalis*) 158
[*Limenitis reducta*] Southern White Admiral 68
*Limodorum abortivum* 141
*Linaria peloponnesiaca* 95
*Linum flavum* ssp. *albanicum* 164, 176
*Linum hologynum* 204
*Linum punctatum* ssp. *pycnophyllum* 4, 122
*Linum tenuifolium* 204
Lion [*Panthera leo europaea*] 81
*Lithospermum goulandriorum* 29
*Lithospermum purpurocaeruleum* (Purple Gromwell) 29
Little Owl [*Athene noctua*] 113, 128, 129

Long-tailed Tit [*Aegithalos caudatus*] 158, 203
*Lonicera caprifolium* 207
[*Loxia curvirostra*] Crossbill 180, 181
[*Lullula arborea*] Woodlark 11, 47, 50, 53
[*Luscinia megarhynchos*] Nightingale 13, 168, 169, 198, 199, 205,
[*Lutra lutra*] Otter 14, 15 67, 68
[*Lycaena alciphron*] Purple-shot Copper 38
[*Lycaena phlaeas*] Small Copper 175
*Lychnis coronaria* 187
*Lysimachia punctata* 218
Lynx [*Lynx lynx*] 113, 115, 126
[*Lynx lynx*] Lynx 113, 115, 126

Macedonia 23, 118, 133, 135, 138, 177
Macedonian Oak (*Quercus pubescens*) 61
[*Macroglossum stellatarum*] Humming-bird Hawk-moth 161
Madonna Lily (*Lilium candidum*) 43, 61
Magoula meadows 134, 136, 154, 156, 162, 169, 176, 197, 198, 202, 206, 215, 217
*Malcolmia graeca* ssp. *bicolor* 165
*Malcolmia orsiniana* ssp. *angulifolia* 42, 155
[*Malpolon monspessulanus*] Montpellier Snake 68
[*Maniola jutina*] Meadow Brown 210
Marbled White [*Melanargia galathea*] 63, 210
Marginated Tortoise [*Testudo marginata*] 51
Markhor [*Capra falconeri*] 127
Mars 48, 85, 113
Marsh Frog [*Rana ridibunda*] 68
Marsh Helleborine (*Epipactis palustris*) 218
Marsh Tit [*Parus palustris*] 188
Mazaria (ravine) 58
Mazarine Blue [*Cyaniris semiargus*] 39
Meadow Brown [*Maniola jutina*] 210
megala leethareeya 108, 139, 147, 148

Megas Lakos (ravine) 56, 74, 77, 86, 93, 101
[*Melanargia galathea*] Marbled White 63, 210
[*Melanargia larissa*] Balkan Marbled White 63
[*Melitaea athalia*] Fritillary, Heath 19, 39
[*Melitaea cinxia*] Fritillary, Glanville 211
[*Melitaea didyma*] Fritillary, Spotted 39, 66
[*Melitaea phoebe*] Fritillary, Knapweed 39
Metsova 114
Middle-spotted Woodpecker [*Dendrocopos medius*] 213
[*Milvus migrans*] Black Kite 123
*Minuartia pseudosaxifraga* 99, 116, 149
Misiou (bridge) 17, 59, 66, 67, 70, 77
Mistle Thrush [*Turdus viscivorus*] 183
Mitsikeli 9, 57, 61, 71, 82, 100, 114, 119
Molossia 23, 75
Molossians 9, 24, 15, 33, 36, 44, 45, 75, 117, 119
Molossus (dog breed) 119
*Moneses uniflora* 215
Monkey Orchid (*Orchis simia*) 208
Monodendri 75
*Monotropa hypopitys* 185
[*Monticola saxatilis*] Rock Thrush 87, 97, 107
[*Monticola solitarius*] Blue Rock Thrush 86, 87, 97
[*Montifringilla nivalis*] Snow Finch 140, 144, 145, 148
Montpellier Snake [*Malpolon monspessulanus*] 64
[*Motacilla cinerea*] Grey Wagtail 20
Moufflon [*Ovis orientalis*] 127
Mountain Small White [*Artogeia ergane*] 57
*Muscari comosum* (Tassel Hyacinth) 19, 211
*Muscari neglectum* 40
*Myosotis alpestris* ssp. *suaveolens* 91, 99

Naiad 45
*Narcissus poeticus* ssp. *radiiflorus* (Pheasant's Eye Narcissus) 100, 178

[*Natrix tessellata*] Dice Snake 15, 68
Nemerska 81, 99
[*Nemorhaedus goral*] Goral 127
[*Neophron percnopterus*] Egyptian Vulture 74, 123
Neoptolemus 9, 23
*Neottia (Listera) ovata* 140
*Neottia nidus-avis* (Bird's Nest Orchid) 184, 220
Nereid 45
Nereid's Spring 199
Nettle-tree Butterfly [*Libythea celtis*] 66
Nightingale [*Luscinia megarhynchos*] 13, 168, 169, 198, 199, 205, 206, 213, 217
Nightjar [*Caprimulgus europaeus*] 48, 50, 53, 169, 200
Noble Crayfish [*Astacus astacus*] 15
Nodding Wintergreen (*Orthilia secunda*) 140, 215
Nose-horned Viper [*Vipera ammodytes*] 24, 103, 121
Nouka 178
Noutsos Kontodimos 16
Noutsos or Kokkorou (bridge) 16
Nuthatch [*Sitta europaea*] 191, 219
[*Nymphalis antiopa*] Camberwell Beauty 63
[*Nymphalis polychloros*] Large Tortoiseshell 212, 218

Oak, Downy (*Quercus pubescens*) 61
Oak, Kermes (*Quercus coccifera*) 21, 61, 63
Oak, Macedonian (*Quercus trojana*) 61
*Olea* 73
Olympos 133, 138, 188
*Onobrychis montana* ssp. *scardica* 130, 165
*Ophrys apifera* (Bee Orchid) 208
*Ophrys scolopax* ssp. *cornuta* (Horned Ophrys) 62, 179
*Ophrys sphegodes* ssp. *helenae* 65
*Ophrys sphegodes* ssp. *epirotica* (Early Spider Orchid) 21
Orange Tip [*Anthocharis cardamines*] 57, 185

*Orchis mascula* 52
*Orchis mascula* (ssp. *pinetorum*) 214
*Orchis pallens* 93, 132, 165
*Orchis provincialis* 141
*Orchis purpurea* (Lady Orchid) 141
*Orchis quadripunctata* 32
*Orchis simia* (Monkey Orchid) 208
*Orchis spitzelii* 140
*Orchis tridentata* 32
*Orchis ustulata* (Burnt-tip Orchid) 53
Oread 45
*Ornithogalum oligophyllum* 90, 99, 147
Orris root 177
Orsini's Viper [*Vipera ursinii*] 103
Orsini's Viper, Greek ssp. [*Vipera ursinii* ssp. *graeca*] 103
*Orthilia secunda* (Nodding Wintergreen) 140, 215
Ortolan Bunting [*Emberiza hortulana*] 111, 116
*Ostrya carpinifolia* (Hop Hornbeam) 72, 93, 216, 225
Otter [*Lutra lutra*] 14, 15, 67, 68
Ottomans 137
[*Otus scops*] Scops Owl 48, 85, 169, 201
[*Ovis orientalis*] Moufflon 127

[*Pachychilon pictum, Barbus peloponnesius*] Cyprinid fish 15
Pades 133
Painted Lady [*Vanessa cardui*] 105, 183
Palaeolithic hunters 87, 92, 93, 102, 109, 110, 150
Palaiokastro 23, 24
Paleosellio 133, 134
Pamvotis Lake 75, 82
Pan (the deity) 45, 87
Panigyri 217, 222
[*Panthera leo europaea*] Lion 81
[*Papilio alexanor*] Southern Swallowtail 68, 6

[*Papilio machaon*] Swallowtail 10, 68
Papingo 28, 36, 118
[*Pararge aegeria*] Speckled Wood (*tircis* race) 191
Parauaea 23, 37
Parga 23, 120
*Paris quadrifolia* (Herb Paris) 198
[*Parnassius apollo*] Apollo butterfly 57, 140
[*Parnassius mnemosyne*] Clouded Apollo 39
[*Parus caeruleus*] Blue Tit 207
[*Parus cristatus*] Crested Tit 193
[*Parus lugubris*] Sombre Tit 31
[*Parus montanus*] Willow Tit 188
[*Parus palustris*] Marsh Tit 188
Passaron 9, 23, 75
Pearly Heath [*Coenonympha arcania*] 64
*Pedicularis graeca* 132, 151
Pelagonian continent 138
Pentasimos 222
Peregrine Falcon (*brookei* race) [*Falco peregrinus*] 160
Perivoli 135, 136
[*Pernis apivorus*] Honey Buzzard 129, 130
Persian Skipper [*Spialia phlomidis*] 66
[*Petronia petronia*] Rock Sparrow 87
Pheasant's Eye Narcissus (*Narcissus poeticus* ssp. *radiiflorus*) 100, 178
Philomela 199
*Phleum alpinum* 88
*Phyllitis scolopendrium* (Hart's Tongue Fern) 104
[*Phylloscopus collybita*] Chiffchaff 185, 205, 206
[*Phoenicurus ochruros*] Black Redstart 105, 122, 155, 159, 202
[*Picus canus*] Grey-headed Woodpecker 190
[*Picus viridis*] Green Woodpecker 190
[*Pieris brassicae*] Large White butterfly 209
Pindar 23
Pindos 23, 37, 71, 103, 133, 139

*Pinguicula crystallina* ssp. *hirtiflora* 190
*Pinus halepensis* Aleppo Pine 10
*Pinus heldreichii* 153, 157, 171, 175, 179-181, 197
*Pinus nigra* (Black Pine) 133, 193
*Platanthera chlorantha* (Greater Butterfly Orchid) 141
[*Plebejus argus*] Silver-studded Blue 64
[*Plebejus idas*] Idas Blue (ssp. *magnagraeca*) 39, 65
[*Plebejus pylaon*] Zephyr Blue (ssp. *sephirus*) 62
Ploskos 150
[*Podarcis erhardii*] Erhard's Wall Lizard 40
*Polygala nicaeensis* ssp. *mediterranea* 28, 172
[*Polygonia c-album*] Comma 222
[*Polyommatus amandus*] Amanda's Blue 65, 66
[*Polyommatus bellargus*] Adonis Blue 39
[*Polyommatus escheri*] Escher's Blue (ssp. *dalmaticus*) 65
*Polystichum lonchitis* (Holly Fern) 104
*Potentilla detommasii* 211
*Potentilla recta* 28
*Potentilla speciosa* var. *discolor* 56
[*Potoman fluviatile*] crab, freshwater 15
[*Prunella collaris*] Alpine Accentor (*subalpina* race) 109, 139, 162
*Prunus* sp. 34, 212
*Prunus prostrata* 108
[*Pseudepidalea viridis*] Green Toad 111
[*Pseudois nayaur*] Bharal 127
*Pterocephalus perennis* ssp. *bellidifolius* 42, 56
*Pterocephalus plumosus* 61, 65
[*Ptyonoprogne rupestris*]Crag Martin 59, 204
Purple Gromwell (*Lithospermum purpurocaeruleum*) 29
Purple-shot Copper [*Lycaena alciphron*] 38
Pydna (battle of) 25
Pyramidal Orchid (*Anacamptis pyramidalis*) 64, 214
[*Pyrgus malvae*] Grizzled Skipper 217
*Pyrola chlorantha* 215

*Pyrola rotundifolia* 215
[*Pyrrhocorax graculus*] Alpine Chough 40, 41, 94, 159
[*Pyrrhocorax pyrrhocorax*] Chough 41, 159
Pyrrhus 9, 23, 25, 44, 96, 133, 138, 177, 195
Pyrsogianni 17

*Quercus coccifera* (Kermes Oak) 21, 61
*Quercus pubescens* (Downy Oak) 61
*Quercus trojana* (Macedonian Oak) 61

*Ramonda serbica* 54, 55
[*Rana graeca*] Greek Stream Frog 15
[*Rana ridibunda*] Marsh Frog 68
*Ranunculus brevifolius* 98, 131, 150, 160
*Ranunculus platanifolius* 172
*Ranunculus sartorianus* 95, 172
Rascianitis (river) 134, 139
Raven [*Corvus corax*] 90
Red Admiral [*Vanessa atalanta*] 214
Red-backed Shrike [*Lanius collurio*] 50
Red Deer [*Cervus elaphus*] 79-82, 192
Red-rumped Swallow [*Hirundo daurica*] 27
Red Squirrel [*Sciurus vulgaris*] 194
[*Regulus regulus*] Goldcrest 97
*Rhamnus fallax* 203
*Rhinanthus pindicus* 210
*Rhynchocorys elephas* 213
Ring Ouzel (*alpestris* race) [*Turdus torquatus*] 178
Robin [*Erithacus rubecula*] 219
Rock Bunting [*Emberiza cia*] 204
Rock Dove [*Columba livia*] 159, 160
Rock Nuthatch [*Sitta neumayer*] 37
Rock Partridge [*Alectoris graeca*] 46, 106, 114, 115, 121, 146, 196
Rock Sparrow [*Petronia petronia*] 87

Rock Thrush [*Monticola saxatilis*] 87, 97, 107
Roe Deer [*Capreolus capreolus*] 114, 167, 168, 192
Rongovou monastery 29
*Rosa heckeliana* ssp. *heckeliana* 105
*Rosa pulverulenta* 175
*Rosa villosa* 172
*Rosalia alpina* 220
[*Rupicapra rupicapra*] Chamois 77-80, 88, 114, 126-128, 130, 133, 192, 196, 222

[*Salamandra salamandra*] Fire Salamander 13
Salamis 195
[*Salmo trutta*] Brown Trout 15, 68
*Salvia amplexicaulis* 218
*Salvia nemerosa* 208
*Salvia sclarea* 65, 207
*Salvia verticillata* 65
Samarina 132, 135, 136
*Saponaria calabrica* 35
Sarakatsani 9, 10, 57, 106, 118, 119, 123-125, 142, 143, 179
Sarantaporos (river) 17
[*Satyrium ilicis*] Ilex Hairstreak 63
[*Saxicola torquata*] Stonechat 115
*Saxifraga marginata* 55, 132, 149, 176
*Saxifraga oppositifolia* 150
*Saxifraga paniculata* 54, 176
*Saxifraga porophylla* ssp. *federici-augusti* 54, 120, 161
*Saxifraga rotundifolia* ssp. *rotundifolia* 189, 206
*Saxifraga rotundifolia* ssp. *taygetea* 177
Scarce Swallowtail [*Iphiclides podalirius*] 34, 182, 212, 224
*Scilla bifolia* 99, 110, 131, 147, 150
[*Sciurus vulgaris*] Red Squirrel 194
[*Scolitantides orion*] Chequered Blue 66
Scorpion Senna (*Coronilla emerus*) 216

*Scutellaria alpina* 152
*Scutellaria rupestris* ssp. *adenotricha* 158, 176
Scops Owl [*Otus scops*] 48, 85, 169, 201
*Sedum acre* 42
*Sedum album* 42
*Sedum atratum* 164
Selio valley 24, 43, 45, 71, 72, 76, 100, 101, 140
*Sempervivum marmoreum* 4, 55
Serin [*Serinus serinus*] 182
[*Serinus serinus*] Serin 182
Serow [*Capricornis sumatraensis*] 127
Shore Lark (*balcanica* race) [*Eremophila alpestris*] 91, 128, 140
Short-toed Eagle [*Circaetus gallicus*] 45
Short-toed Treecreeper [*Certhia brachydactyla*] 221
*Sideritis raeseri* 30
*Silene caesia* 160
*Silene chromodonta* 99
*Silene fabarioides* 22
*Silene parnassica* 56
Silver Fir (*Abies alba*) 24, 25, 93, 194, 225, 226
Silver-studded Blue [*Plebejus argus*] 64
Silver-Y moth [*Autographa gamma*] 31
[*Sitta europaea*] Nuthatch 191, 219
[*Sitta neumayer*] Rock Nuthatch 37
Skala 58
Skamneli 11, 22, 24-27, 37, 43-46, 76, 99, 102, 108, 111, 118, 123, 124, 133, 134, 140, 179, 215
Skamneliotikos 10-12, 14, 16, 34, 37, 43, 44, 48, 59, 67, 70-72, 100, 118, 123, 126, 14
Skamnellian (glacial phase) 73, 76, 101, 156, 226
Skamnellian (glaciers) 12, 72
Skylark [*Alauda arvensis*] 107, 122
Small Copper [*Lycaena phlaeas*] 175
Small Heath [*Coenonympha pamphilus*] 64

Small Skipper [*Thymelicus sylvestris*] 210
Smiksi 135
Smilax 147
Smolikas 84, 98, 133, 135, 137-139, 152, 155, 170, 176, 209
Snow Finch [*Montifringilla nivalis*] 140, 144, 145, 148
*Soldanella pindicola* 132, 172
Sombre Tit [*Parus lagubris*] 31
Southern Festoon [*Zerynthia polyxena*] 69
Southern Grayling (*senthes* race) [*Hipparchia aristaeus*] 194
Southern Nettle Tree (*Celtis australis*) 66
Southern Swallowtail [*Papilio alexanor*] 68, 69
Southern White Admiral [*Limenitis reducta*] 68
Sparrowhawk [*Accipeter nisus*] 183
Speckled Wood (*tircis* race) [*Pararge aegeria*] 191
[*Spialia phlomidis*] Persian Skipper 66
Spotted Hyaena [*Crocuta crocuta*] 81
Spreading Bellflower (*Campanula patula*) 19, 210
Stanee 28, 110, 118, 123, 124, 141, 142-144, 153
St. Demetrius Day (Oct 26th) 135
St. George's Day (Apr 23rd), Feast of 124, 135
St. John's Wort (*Hypericum rumeliacum* ssp. *apollinis*) 35, 148, 210
St. Pandelis, Panigyri of 217
St. Paraskevi, Panigyri of 217
Stonechat [*Saxicola torquata*] 113
Stouros 55, 75, 84
[*Strix aluco*] Tawny Owl 170
Summer Triangle 114
[*Sus scrofa*] Wild Boar 187, 196, 199
Swallowtail [*Papilio machaon*] 10, 68
Syrian Woodpecker [*Dendrocopos syriacus*] 179

Tassel Hyacinth (*Muscari comosum*) 19, 211
Tawny Owl [*Strix aluco*] 170
[*Testudo hermanni*] Hermann's Tortoise 69, 208

[*Testudo marginata*] Marginated Tortoise 51
*Thalictrum aquilegiifolium* 205
Tharypas 75
Theofanis Tsavalias 27, 221
Thesprotia (Thesprotians) 61, 75
Thessaly 23, 118, 135, 136
*Thlaspi microphyllum* 152
*Thlaspi perfoliatum* 42
Thrace 118
Thyamis (river) 75, 82
[*Thymelicus sylvestris*] Small Skipper 210
*Thymus boissieri* 96
*Thymus leucospermus* 96
[*Tichodroma muraria*] Wallcreeper 125
*Tilia* 73
Tomaros 9
*Tordylium apulum* 167
Touberieki (drum) 222
Toubkal 127
Treecreeper [*Certhia familiaris*] 221
Trikkala 136
[*Triturus alpestris*] Alpine Newt 184
Troy 23
Tsepelovo 10-14, 21, 22, 26, 27, 30, 31, 36, 45, 46, 53, 64, 64, 71, 84, 99, 101, 108, 109, 112, 113, 118, 123, 174, 177, 178
Tsepelovo glacier 102, 139
Tshelniku (tshelnikadzi) 136
Tsouka Rossa 149, 154-157, 159, 162, 166, 170, 173, 196, 204, 206, 222, 223
Tufted Vetch (*Vicia cracca*) 210
*Tulipa australis* 108
[*Turdus merula*] Blackbird (*aterrimus* race) 186
[*Turdus torquatus*] Ring Ouzel (*alpestris* race) 178
[*Turdus viscivorus*] Mistle Thrush 183

Tymphaean glacial phase 76, 77, 226
Tymphaean massif 4, 10, 24, 36, 59, 75, 77, 116, 117, 171
Tymphaeans 9
Tymphi 4, 5, 9, 10, 25, 27, 29, 34, 55, 57, 61, 65-67, 70, 71, 73, 76, 84, 95, 98, 116, 118, 119, 124, 126, 127, 133, 134, 154, 152, 177, 181, 225, 226
Tzoumako 37

*Ulmu* 72
[*Upupa epops*] Hoopoe 53
[*Ursus arctos*] Brown Bear 140, 166, 192

*Valeriana crinii* ssp. *epirotica* 132
*Valeriana tuberosa* 100, 105, 120
[*Vanessa atalanta*] Red Admiral 214
[*Vanessa cardui*] Painted Lady 105, 183
Vega 114
Venus 48, 85, 113, 170
*Veratrum album* 184
*Verbascum longifolium* ssp. *samaritanii* 40
*Vicia cracca* (Tufted Vetch) 210
Vikaki (ravine) 12, 16, 59, 72, 83, 123, 129
Vikos canyon 14, 15, 31, 34, 36, 52, 55, 70, 72, 74-76, 86, 101, 102, 118, 119, 123, 129, 160, 178, 179, 196, 225, 226
Vikos (river terrace) 76
*Viola albanica* 98, 131, 146, 148, 158, 203
*Viola epirota* 95, 120, 148, 154
*Viola tricolor* ssp. *macedonica* 207
[*Vipera ammodytes*] Nose-horned Viper 24, 103, 121
[*Vipera ursinii*] Orsini's Viper 103
[*Vipera ursinii* ssp. *graeca*] Orsini's Viper, Greek ssp. 103
Viryinadha (song) 222
Vitsa 24, 67, 75, 76
Vlakhi (see Arumani) 135

Vlasian cold phase 71-73, 76, 226
Vlasian glacier 71, 72, 101
Voidomatis (river) 10, 14-16, 55, 57-59, 61, 67, 69-71, 137, 228
Vradeto 10, 58, 87, 118
Vrisochori (see Leshinitsa) 28, 134, 136, 155, 156, 165, 198, 209, 214, 217, 222


Wallcreeper [*Tichodroma muraria*] 125
Walnut (*Juglans regia*) 31
Wheatear (*libanotica* race) [*Oenanthe oenanthe*] 110, 148
White-backed Woodpecker (*leucotos* race) [*Dendrocopos leucotos*] 220
White-backed Woodpecker (*lilfordi* race) [*Dendrocopos leucotos*] 220
Wild Boar [*Sus scrofa*] 187, 196, 199
Wild Strawberry (*Fragaria vesca*) 207, 217
Willow Tit [*Parus montanus*] 188
Wolf [*Canis lupus*] 10, 126
Woodland Ringlet [*Erebia medusa*] 222
Woodlark [*Lullula arborea*] 11, 47, 50, 53
Wood White [*Leptidea sinapis*] 185
Wryneck [*Jynx torquilla*] 31-33, 53


Xatsiou (bridge) 11, 13, 15, 17, 101


Yellow-bellied Toad [*Bombina variegata*] 13, 111, 184
Yiftokambos 124, 174


Zagori 4, 10, 11, 21, 25-26, 46, 57, 118, 135, 136, 137, 222
Zeibekiko (dance of the eagle) 44
*Zelkova* 72
Zephyr Blue (ssp. *sephirus*) [*Plebejus pylaon*] 62
[*Zerynthia polyxena*] Southern Festoon 69
Zeus 9, 32, 45
Ziogas Frontzos (bridge builder) 17
[*Zygaena trifoli*] Five-spot moth 183

# Other Nature Books by Brambleby Books

*Sheer Cliffs and Shearwaters – A Skomer Island Journal*
Richard Kipling
ISBN 9781908241214

*Walking with Birds*
Colin Whittle
ISBN 9781908241351

*Scilly Birding – Joining the Madding Crowd*
Simon Davey
ISBN 9781908241177

*Gardening with Nature* series by Jenny Steel
*Making Garden Meadows*
ISBN 9781908241221

*Butterfly Gardening*
ISBN 9781908241436

Making Wildlife Ponds
ISBN 9781908241481

*Is no Problem*
Simon Davey
ISBN 9781908241405

The Five-year Butterfly Hunt
Phil Hall
ISBN 9781908241467

www.bramblebybooks.co.uk